BY JOSEPH FOSTER

In the Night Did I Sing

The Great Montezuma

A Cow Is too much Trouble in Los Angeles

Street of the Barefoot Lovers

Flower of a Day Café

Stephana

D. H. Lawrence in Taos

frontispiece: Portrait of Lawrence by Knud Merrild

D. H.
LAWRENCE
IN TAOS

BY JOSEPH FOSTER

UNIVERSITY OF NEW MEXICO PRESS

PERMISSIONS

Excerpts from *The Autobiography of Bertrand Russell*, Vol. II, by permission of George Allen and Unwin Ltd., London; and Atlantic-Little Brown and Co., Boston, Mass. Copyright © 1951, 1952, 1956 by Bertrand Russell. Copyright © 1968 by George Allen and Unwin Ltd.

Excerpts adapted from Knud Merrild: *With D. H. Lawrence in New Mexico*, Barnes and Noble, Inc., New York, N.Y.; and Routledge and Kegan Paul Ltd., London, by permission of the publishers.

Excerpts from *Journey with Genius* by Witter Bynner are reprinted by permission of the John Day Company, Inc., New York, N.Y. Copyright © 1951 by Witter Bynner.

Passages from "Ghost Dance Song" and "Song of Healing" from *The Indians' Book* by Natalie Curtis. Reprinted by permission of Dover Publications, Inc., New York, N.Y.

Excerpts from *The Intelligent Heart* by Harry T. Moore by permission of Farrar, Straus & Giroux. Copyright 1954 by Harry T. Moore.

Excerpts from *Shakespeare and Company* by Sylvia Beach by permission of Harcourt Brace Jovanovich, Inc., New York, N.Y.

Excerpts from "David" in *The Complete Plays of D. H. Lawrence* by permission of Curtis Brown, Ltd., New York, N.Y.; and Laurence Pollinger Ltd., London; and the Estate of Mrs. Frieda Lawrence [Ravagli].

Excerpts from *Frieda Lawrence: Memoirs and Correspondence*, edited by E. W. Tedlock, Jr., by permission of Laurence Pollinger Ltd., London; and the Estate of Mrs. Frieda Lawrence [Ravagli].

Excerpts from "*Not I But the Wind . . .*" by Frieda Lawrence by permission of Laurence Pollinger Ltd., London; and the Estate of Mrs. Frieda Lawrence [Ravagli].

Excerpts from *The American Rhythm* by Mary Austin by permission of Houghton Mifflin Company, Boston, Mass.

Excerpts from *Lawrence and Brett: A Friendship* by Dorothy Brett (published by J. B. Lippincott Company, Philadelphia, Pa.) by permission of John Manchester, Attorney-in-Fact and Literary Executor for the Honorable Dorothy Brett, Taos, N.M.

Excerpts from *Intimate Memories* [V. 3 *Movers and Shakers*] by Mrs. Mabel (Ganson) Luhan by permission of Curtis Brown, Ltd., New York, N.Y. Copyright © 1936 by Harcourt Brace and Co.

Excerpts from *Lorenzo in Taos* by Mabel Dodge Luhan. Copyright © 1936 by Alfred A. Knopf.

Quotations from *Leon Gaspard* by Frank Waters by permission of the publisher Paul Weaver of Northland Press, Flagstaff, Ariz.

iii

iv

To the memory of

MARGARET HALE FOSTER

ACKNOWLEDGMENTS

I am greatly indebted to the late Frieda Lawrence for many profound conversations with her about Lawrence after his death.

My special insights into Lawrence could not have been so clearly realized without a lifetime of discussions about Lawrence and literature in general with the late Margaret Hale Foster.

Conversations with Witter Bynner, Richard Aldington, Mabel Dodge Luhan, Professor Harry T. Moore, David Garnett, Dr. Keith Sagar, and many of the members of the discussion panels of the D. H. Lawrence Festival in Taos— notably Dr. Ernest Tedlock, Jr., Enid Hilton, Helen Corke, Dr. James Cowan, and Dr. N. Scott Momaday—have strengthened me in my belief that Lawrence transcends the present meaning of European Culture. We must reassess our entire civilization in Lawrence's terms, not our own.

I wish to thank the Harwood Library and its Director Mrs. Thomas Tarleton for permission to reproduce the photograph of Frieda Lawrence.

Mr. Saki Karavas of Taos has kindly given me permission to use Knud Merrild's portrait of Lawrence.

I am especially grateful to my friend Dr. F. Warren Roberts, Director of the Humanities Research Center of the University of Texas for patiently answering my many questions and granting me permission to reproduce several pictures from the University's D. H. Lawrence collection.

I am indebted to Miss Mariana Howes for her photograph of Mabel, Frieda, and the Brett—the only one in which the three women ever appeared together; to Mrs. Jenny Vincent for a rare, newly discovered photograph of Lawrence as a young man; and to Frank P. Chase for his photograph of Tony Luhan taken in 1957. The picture of the Brett as a young woman is used through the courtesy of the Manchester Gallery, El Prado N.M. The photograph of Mabel Dodge is by Laura Gilpin.

The famous photograph of Lawrence was taken by Edward Weston, and is used on the jacket by permission of his son, Cole Weston.

I am indebted to Professor Harry T. Moore for a sympathetic reading of the original manuscript.

I wish to thank Mrs. Raphael Hayes for her sympathetic reading and suggestions about an earlier version of the manuscript.

I am indebted to Col. Herschel Colbert for permission to quote from his monograph on early Taos doctors; and to Mrs. Rowena Meyers Martinez for her letter containing Mr. Ralph Meyers' characterization of Lawrence.

CONTENTS

Illustrations

DRAMATIS PERSONAE

Albidia. Mabel Luhan's Indian maid.

Archuleta, Trinidad. Lawrence's Indian helper who used to work on the ranch. A famous dancer at the Pueblo, he is still alive today. Friend of the author.

Austin, Mary (1868–1934). American novelist, playwright, short story writer. Knew Lawrence, Frieda and Mabel in summer of 1924. *The Land of Little Rain.* Onetime friend of the author.

Berninghaus, Oscar (1874–1952). Artist. Came to Taos in 1898. A national figure in western art. Honors: elected an Associate of the National Academy of Design, 1925; Altman Prize. Decorated State Capitol Building of Missouri. Friend of the author.

Brett, The Honorable Dorothy Eugenie (1883–   ). Daughter of 2nd Viscount of Esher. Painter. Wrote *Lawrence and Brett.* Friend of Lawrence, J. Middleton Murry, Katherine Mansfield, Virginia Woolf, Lytton Strachey, Bertrand Russell, Mark Gertler, Mabel Dodge Luhan, Alfred Stieglitz, Georgia O'Keeffe, Robinson Jeffers, Leopold Stokowski. Became American citizen in 1938. Lives in Taos. Friend of the author.

Brill, Dr. A. A. (1874–1948). Mrs. Luhan's psychiatrist, born in Austria. Chief of the clinic of psychoanalysis and psychosexual sciences at Columbia University.

Bynner, Witter (1881–1968). American poet, born in Brooklyn, N. Y. Graduated from Harvard 1902. Assistant editor of *McClure's* magazine. Traveled with Lawrence in Mexico in 1923. Also traveled extensively in China. Author of many volumes of poetry including the hoax *Spectra* (1917). Faithful friend of Frieda. Author of *Journey with Genius: Recollections and Reflections Concerning the D. H. Lawrences* (John Day Co., 1951). Bynner left an estate of more than a million dollars. Friend of the author.

Cather, Willa (1876–1947). U.S. novelist. Miss Cather stayed with Mabel during the summer of 1925. Author of *Death Comes for the Archbishop*. Miss Cather visited Lawrence at the ranch. "Everybody said she was blunt and abrupt, but we got along famously," said Frieda.

Cottam, Mr. and Mrs. Louis. Friends of the Lawrences, 1922–25. Mrs. Cottam is the daughter of Mr. and Mrs. A. D. Hawk and the sister of William and Mrs. Joseph DuBarry, the former Bobby Hawk. Friends of the author.

Couse, E. Irving (1866–1936). Painter. National Academician. Came to Taos in 1902. Hon. men., Paris Exposition 1900. First prize, National Academy of Design, 1902. Gold Medal, National Academy of Design, 1911. Carnegie Institute Prize, National Academy of Design, 1912. Altman prize, National Academy of Design, 1916. Friend of the author.

Covarrubias, Miguel (1902–57). Mexican painter. Showed Lawrence the Rivera frescoes in Mexico City. Later illustrator for *Vanity Fair* in New York. Visited Mabel in Taos in 1930.

Dasburg, Andrew (1887–   ). Painter, born in Paris. Studied at Art Students' League, New York, with Kenyon Cox; also with Robert Henri at New York School of Arts. Exhibited in famous First Armory Show in New York

(1913). Guggenheim Fellowship, 1932, 1960. Honorary Doctor of Fine Arts, University of New Mexico. Friend of Mrs. Luhan in New York. Painted the *Absence of Mabel Dodge*. Marsden Hartley said of Dasburg: "He has pushed himself into his own high place of the mind, and I know he will stay there." Luhan, *Movers and Shakers*, p. 250. Dasburg still paints the landscape around Taos. Friend of the author.

de Angulo, Jaime (1887–1950). Born in Paris. Received an M.D. from Johns Hopkins. Served in Medical Corps, World War I. Was once an overseer of a convict camp in Honduras. A brilliant eccentric Lawrence did not care to understand. A linguist in Indian languages; equally at home in Spanish, French and English. He was always entertaining. His *Indian Tales* (Wynn, 1953) has become a modern classic. Friend of the author.

Dunn, John (1857–1954). Early pioneer. Stage driver from Taos to Taos Junction. Friend of the author.

Dunton, Herbert (1878–1936). An illustrator of the old West. Came to Taos in 1912. Original member of Taos Society of Artists organized in the home of Dr. T. P. Martin in 1912. Dunton showed annually in all important national exhibitions. Also invited to exhibit in the Bi-Centennial in Venice.

Evans, John Ganson (1902–   ). Novelist, government administrator, son of Mabel Luhan. Student at Yale, 1920–21. Married Alice Henderson, 1922. In 1933 married novelist Claire Spencer. Foreign correspondent in Portugal, Spain, France for Newsweek, Inc., 1941. Acting chief of the Alaskan Branch, Division of Territories and Island Possessions, Dept. of Interior, 1943–44, General Superintendent of Indian Service, Albuquerque, N.M., 1944–46. Director of Rural Improvement, Iran—U.S., Tehran, 1952. Chief, Egypt—Jordan Division, Foreign Operations Administration, 1953. Also many other government assignments. Friend of the author.

Fechin, Nicolai (1881–1955). Painter, born in Kazan, Russia; of Tartar ancestry. Studied at Imperial Academy of Fine Arts at St. Petersburg. First Prize, Imperial Academy of Fine Arts, St. Petersburg, 1908. Gold Medal, International Glass Palace, Munich, 1909. Studied under the famous Ilya Repin. During the Bolshevik revolution Fechin hid with his wife and daughter Eya in the forests along the Volga for several years. Eventually Mabel Luhan invited Fechin to Taos. Fechin was one of the great colorists of our time, a master craftsman and portrait painter. Willa Cather selected Fechin of all others to do her portrait. Fechin was a silent, contemplative man. The author once spent an hour trying to get Fechin to talk. He merely sank deeper into his Asiatic-Russian self. I then mentioned Dostoievski. His eyes lightened: *"You* know Dostoievski?" Fechin lived only in Russia no matter where he happened to be in the world.

Foster, Margaret Hale (1891–1962). Wife of the author.

Gaspard, Leon (1882–1964). Born in Vitebsk, Russia. Studied at Odessa and Moscow. Friend of Chagall in Russia. Went to Paris at the turn of the century where he was part of the Bohemian life. Friend of Renoir, Proust, Degas, Monet, Modigliani, Pascin, Matisse and Utrillo. He also knew the writers Verlaine and Maeterlinck, the poet Apollinaire and the composers Puccini and Massenet. He knew Rodin and once shared a studio with the pianist Gabrilowitsch. He also shared a studio with Nijinsky, the star of Diaghilev's famous Russian dance troup. Gaspard and Nijinsky sat up playing chess all night. In spite of Gaspard's extraordinary talent and background he was rejected by the Taos artists—which is a comment on *them* not him. Lawrence knew Gaspard and admired him. They were both Europeans and could understand each other. "I can think of no one who paints forests as you do, Leon," said Lawrence. "Yes, you know an entanglement of trees!" Mabel Luhan was Gaspard's friend for life. Gaspard was Taos' greatest painter. Friend of the author.

Gillett, Barbara Hawk, younger daughter of Mr. and Mrs. A. D. Hawk, owners of the Del Monte Ranch. Now Mrs. Joseph DuBarry and lives in Granada, Spain. Friend of the author.

Götzsche, Kai (1886–   ). Danish painter, born in Aarhus, Denmark. Studied in the Royal Academy of Fine Arts, Copenhagen, 1908–12, with Knud Merrild. Shared life with Lawrences at Del Monte Ranch, winter of 1922–23. In 1923 Götzsche traveled down the west coast of Mexico to Guadalajara with Lawrence. His letters to Knud Merrild concerning Lawrence are included in Merrild's *With D. H. Lawrence in New Mexico*. Lives with his wife Esther Anderson in Denmark.

Hale, Swinburne (1884–1937). Poet, lawyer. Graduated from Harvard, 1905. Twice editor of Harvard *Advocate*. Husband of Beatrice Forbes-Robertson of England. Friend of Frieda Lawrence during the summer of 1924. Brother of Margaret Hale Foster.

Hale, Professor William Gardner (1849–1928). Co-founder, with Dr. William Rainey Harper, of the University of Chicago. Professor Hale was considered the foremost Latin scholar of his time. Father of Swinburne Hale and Margaret Hale Foster.

Hawk, William, son of Mr. and Mrs. A. D. Hawk, owners of the Del Monte Ranch. Husband of Rachel. Rachel and Bill Hawk still live on the Del Monte Ranch where Frieda and Lawrence stayed with them the winter of 1922–23. Friends of the author.

Henderson, William Penhallow (1877–1943). Santa Fe artist. Friend of Mabel Luhan. Father-in-law of John Evans.

Higgins, Sara (1901–   ). Former wife of Victor Higgins. Now Mrs. Robert Mack of Santa Fe, N.M. Friend of Lawrence, 1922–25. Friend of the author.

Higgins, Victor (1884–1949). Taos painter. National Academician. Awards: First Altman Prize (for figure), National Academy of Design, 1918. First Altman Prize (for landscape), National Academy of Design, 1927. First Altman Prize, National Academy of Design, 1932. Lawrence called on the Higginses frequently but Higgins was embarrassed and could not speak in Lawrence's presence. Lawrence referred to Higgins as "—a lost soul." He was in reality very famous in America as an artist. Friend of the author.

Jeffers, Robinson (1887–1962). American poet. His works stress modern man's alienation from nature. Wrote *Tamar and other Poems*, adapted *Medea* for the stage. It was to Robinson Jeffers that Mabel Luhan addressed her book *Lorenzo in Taos*. Visited Mabel in Taos.

Johnson, Willard [Spud] (1897–1968). Journalist. Friend of Lawrence, Frieda, Dorothy Brett and Witter Bynner. Secretary to Mabel Luhan. Onetime editor of *El Crepusculo*, Taos newspaper. Also on staff of *The New Yorker*. Printed the famous Lawrence criticism of Ben Hecht's book *Fantazius Mallare* in his little magazine *Laughing Horse*. Johnson's remains were donated to the University of New Mexico School of Medicine. Friend of the author.

Joyce, James (1882–1941). Irish novelist born in Dublin. A major figure of world literature, he wrote *Ulysses* (1922, banned in U.S. for indecency). His labyrinthine prose explores many levels of both conscious and unconscious meaning, and employs many linguistic neologies and many-faceted images. A brilliant virtuoso who saw man humorously, a pathetic, fragmented being at the mercy of the trivia of his mind. Joyce's dark world of the subconscious (*Night Town*) has less depth than Lawrence's insistence on life itself as the only reality. Joyce is a poetic psychologist, whereas Lawrence is a metaphysician who believes the eternal fires of the universe have burned out in man, passed on—leaving man forsaken, waiting for a resurrection that perhaps will never come to us but rather to some other form of life on earth. Lawrence and Joyce were intolerant of one another's work.

Lawrence, David Herbert (1885–1930). Born in Eastwood, Nottinghamshire, on September 11, and died March 2 at the Villa Robermond, Vence, Alpes-Maritimes, France. His ashes were later taken to the Lawrence Ranch in Taos, N.M.

Luhan, Antonio (?–1963). Indian husband of Mabel Luhan.

Luhan, Mabel Dodge (1879–1962). Patroness of the arts. Author of *Lorenzo in Taos, Winter in Taos, Movers and Shakers* and other books. Her writing reflects her remarkable insight into people's character. A controversial yet dynamic personality, Mrs. Luhan had one of the most powerful desires for life ever known, but it remained imprisoned within the walls of her negativity. Brought Lawrence to Taos.

Marin, John (1870–1927). American landscape painter. A supreme water-colorist. One of Alfred Stieglitz's discoveries. Visited Mabel Luhan in Taos and lived in her two-story house across the alfalfa field. Like Georgia O'Keeffe, Marin prefered a people-less world. The desert landscape of the Southwest awed him: "My God! My God! That such a place exists," he cried. "It engulfs you. . . . It's the best possible place to come alive. . . . You've got an intangible world out here. What opposes what? . . . Space—

it's unbounded. How do you paint the drama of space? . . . And that sky—it's a blank empty wall—the most powerful emptiness I've ever known. . . . I'd like to paint lots of deserts. Go down in my guts and haul up light. Oh, to be bold."

Martin, Dr. T. P. (1864–1935). Dr. Martin was the first practicing physician in Taos. He was almost a legendary figure. He arrived in the village of Taos in 1890 after graduating from the College of Physicians and Surgeons of Baltimore in 1887. The primitiveness of Taos in the 1890s cannot be imagined today. Dr. Martin often used Indian guides to lead him to remote villages in the mountains. A doctor could do very little in those days. Pneumonia and appendicitis were always fatal. The only preventative against infection from an ax wound in the leg or a sore throat was to swab generously with iodine. Martin covered almost 500 square miles including Peñasco, Costilla, and Questa and the Picuris and Taos Pueblos. It was an insurmountable task. He went everywhere by horse and buggy. Strangely enough he wore a short, tan, opera coat in winter. When calls came from across the Rio Grande, he would drive down to Pilar on the river (15 miles). Then he would climb into a dugout canoe and paddle across the river and walk to the home of his patient. Often he was paid in produce—chickens, vegetables, livestock. Often he received no pay. Such a pioneer life resulted in a gruff, rugged man. Dr. Martin was the author's family doctor for ten years. He treated the author's wife, daughter and the author himself during that time. He was truly a horse-and-buggy doctor. Later he drove a touring car rather jerkily and always in "second." He was a very weary, garrulous man and talked exactly as the author has characterized him. He was fascinated by Mabel Luhan; he talked of her everytime you met him. He was an entertaining gossip. This was the doctor who came up the

above: Lawrence and cat on ranch porch
below: The three women—Mabel, Frieda, the Brett

Ranch kitchen

mountain in the summer of 1923 to examine D. H. Lawrence's chest.

Merrild, Knud (1894–1954). Painter, born in Odum, Denmark. Studied in the Royal Academy of Fine Arts, Copenhagen. Came to New York in 1921. With Kai Götzsche, shared life with the Lawrences at Del Monte Ranch winter of 1922–23. Exhibited widely in Europe and America. Settled in Los Angeles in 1923. Author of *A Poet and Two Painters: A Memoir of D. H. Lawrence*. The title was later changed to *With D. H. Lawrence in New Mexico*. Friend of Henry Miller.

Meyers, Ralph (1885–1948). Taos artist, writer. A profound and sensitive man. Friend of Lawrence, Mabel Luhan and all the early artists. Meyers experienced the meaning of Taos—its beauty, its spiritual importance —more deeply than any of us. In his time he was the only white man respected by the Indians. It was to Ralph Meyers that Lawrence's famous Pips was entrusted when Lawrence left Taos in 1923. Mrs. Rowena Martinez in a letter to the author said of her late husband: "I do remember Ralph saying that Lawrence really didn't care much for women; he felt he [Lawrence] really liked men better." Friend of the author.

Mozely, Loren. Friend of Mabel Luhan and Spud Johnson in the '20s. Now professor of Art at the University of Texas. Onetime friend of the author.

Murry, John Middleton (1889–1957). English author, editor, critic. Husband of Katherine Mansfield. Met Lawrence in London, 1913. Witness at Lawrence and Frieda's marriage (13 July 1914). Editor of *Westminster Gazette, Adelphi, Athenaeum*. Educated at Oxford. Lifelong stormy friendship with Lawrence—full of hatred. Twenty-five years after Lawrence's death, Frieda wrote to Murry:

"There was a real bond between you and L. . . . he wanted so desperately for you to understand him. I think the homosexuality in him was a short phase out of misery— I fought him and won. . . . Maybe after all L.'s hatred was love." Frieda Lawrence to J. M. Murry, from El Prado, New Mexico, 6 August, 1953. Tedlock, *Frieda Lawrence: The Memoirs and Correspondence* p. 360.

O'Keeffe, Georgia (*Mrs. Alfred Stieglitz*) (1887–   ). Nationally famous artist, born in Sun Prairie, Wis. Honorary Doctor of Fine Arts, William and Mary College, 1938. Honorary Doctor of Letters, University of Wisconsin, 1942. Visited Mabel Luhan in Taos, but wisely took herself across the river to the Penitente town of Abiquiu. Like Lawrence, Miss O'Keeffe believed the last reality was in aloneness. She has progressed from absolute non-objectivity to the absolving grace of man-less, God-less landscapes. "My pleasant disposition likes the world with no one in it." Miss O'Keeffe has an immaculate eye—but the philosophic meaning in her canvases is illusory—still missing, in fact. Onetime friend of the author.

Phillips, Bert Greer (1868–1956). Artist. Came to Taos in 1898 with Ernest L. Blumenschein in a wagon. It was an unforgettable experience for them both—Taos seventy-three years ago. Friend of the author.

Quintanilla, Dr. Luis (1900–   ). Mexican poet and diplomat, born in Paris. Educated in the Sorbonne. Ambassador to the Soviet Union, 1943–45. In spite of their quarrel, Dr. Quintanilla said of Lawrence: "Perhaps the outstanding feature of D. H. was, besides his genius, his kindness of heart and his absolute modesty. His physical aspect was that of a monk: tall, slender, of pale complexion, auburn hair and clear blue eyes; with a delicate head bent forward as if in constant meditation. He always spoke softly, rather timidly." Dr. Quintanilla was present at Lawrence's bedside in Mexico City when Dr. Uhlfelder told Frieda that Lawrence had an advanced case of tuberculosis. Nehls, *D. H. Lawrence: A Composite Biography*, pp. 368, 396.

Rauh, Ida (1878–1970). Actress. Wife of Max Eastman, writer; and later of Andrew Dasburg, artist. Knew Lawrence in Taos, 1922–25. Also with Frieda when Lawrence died in Vence in 1930. Mabel Luhan said of Ida: "—noble looking, like a lioness." *Movers and Shakers*, p. 199. Friend of the author.

Ravagli, Mrs. Frieda Lawrence (1879–1956). Second daughter of Baron and Baronin Friedrich von Richthofen of Germany. Married Ernest Weekley, 1899. Married D. H. Lawrence, 1914. Married Captain Angelino Ravagli, 1950. Buried at the Lawrence Ranch. Wrote *"Not I, But the Wind . . ."* after Lawrence's death.

Russell, Bertrand, O.M., 3rd Earl (1872–1970). English mathematician and philosopher, an academic firebrand. Fellow of Trinity College, Cambridge (to 1916); dismissed because of pacifist beliefs and opposition to World War I. Sentenced to six months in prison for article called "The Tribunal." Russell and Lawrence were at first great friends. But they quarreled bitterly. After Lawrence died Russell attacked him and called him a Fascist. To which Frieda replied: "As for calling Lawrence an exponent of Nazism, that is pure nonsense. You might as well call St. Augustine a Nazi."

Secker, Martin (1882–   ). Lawrence's English publisher from 1921–30. Secker refused to publish *Lady Chatterly's Lover*. Later Lawrence was published in England by Heinemann.

Seltzer, Thomas (1873–1943). Lawrence's chief American publisher in the 1920s. Visited Lawrence at the Del Monte Ranch in December 1922. Although Seltzer subsequently went bankrupt he always thought of Lawrence as "the greatest living writer."

Sharp, Joseph Henry (1859–1953). Artist. First visit to Taos, 1883. In Paris in 1895 he met Phillips and Blumenschein. He spoke to them with great enthusiasm about the mountains and the Indians of Taos. Out of this chance meeting of three American artists the Taos Art Colony was born. Mr. Sharp always used to greet the author with the words, "Welcome, stranger."

Steffens, Lincoln (1866–1936). American editor and author. Managing editor of *McClure's* when Willa Cather was discovered. Counselor of Mabel Luhan. She says of him: "He had invented 'muckraking' and had gone from city to city cleaning up politics. . . . He was a delicately built little man . . . with rapier-keen mind." *Movers and Shakers*, p. 66.

Stein, Gertrude (1874–1946). American author of *The Autobiography of Alice B. Toklas* and other books. Through her salon in Paris she influenced many artists and writers including Picasso and Hemingway. Her style is notable for repetitions. "A rose is a rose is a rose." Warm friend of Mabel Luhan.

Stone, Mrs. Idella, née Purnell (1901–   ). Born in Guadalajara. Editor of famed little magazine *Palms*, to which Lawrence contributed. Knew Lawrence in Guadalajara and Lake Chapala, 1923.

Thompson, Clarence. Protégé of Mabel Luhan. Knew Lawrence in Taos summer of 1924, but later they quarreled. Thompson was a graduate of Harvard and later a screen writer. Lawrence bore him no ill will. From Oaxaca he wrote, "In me there is no change, and never will be: only surface adaptations." D.H.L. to Clarence Thompson, from Hotel Francia, Oaxaca, 17 November

1924. Moore, *Collected Letters*, p. 820. Onetime friend of the author.

Toomer, Jean (1894–1967). American poet. Perhaps the first Negro literary figure to realize the plight of his people in America. Author of *Cane*, a classic novel of Negro life. Gave a lecture on Gurdjieff (a Middle East mystic) in Mabel Luhan's drawing room in the '20s. Tony Luhan was very jealous of Mabel's attraction to Toomer. Of Gurdjieff's philosophy, Tony said, "It is without foundation." Friend of the author.

Ufer, Walter (1876–1936). Early Taos painter. Studied at National Academy in Dresden. Represented in major museums throughout America. Elected to National Academy of Design in 1926. Friend of the Lawrences, 1922–23. Friend of "the Danes." Introduced D. H. Lawrence to the author.

Weston, Edward (1886–1958). Perhaps America's most famous photographer. From Weston's diary: "The sitting of Lawrence this morning. A tall, slender, rather reserved individual, with reddish beard. He was amiable enough and we parted in a friendly way, but the contact was too brief to penetrate another more than superficially . . . now I lack sufficient interest in developing films." Nehls, *D. H. Lawrence: A Composite Biography*, p. 370.

D. H. LAWRENCE IN TAOS

1

LAWRENCE CAME TO TAOS THAT YEAR.

Mabel thought it was her doing. Mabel was Mabel Dodge Luhan—the millionairess from Buffalo, patroness of the arts, a Head Hunter.

"I sent him a powerful letter. I used a lot of willing on him."

The letter was several feet long—and done up like a roll of papyrus. She also sent Frieda an Indian necklace she thought carried some Indian magic and would draw Lawrence to Taos.

Lawrence was in India. He had cut himself loose from his moorings. England had burned his books, repudiated him. Consigned him to that same oblivion it reserves for all its great—Keats, Blake, Shelley, Byron.

He had become a spiritual nomad. He had to get out of Europe. Europe was always a special anguish of love and hate to Lawrence. He was always at the end of his tether in Europe.

He wanted to go away from England forever. "I want to

go to a country of which I have hope, in which I feel the new unknown . . . in short I want to transfer all my life to America."

To Mabel Dodge Luhan he wrote, "Truly I would like to come to Taos. I want to leave Europe. I want to take the next step. Shall it be Taos?"

Taos was one of the famous lost cities of the world. After languishing 1000 years in the forgetfulness of history Taos was rediscovered by two wandering artists at the turn of the century. It was buried high in the Rocky Mountains of New Mexico. A place of unspeakable grandeur.

Lawrence wrote of New Mexico, "It was the greatest experience of the outside world I ever had. It certainly changed me forever."

The strangest, most wonderful thing about Taos, the most enduring, are the Indians. The Indians claimed the valley as far back as the twelfth century. A straggling tribe of scarce two hundred crossed the Rio Grande in A.D. 1200 and built two brown-terraced pyramids to live in under Taos Mountain. They were windowless, stepped-back apartment houses of mud. The Taos Pueblo Indians are a miracle of survival. Kings and Queens cross the ocean to see these prehistoric people who live as primitively today in their mud Pueblo as they did 800 years ago.

The spirit of Taos is Indian.

As soon as you are near Taos Mountain you will see Indians everywhere on their frisky little horses, or small wide-faced warriors hoeing corn in the fields.

Here and there are summer brush-huts of the Indians.

4

There are patios filled with piles of yellow corn, and women in tight-waisted black skirts stringing red chili and men seriously skinning the bloody carcasses of sheep. Green farm wagons of Indians pass you on the road to the Pueblo, whole families of smiling Indians squatting in their orange-wheeled wagons singing as they go back to the Pueblo along the dusty road.

Ai Yo Ai Yo Aiiii Yo

The men are all singing in their strange Chinese falsetto, happy their beautiful soft-voiced women were with them and they were all on their way back to the Pueblo.

"To the Indian the Universe and Song are one," Margaret once told me.

Everyone in Europe is intrigued by the Red Indian. They still think of him as naked and warlike.

Lawrence too was drawn to the Indians in Taos: "I also believe in the Indians.... I do hope I shall get from [them] something which this wearily external white world cannot give.

"We are so keen on coming.... I build a lot on the Pueblo. I shall be so glad if I can write a novel from that center [The Indians']."

Taos, still ancient, unspoiled, lost, was seventy miles north of Santa Fe. When Mabel "discovered" it in 1917 she immediately set about building an enormous adobe hacienda at the edge of town—and sought happiness in extremism, fanciful behavior. She took an Indian lover, Tony Luhan.

Mabel was to make Taos famous throughout the world.

But Lawrence, although he was drawn to Mabel, her wealth, her daring, could not go West to America. He must first go *East* to India.

5

Mabel was annoyed. "This silly detour to India. You see how he follows his impulses."

But once in India—! He drew back. He didn't like India. "One sees a darkness, and through the darkness the days before the Flood, marshy with elephants mud-grey, and buffaloes rising from the mud and soft boned voluptuous sort of people, like plants under water, stirring in myriads."

He was overwhelmed with the heat. "I don't feel at all myself." He could not relate to India.

"We made a mistake forsaking England.

"I really think the most living clue to life is in us Englishmen in England.

"So I am making up my mind to return to England."

He would give up going to America: "America exhausts the springs of one's soul," he decided without ever having seen it.

And yet there was a check in the mail for $1000 from Mr. Hearst for *Captain's Doll*.

"If America will accept me and England won't I belong to America."

There was also a letter from Mabel Dodge at Thirroul, New South Wales, "willing" him to come.

But he put her off. "I have started a novel [*Kangaroo*]. It's a funny sort of novel where nothing happens and such a lot of things *should* happen. Scene Australia. I shall stay till I've finished it—till about the end of August."

So they weren't coming yet. Mabel was enraged. She became adamant. She'd sit in Taos until he came. She'd go down inside herself and call Lawrence until he *had* to come.

Lawrence wrote again, "Am stuck with my novel. Gone at it full tilt to page 305, but it has come to a stop and kicks."

6

Mabel waited. She was almost evil in her power to wait. But then perhaps it was *strength*. All of Mabel's traits depended upon how you looked at them. She confounded everyone—even Lawrence. She created and she destroyed. But you were never certain which mood was in the ascendancy. She defied analysis—even her own. Hutchins Hapgood said of her, "There was no mental form to her surging and changing inner existence."

Lawrence said of her, "You were born without any center—only a vortex of an ego."

Yet Mabel was very nice. She charmed everyone. Her silence made you defer to her. They were *knowing* silences. They affirmed the deepest thing in you. You *wanted* to be near Mabel.

Lincoln Steffens said to her, "You have a certain faculty. It's a centralizing, magnetic, social faculty. You attract, stimulate, and soothe people. And men like to sit with you and talk. You make men think more fervently and they feel enhanced."

Still no one liked Mabel. What she gave she would eventually take away. Even fine experiences became tiresome. Yet though she was bored by everything she was also excited by everything. It was a strange paradox—her boredom, her ebullience that transformed her into something inspiring. Yes, she surged with life—yet was tired to death with her own.

She was intensely unhappy. It was her essential reality. She could not relate herself to anything. She sought violently, evilly, humbly, excitingly to relate to a deeper, finer thing in life than that of which she was capable. And she failed—utterly. Even her relationship with Tony was a failure. Tony's religious world excited her. She wanted to

7

get into it. But fortunately for Tony she could not.

Perhaps Lawrence's role for her would have been the best: "Eve who is voiceless like the serpent—yet communicates."

Mabel was tremendously wealthy. She had a salon at 23 Fifth Avenue in New York. She wrote, she painted (badly), she shocked society with her strange affairs.

She had known the most famous people of her time. Eugene O'Neill; Robinson Jeffers, the misanthrope from Carmel-by-the-Sea; Marsden Hartley; John Marin; Isadora Duncan, the erotomaniac, whose dances were extravaganzas of release; Jean Toomer, the Negro poet; Arthur Brisbane, the great editorialist of yellow journalism in the twenties; John Reed, her lover, the revolutionary who wrote *Ten Days That Shook the World* and is buried within the walls of the Kremlin; Willa Cather, famous, dull, self-important; Georgia O'Keeffe, painter of bleached bones in the desert and macrocosmic genitalia disguised as red fuchsia; Max Eastman, the Leftist, and his wife, Ida Rauh; Edward Arlington Robinson, a great poet, retiring, civilized, finest of all Mabel's friends.

Mabel knew Eleanor Duse, also Leopold Stokowski; Dr. A. A. Brill, Sinclair Lewis, John Galsworthy, Lillian Gish, Thornton Wilder, and Gertrude Stein who was to write "Portrait of Mabel Dodge; at the Villa Curonia."

Mabel also knew Gordon Craig, the English stage designer, Henri Bergson, the French philosopher, Jo Davidson, the sculptor, Emma Goldman, the anarchist, Walter Lippmann, the columnist, Margaret Sanger, a madonna type of woman who advocated birth control, Boardman Robinson, the painter, and Alfred Stieglitz, who opened the famous gallery "291" and introduced Cézanne and Picasso to America in 1905. Mabel knew everyone of intellectual or creative importance on both sides of the Atlantic.

Many of these celebrities were to visit Mabel in Taos—including Thomas Wolfe, who cursed her from the bottom of the staircase at midnight because she did not await his drunken arrival.

Her greatest desire was to add D. H. Lawrence to her list of conquests.

The town of Taos knew Lawrence was coming. He was a celebrity, the most widely discussed novelist in the world. Few of the Taos artists read books but they all wanted to meet Lawrence. Mabel, however, intended to keep him to herself.

All that summer we waited.

"Do you think we'll ever be able to meet him?" I asked my wife, Margaret.

"There will be a way," said Margaret. "We'll meet him somehow."

II

MARGARET AND I LIVED ON A RUINED old ranch near Taos. The ranch was a failure—but not our love. Margaret saw to that. We were happy.

Four miles away under the mountains was Taos—just a little adobe town. Indians, Mexicans, artists—

We lived alone—Margaret and I. It was a frontier life—austere, frightening. The hardships in winter unbearable. But our lives were dominated by the beauty around us. The sky was so vast, the mountains so everlasting. And Margaret the heroine of it all.

Our small adobe house was lost in the sage.

I liked the dimly lighted peasant kitchen at night, the thick walls, the soft white-earthen floor, the sweet-smelling cedar crackling in the old-fashioned wood stove. Outside there was the ancient moonlight—and the resounding silence of the desert. I could even smell the sage through the open door.

"It's so strange here," I would say to Margaret. "Bygone. I feel I'm looking back."

"Isn't it wonderful?" she would agree.

"But what is it about Taos that makes it so wonderful?"

"Well, we're isolated. And everything is true here. The nonsense of the world has not crept in."

We had both fled the world to live in this beautiful nowhere. I had been working on a newspaper back East, a boy wonder—writing editorials for William Randolph Hearst who owned the largest string of newspapers in the world—and great things were expected of me.

But suddenly I wanted to write. It became an overpowering resolution, this desire to write, and I gave up a brilliant career and came West.

Margaret and I had met by accident and fallen in love. And our reality was forever.

Margaret Hale had been brought up in London, Paris, Rome. Her father was co-founder of the University of Chicago and head of the Classical School of Rome. But after Europe, Margaret's vitality, her maturity, had been wasted in thoughtless America. She had rebelled and came to Taos.

How I was drawn to Margaret. Every moment we were together was an intoxication. We were entranced with each other—our minds, our bodies.

We had worlds and worlds to talk about: Literature, Life, People—the beautiful woman of thirty and the shy young man scarcely out of his teens.

In summer Margaret and I would stand outside in the moonlight against the mud wall and look at the moon-flooded valley. The slopes of the mountains were as white as day. Below us were the green fields in the moonlight, the wandering narrow strips of yellowing wheat that had been cultivated since the year 1200 by the prehistoric Indians. The darkened mud houses of the Mexicans. The silver haystacks, the staggering silver fences. The phantom trees blooming whitely in the cold summer night.

"Everything out here—the scene itself—forces itself upon you," I said.

"Yes," she said. "The beauty of it. It's so powerful—it rouses you."

I saw the small timid lights in all the adobe houses around us in the sage, like little boats tossing far off on a sea of darkness. We were alone in this foreign land.

"It's so silent," I said.

"Yes. Silence is a sort of luxury in the world today. A lost beatitude. We have so much of it," she said, nodding toward the moon-frosted mountains on our left. "Those are the Sangre de Cristos."

But I was in agony. "I feel as though the pins had

been knocked out from under me," I confessed.

"But were they very good pins?" she asked. "A job, Mr. Hearst, the Loop, Chicago, meaningless drive—where? You weren't happy. You wanted to write."

We stood another long time in the silence looking at the white undulating desert in the moonlight.

The next afternoon we rode in to Taos.

I went out to the large alfalfa field to catch the horses. But I was not a very good ranch hand. It took two hours to catch the two strawberry roans and lead them back to the ranch house.

"Oh, that's wonderful that you caught them." Margaret had changed to brown suede riding breeches, black boots, a blue velvet smock, and a huge Navajo silver belt. Her face was radiant. Her large eyes inquiring, intelligent. She was tall. There was a splendor to her body. Classic. She wore a white bandeau against her sun-blackened forehead. She had a striking Greek profile, a beautiful smile.

Almost as soon as we were in the sage the horses started to gallop toward Taos. There were no fences between the ranch and Taos in those days. Just the level desert of sage rising gently toward the sharp mountains, and over it all the blue transcendent sky. It was a bottom-of-the sea world —cracked crookedly here and there with dry red arroyos.

I saw how happy she was, a joyful part of this world we were galloping across. I turned in my saddle and looked toward the West at the undulating horizon of volcanic lava forty miles away.

"The distance—?" I said vaguely.

12

"Yes, isn't it beautiful—? Just space."

"It's so intense."

"And so beyond knowing."

The West!

The eternalness of the scene invaded you, the cloud shadows on the mountains, the everlasting silence of the afternoons, the far lonely horizons, the abyss of black beauty the whole round world dropped into each night.

The West wasn't mysterious. It was clear, finished, great. Dawn made it great—the far red mesas. Man could not impose his stupidities upon its grandeur. Each dawn was a pale genesis. Each nightfall the last day of the world.

The West!

We trotted through the plaza of Taos. There were horses tied all around the square. And Indians in white, lounging against the adobe walls. And Mexicans—*politicos*—talking excitedly before the courthouse. There were a lot of shabby adobe trading posts with ponies tied outside. The bank looked old and grey, waiting for a holdup in a William S. Hart Western. There were no cars. Taos—fifty years ago.

"Mabel gave them the bandstand," Margaret said as we trotted round the square.

I could not keep my eyes off the great quartz-glinting mountains above the ramshackle roofs of the town.

"Don't you love it!" Margaret cried. "It's sort of a run-down paradox in the middle of the desert's grandeur. But it's really the West! Those chili restaurants. The ranchers and the cowboys. The Mexican barbers. And the saloons. It has the elemental harshness of the West."

We tied our horses at the rail and went under the arcades and joined the crowds. There were Indians everywhere coming toward us—in white and whiter sheets—laughing, laughing, chattering to themselves in their strange Chinese-like language. There were lovely Indian girls in blue coming out of the stores with their purple shawls arranged madonna-like about their soft flat faces. I was drawn to the wonderfulness of the afternoon, of life, with Margaret—to the golden summer crowds of Mexicans and Indians milling about the plaza, going in and out of the trading posts, the bakery, the butcher's, the guitar-tinkling tavern. Everywhere Margaret's Indian friends were laughing their happy Indian laughs. And above it all the rose-breasted peak of the Pueblo mountain.

Toward evening we rode again through the sage toward the ranch, the vast sunset towering above us, yellowing the desert—a low alluvial flow of gold.

When we got back to the ranch the horizon was one vast stratum of luminous yellow. The summer night was sharp.

I unsaddled the horses and turned them loose. I got the old lantern and went out to the corrals and did the chores. I threw a dozen forkfuls of alfalfa to the horses. The stack was getting low. It wouldn't last much longer. I came back and chopped some wood and took several armfuls to her in the dim kitchen.

She was making supper.

"Beets," she said, "and bacon."

And she had had time to make some baking powder biscuits. The table was neatly set in that little ranch kitchen —fifty years ago.

"Sit next to me," I begged.

Her face was striking, sensitive, her being constant. Margaret was unbelievable—her strength, her gentleness, her high-mindedness.

We washed the dishes in silence. She handed each large plate to me and smiled. "You are *so* emotional. You are always being moved."

"But why?" I asked.

"Perhaps it's Taos. There's something deeper here—an invisible fire."

She took the dishpan of water and flung it through the doorway into the sage. She hung the dish cloth up to dry.

"Shall we look at the stars awhile?"

We went outside.

The air was sharp. The new moon, an enormous orange arc balanced delicately for the last moment on the western horizon.

We leaned against the adobe wall of the house and looked at the stars—Venus, Arcturus, the Pleiades, Orion. They were her stars, their beauty in the black void gleamed for her alone. I worshipped her. I wanted to cry out at the unavailingness of everything. All beauty, all life, all urge was futile.

But she was looking at the stars.

The arc of the moon lowered itself slowly below the horizon. Only the greatness of the universe was left.

But there was only one thing in our life beside the urgency of our love: I wanted to write. I had a powerful desire to be drawn into the maelstrom of literature. Each morning I would go to my tent under the locust tree, sit down, and look at the yellow leaves of copy paper Margaret had given me. After gazing five hours at the blank pages and without writing a single word I would go back to the kitchen.

Margaret was drinking tea. She sat in the swing seat in a yellow corduroy dress and silver belt waiting for me.

"I can't do it," I cried, flinging myself down beside her.

"Of course, you can."

"But why, why can't I—?"

"Because you're *thinking*—and not writing."

"Oh—?"

"Writing is not thinking. Writing is *writing*. It's a special talent. Everyone thinks. *I* think. But I cannot write."

"Nor can I."

"You were made to write. Stop thinking. *Write*."

Margaret was sensitive to these first efforts. She was patient with my failure. She was beyond discouragement. She saw the nobility of our effort and accepted defeat all along the way—strangely, as a kind of reward.

III

THE FIRST TIME I SAW MABEL was the summer before Lawrence came to Taos.

It was June, and Mabel and Tony had galloped up to the ranch on two magnificent horses. They must have come very fast across the sage, the four miles from Taos, for Mabel's horse was covered with white lather—reeking with sweat.

"She crazy," said Tony. "Gallop all the way." Tony was young and strong and savage as he sat on his big black horse.

"Of course!" Didn't a queen gallop?

16

She had the strangest costume. I couldn't quite make it out. Veils and veils. Isadora Duncan on horseback.

She clutched an enormous bouquet of lavender and white sweet peas. She had galloped across the desert with all those flowers in her arms. "For Margaret," she said, slipping from her horse and pressing them to Margaret. Her face was radiant with life, with the day, with Tony. Tony was her new lover—a magnificent young Indian from the Pueblo.

"Oh, thank you," said Margaret, taking them.

Mabel was breathless with delight.

"Won't you come in?" asked Margaret.

"No," said Mabel, "we just came to give you the sweet peas."

I saw her question Margaret, demand of her, her deepest confidence. But Margaret gave no one her confidence—just her beautiful serenity. And Mabel was piqued.

"Tony, get down, we're going to stay awhile."

"No, we go," he insisted. He was as stubborn as she. They were evenly matched. What did she see in him—an Indian? An outlet for her insatiable ardor for life?

Tony tied the sweating horses to the straw-roofed pergola. He wore a dark green shirt and a white sheet twisted sash-like around his strong hips. His black braids were very long and glistened in the sunshine.

They came toward us in the doorway.

"This is Joseph Foster," said Margaret.

"Oh," said Mabel, by way of greeting.

Tony ignored me. I was just a white man.

We went inside and Margaret put the sweet peas in a pail of water. Then she made tea on the old-fashioned wood stove.

17

Mabel was nervous, impatient. She sat in the swing seat beside me, ignoring me, yet furiously one with me.

Tony took up Margaret's big red drum from the floor and sang:

Hi ne ya
Dal tso ho zho ni
All is beautiful, beautiful
Dal tso ho zho ka
All is beautiful
Dal tso ho zho ni
All is beautiful, indeed,
Dal tso ho zho ni
All is beautiful
Ko la ra ne

"Navajo," he said quietly.

Mabel turned to me suddenly. "What makes you so silent!"

She hated me—for no reason. Things, people, should not exist if the queen did not wish them to.

"He just came from the East and the altitude has got him," explained Margaret.

Tony went on singing softly—to Mabel, I'm sure, not to us.

Ahou! Ahou! Ahou!
Your face is strange
And the smell of your garments
But your soul is familiar
As if in dreams we had visited one another
Ahou! Ahou! Ahou!

No one existed in life for him but Mabel. Ah, what a

king was Tony, his strong arms, his graceful shoulders, his impassive beautiful face that knew all our secrets.

Then he turned to me. "You go back," he said.

"I don't know," I said. I didn't know how to talk to an Indian. In the school books no one ever *talked* to an Indian. Just shot at them from behind an overturned wagon. And they fell from their horses—warbonnet and all. I realized I was a little in awe of Tony, of his powerful self-assurance.

"White folks," laughed Tony. "Come in car yesterday. Stays today. Goes tomorrow," and he laughed knowingly.

I was unprepared for such frankness.

"Hello-Goodbye people. White folks," he laughed.

"Maybe not," I said.

"Oh, yes," he said. "You go back. You're afraid out here."

"He's not afraid, Tony," said Margaret. "He's enchanted."

Tony didn't know the word, although he himself led a life of enchantment. To him white people had no feeling.

Mabel turned to me hostilely. "What are you thinking about so much?"

"Well, I—?" The altitude had really got me.

"You're thinking, you're thinking, you're thinking," she said, annoyed. Her blue eyes blazed.

I could not understand such a direct affront. But Mabel always attacked. Upset you.

"Isn't what he is thinking his own affair?" said Margaret. She poured the boiling water in the brown teapot—and smiled.

"Yes, but to think so intensely—it's not good whatever it is he is thinking—and about what?"

19

"Perhaps he is experiencing something new in his own way," said Margaret, still not disturbed.

"Well, *what?*"

It was a terrible situation now. And I did not understand it. Her impatience, her irritation with me. I had said nothing. Yet I had enraged her.

"Come on, Mabel. We go," said Tony. And it was a command.

They had not touched the tea.

Still Mabel was very happy. She had had a fight. Her face was radiant. She was exhilarated.

She started to talk to Margaret. "I wrote him again last night."

"You did!" said Margaret.

"I told him how much I wanted him to come and know this country—before there are roads and it becomes exploited and spoiled. I tried to tell him the simple things. Taos has something wonderful about it—like the dawn of the world."

There was a wonder about her suddenly. A soft deep self that had escaped her own impatience. Her voice was low and cultured. "He is the only one who can *see* Taos, the Indians, who can describe it so that it becomes alive."

"Perhaps," said Margaret.

"He can see and feel and wonder."

"Yes."

"Before I went to sleep I drew myself into my core. I willed him to come. I leaped into space joining myself to the central core of Lawrence. Come, Lawrence! Come to Taos!"

Mabel always talked that way. "If there is anyone living who can give me feeling, meaning, a *heart*, it's Lawrence."

20

"Have you heard from him?" asked Margaret.

"He's in Australia. Another novel! He knows I want him to come."

"Perhaps he will."

"I need a center," confessed Mabel. "I was born without one."

"Goodbye, Margaret," said Tony, giving her his big hand.

"Goodbye, Tony. Don't you want to wait for the tea?"

"We go," he said, but not rudely.

Mabel rose. She knew that when Tony wanted to go, they went.

You were never through having thoughts about Mabel and Tony. They were royalty, or so they thought—each in his own way. Tony knew about the sun and the moon and the earth and the rains and the stars. He knew a certain magic about life, and he assumed you did not. He was very gruff with you—he pitied you. His knowledge ennobled him.

And Mabel? Mabel never knew anything, never experienced anything—and acted as importantly as though she did. It was her tragedy to have been born without feeling, without relatedness, without love.

"Well, goodbye, Margaret. Do you think he will come?" asked Mabel.

"I don't know, Mabel. Goodbye. Thanks for bringing me the sweet peas."

"Come and see me sometime," said Mabel. Her glance did not include me.

"We shall," said Margaret. And she let it be understood once and for all that she and I were in love.

Mabel didn't like it.

"Come on, Mabel," said Tony. He was already outside in the sage and on his horse, waiting. He was always waiting for Mabel, always superior to her, always in love with her. She knew that.

The sun had gone down. Taos peak was a prismatic rose flushing upwards into an outer-space blue.

We watched Mabel try to mount. The huge sweating horse wheeled round and round.

"What's the matter with you?" scolded Tony. He laughed and laughed at Mabel trying to mount her huge, spirited horse. Finally Mabel was in the saddle.

Tony turned to me. "Goodbye, Gringo. Too many stories in your head," pointing to his forehead. "Throw some away and then you'll be happy."

"Goodbye," I said.

Mabel said nothing.

They were already dashing across the sage—Mabel ahead, at a breakneck speed. Tony was holding his horse in so that she appeared the stunning madcap woman she was. They were very much in love that summer long ago.

"Mabel rides like a Valkyrie—and Tony after her."

"Yes," I said.

"She is really a magnificent woman."

I saw how much Margaret was taken with Mabel.

"And, of course, Tony is the handsomest Indian in the Pueblo."

I couldn't understand an Indian and a white woman.

"Mabel and Tony are strangers. Wonderfully strange to one another," Margaret explained. "That's why they're in love. Two separate worlds."

"Does she always attack?"

"She likes to start things. But you handled her beautifully. Oh, look at the sunset!"

The shadows were deep on the summer mountains now. There was a golden dust storm on the mesa opposite. A herd of sheep, no doubt. The purple volcanic peaks on the horizon were a surge of gold.

"Wouldn't it be wonderful if D. H. Lawrence came to Taos?"

"Oh, was that what she was talking about? All this stuff about willing?"

"She has a pretty strong will, Joe."

We talked a great deal about Mabel because everyone did in Taos. People were proud to know her and boasted that she had talked to them.

As a matter of fact Mabel rarely talked. She thought of herself as someone who could influence great men through her silence. She was never seen in the Plaza. If you passed a car with the curtains drawn, it was Mabel. She took the back roads.

The more she withdrew the more fascinating she became. Her legend was so enormous that she could not go anywhere. It prevented her from knowing anyone. It was a lonely house on the hill under the big cottonwoods. The tourist cars circled it daily hoping to get a glimpse of her. But the big carved gates were always closed.

Yet when you met Mabel you were disappointed. She gave nothing. She studied you. Were you or weren't you important? Could you or couldn't you be broken to her needs? But her needs weren't always clear to herself. She was superior to understanding you. She refused to understand anyone. If she couldn't influence you she wasn't interested. In spite of the apathetic female Buddha face there was nothing still about her. She could not be still—yet she would not do things herself. A queen—a very, very unhappy queen.

All her life she was hoping, searching, waiting. She sought and sought and was to know only unhappiness. Perhaps Lawrence would bring her peace.

Margaret and I read everything we could of Lawrence. *Sons and Lovers* became a profound experience for us. *Sons and Lovers* was living. It was devoid of all technique. It was all new—deep, simple, valid. Yet Lawrence used the old methods of writing to say something new. Not like Joyce who thought it necessary to destroy the language to bring a new message. Lawrence was a power speaking from beyond his own human limitations. A prophet.

It was the exquisite intimacy of Lawrence's dialogue—the brooding reality of a character that first moved us.

"How *can* he make dialogue imply so much?" I asked Margaret.

The intense clashes of emotions in Lawrence's novels—a new darkness of understanding—a *living*, beyond the grasp of anyone who had written before him.

It was England, of course, the fields, the farms, the sensitivity, the silent knowledge of life, of the people. Perhaps it was Lawrence—but, no, it was England. Not their brusqueness, their frightened aloofness, but their deeper, gentler forbearance, they themselves were ashamed of.

We read and read, absorbed in the beauty of England, of Lawrence. Never had anyone worded it all so well before—the anguish of the spirit, the tragic ecstasy of man and woman's irreconcilableness. The deeper, deeper unknowns carrying his tide of meaning along effortlessly.

The Rainbow was a new stream of life. The tempestuous unfolding of a new depths of man together with the richness of life, life washing over one darkly in huge waves, sparkling with poetic stars—all new stars.

Lawrence was being violently attacked in the world for his mysticism. They scoffed at his blood-philosophy. "The heart's mysterious resonance . . . the dark powerful source whence all things rise into being. . . ."

The whole world of critics admitted his greatness, but was against him. Margaret and I were angry to hear him belittled. A great new approach to life belittled. The critics seemed intentionally to misunderstand him. They jeered at him, insulted him. He was sexually depraved, they said. Literary England said he was redundant, didn't know how to write. Joyce after reading two pages of *The Rainbow* said it was sloppy writing.

The magistrates suppressed the sale of *The Rainbow*, ordered all existing copies destroyed. His friends began to desert him. All England hated Lawrence. And he fled their fury—to America.

The rumors were thick now in Taos. Lawrence was coming. Mabel had received a letter from San Francisco.

I think we shall leave Thursday—perhaps even Wednesday. I fondly hope. . . . We ought to be with you by Saturday. It all sounds so delightful. *Tante belle cose di noi due.*

                    D. H. Lawrence

I finished *Kangaroo.*

This was September 1922—almost fifty years ago.

Mabel met Lawrence in the old Santa Fe station at Lamy one evening in September of 1922.

It was an embarrassing meeting. Lawrence, fragile, nervous, fussy, giggling. Frieda overexpansive, vociferous.

Tony, the Indian, aloof, unperturbed.

Mabel, stolid—still "willing" the relationship.

Mabel, however, was very astute. In that first moment the two women sized each other up. Mabel realized how powerful was her rival. And, of course, Frieda did the same. Neither woman was a fool.

Lawrence was keyed to Frieda—felt things through her. Although he hated it he must *see* through her. And it irked him.

On the other hand Mabel, even in the stuffy little lunch room in the Santa Fe station in Lamy fifty years ago was already imposing her will on Lawrence, on his mind, his body, his conceptions of life.

"He was through with Frieda," at least so Mabel hoped. "He needs another kind of force to propel him. . . . He was ready to receive from woman" (that is, Mabel).

"I longed to help him—to be used—to be put to his purpose."

26

Margaret Hale Foster
right above: Joseph Foster   below: Swinburne Hale

above: Lawrence as a young man
below: Willard Johnson, Witter Bynner, Lawrence

It was questionable if she felt anything for anyone ever. Lawrence sensed that when he hid behind Frieda's big body at the lunch counter.

Lawrence was really only interested in the beauty of the universe. Man he eternally anathematized. "Oh! Look how the stars hang in the southern sky!" he said when he left the station.

This was the beginning of the awkward drama of Mabel and Lawrence in Mabel's big house on the hill under the cottonwoods in Taos.

Mabel was never to let things "flow" between them. She would not let him be. She wanted to change him. His greatness she never understood. The tremendous thing he had done in creating and ordering a new spiritual universe passed over her completely. She saw only Lawrence's eccentricities—which needed correcting. Eccentricities born of creative fatigue, of the criticism and vituperation of the whole world, and a frail breathless body that weighed scarcely ninety-eight pounds.

This delicate organism she wanted to *do* something to, destroy.

Lawrence liked Taos.

"Taos in its way *is* rather thrilling. . . . It is a tiny place 30 miles from the railway, high up—7000 feet in the desert so one's heart pit-a-pats a bit. We have got a pretty adobe house with furniture made in the village and Mexican and Navajo rugs and some lovely pots. It stands just at the edge of the Indian reservation: in front, the so-called desert, rather like a moor covered with whitish sagebrush, flowering yellow now. Some five miles away the mountains rise . . . on the North the sacred mt. of the Indians, sits massive on the plain . . . toward the foot of the mt. three miles off a big adobe Pueblo, like two great heaps of earthen boxes, cubes. There the Indians all live together. I have already learned to ride one of these Indian ponies, with Mexican saddle. Like it so much. We gallop off to the Pueblo or up one of the canyons. Frieda is learning too. Last night the young Indians came down to dance in the studio with two drums: and we all joined in. It's fun and queer. In the Spring I want to come to England. But I feel England has insulted me . . . *Pero son sempre inglese* [But I am always English]. . . . Perhaps it is my destiny to know the world. The desert has a fascination—to ride alone—in the sun in the forever unpossessed country—away from man."

Of his first impressions of Mabel he wrote: "—so childlike . . . the bright candour of unquenchable youth . . . a seductive serpent of loneliness . . . heavy with the energy like a small bison . . . young looking, the soft crudeness as if she were sixteen . . . feminine."

And so he was intrigued.

But, of course, Mabel insisted that the drama between them should begin.

They would write a book together!

It was for this she had called him from across the world —to give him the truth about America—and herself.

One could never quite understand Lawrence's fascinations for upper-class women. Their wealth, their status? Lady Asquith. Lady Ottoline Morrell—and he, the Nottingham miner's son.

28

And now Mabel Dodge Luhan.

What could she possibly have in common with a man like Lawrence? A book with such a man? One wonders at her crass ignorance, her total blindness to his tremendous genius. That she should intrude her fraudulent mysticism into his world—bother him with her faint merits—her silly reminiscences.

But there was a sexual necessity between Mabel and Lawrence. Almost a conspiracy of which Frieda was well aware. How far the affair went we will not know until the seals of the archives are broken twenty years from her death (1962). Mabel's stipulation.

But a book—! She was thrilled at the thought. And so they started.

Lawrence came across the alfalfa field in the morning ready to begin their work together.

Mabel was taking a sunbath on the long flat roof outside her bedroom. She called him to come up. She quickly put on a long white cashmere thing like a burnous.

Lawrence averted his eyes. The sight of the unmade bed was repulsive to him.

They squatted on the hot earth of the roof—Mabel and Lawrence. All around them was the piñon-covered foothills of Indian land. The sun shone on Lawrence's red beard, made it a flame. He dropped his chin on his chest in gloomy silence.

"I don't know how Frieda is going to feel about this?"

"Well, surely she will understand. . . ."

"Understand! She can't understand anything! It's the German mind. The blonde conquerors . . . strong because it does *not* understand."

29

In that hour, thought Mabel, she and Lawrence became more intimate psychically than she had ever been before with anyone else. "In that first long long talk together he repudiated Frieda."

Ah, but did he? Did he not act out a thousand possibilities of his life—with such sincerity as to throw Mabel off the track?

A great desire to save him surged up in Mabel. She would save him.

Lawrence went downstairs and Mabel stayed to throw on her dress and stockings.

Frieda did not like Lawrence writing a book with Mabel. She did not want it. She had always regarded Lawrence's genius as given to her. She felt deeply responsible for what he wrote.

The next day he went across the fields again to see Mabel. He looked diminished.

"Frieda thinks we ought to work over in our house."

"With her *there*?" asked Mabel. How could she talk to Lawrence and tell him her feelings with Frieda in the room? "If we can't do this book my way, in my house, I won't do it at all."

"Very well," said Lawrence.

Nevertheless, Mabel did go over to the Lawrences in the morning and she and Lawrence sat in a cold room with the doors open and Frieda stamped around, sweeping noisily, and singing in loud defiance. Nothing passed between Lawrence and Mabel.

30

"She is inimical to the spirit," complained Lawrence. He was merely characterizing Frieda not repudiating her.

Mabel thought otherwise. She stormed into the other room and faced Frieda. "He needs something new and different. He's done with you. You have mothered his books long enough. He needs a new mother. You are not the right woman for Lawrence."

Frieda was thoroughly roused. "Try it then yourself, living with a genius, see what it is like and how easy it is. Take him if you can."

And so it was a wonderful fight—on those September days when they were getting to know each other.

IV

EVERYONE IN TAOS WANTED TO MEET Lawrence, especially the artists. Mabel carefully protected him. Mabel herself had a contempt for the early artists. Perhaps she communicated her distaste for Taos artists to Lawrence.

Most of the artists in Taos painted landscapes without any drama in their canvases. The West was dramatic in a subtle, powerful way. The early artists missed the characteristics of the country—a transcendent stillness to the mountains, to the sky. They deadened the beautiful scene they painted. There was an emptiness in everything they did.

Lawrence didn't want to meet them. "Keep us dark—

terribly dark," Frieda had cautioned in a letter to Mabel from Australia.

Few saw him after he arrived in Taos. Rachel and Bill Hawk, of course, from whom Lawrence got milk. Rachel was his favorite.

Walter Ufer, the painter, tried without success to meet Lawrence. Later Lawrence and Ufer became half-friends.

Lawrence knew Gerson Gusdorf, owner of a Taos trading post, from whom Lawrence bought putty and nails. He knew Cummings, the butcher, a sallow-faced man who sold meat at 20 cents a pound—any cut. He saw Trinidad, the sweet young Indian, the best dancer in the Pueblo, who is still alive today.

Sara Higgins, the young wife of Victor Higgins, the painter, knew Lawrence very well. Sara Higgins interested Lawrence very much. Her youth, her intuitions, her magic awareness of life.

Sara and Lawrence took rides together back of Mabel's house in the sage.

"He's simply wonderful," Sara told us. "He talks beautifully—for a whole afternoon. It just pours out of him. He's brilliant. You know him immediately. We have a marvelous *rapport.*" And her eyes shone. Was Lawrence in love with her?

"When you are with Lawrence you are something *more* than yourself instantly," Sara said. "And everything around you comes to life. He points out things in the sage—and the mountains. Lawrence doesn't talk like other people. He brings everything alive around him—and he brings *you* alive. It's wonderful what he does to a person. You feel you are living for the first time. Today we rode for miles across Indian land to the mountains. I saw everything, everything for the first time. It was marvelous to be with him."

The first time I saw Lawrence was on the afternoon of September 30, 1922 at the Indian Pueblo. It was the San Geronimo Fiesta.

Margaret and I were leaning against the wall of the whitewashed church watching Juanito—naked in loincloth —climb the huge slippery pole.

There were crowds and crowds of Mexicans and Indians laughing at the naked chifonete shooting straw arrows at the beribboned dead sheep suspended high on the pole in the rare blue sky.

The terraced Pueblo was crowded with red and blue and yellow costumed throngs. There were buggies, wagons, Mexicans on horses, Navajos, Apaches. One car—Mabel's.

Every so often a shout would go up and the huge circle of people around the pole would break and the wild-eyed clowns would come dashing after some poor Mexican. They would catch him and throw him into the river. The crowd would roar their delight.

Suddenly I saw him with his back to us—not ten feet away. He was laughing with everyone. I saw only his back and that was very stooped, and the huge ten-gallon Stetson worn too far down over his ears. His clothes fitted poorly. The grey suit was too large, too long, and he kept his hands in his pockets.

"That's D. H. Lawrence," I said to Margaret.

We both looked now at the stooped back wedged in the laughing crowds.

He didn't look like a very strong man. It was ridiculous, that huge hat crushed down on the head of an Englishman hemmed in by a crowd of Indians and Mexicans in New Mexico. He was enjoying the antics of the naked clowns trying foolishly to climb the white pole.

Suddenly Lawrence turned around and frowned at us. He had sensed someone was looking at him. And there was hatred in his eyes for both of us. When he had given us a moment of his wrath he turned again to the white pole and watched the naked Indians trying to climb it.

"Oh, dear," said Margaret.

But I had seen the heavy red beard, the crudely bulbous nose, the Jehovah-like wrath, the supreme self-confidence of the man.

We didn't dare stare at him after that. We led our horses through the crowds toward the other side of the circle. We felt very guilty, we had embarrassed him.

Juanito, the chifonete, shinnied to the very top of the pole, waving his arms and lecturing the crowds in sing-song Indian. A shout went up from everyone.

Lawrence stood in the circle opposite us, his face raised, a smile on his sunken cheeks.

Lawrence looked casually at things, but he always created in his writing something larger than what he saw. The early books, *Twilight in Italy* and *Sea and Sardinia*, have a tenderness of response that he somehow lost when he became a world traveler. When Lawrence traveled he became more irritable, more prejudiced in his observations. *Kangaroo* was not so much an aesthetic response to Australia but rather an act of will in his plan to write a book about each of the five continents. Yet in *Kangaroo* Lawrence has left us the unforgettable cosmic magnificence of the sea.

Mabel wanted Lawrence to write about New Mexico and the Indians. It was almost a command. Yet Lawrence never wrote a real novel of America—to spite her, Mabel would have you believe. The American Indians he avoided —made feints toward understanding them with his own sensitive intuitions. "The Indians are very American—no inside life," he wrote mistakenly to Catherine Carswell. The Indians intrigued Lawrence, amused, annoyed, baffled him. But no major work came from Lawrence's pen about the Red Man.

Mabel—? Perhaps.

Lawrence *was* perverse. And the hopelessness of ever making Mabel sensitive to life angered him to the point of repudiating *all* of America. This could be a sign of the depths of his feeling for her—and his disappointment.

Still there was the novel he was writing with Mabel— about Mabel. And Frieda's jealousy. The three of them fought violently. Frieda was aware her deepest life with Lawrence was threatened. It wasn't a book they were writing, it was a love affair.

Frieda was miserable. Mabel was conscienceless. And Lawrence was amused. Again the perverse delight in nettling Frieda. One doesn't understand this pettiness in Lawrence. He seemed to set Frieda and Mabel at each other. He would talk against Mabel to Frieda. "All women are alike, bossy, without decency."

And of Frieda he would say to Mabel, "You cannot imagine what it is to feel the hand of that woman on you if you are sick...."

It was treacherous of Lawrence to play the two women off against each other. Mabel was only a useful foil in the lifelong battle between Frieda and Lawrence. Did Mabel for one moment believe Lawrence could care for her? Years later he summed up Mabel, "You never really trusted anybody. And you have never felt any real togetherness with anyone."

Lawrence had already written a chapter of Mabel's life. "I have done your train episode and brought you to Lamy at three in the morning."

Mabel, of course, couldn't write. She couldn't start "the flow" of herself. Of course, she didn't want to write. She wanted to dominate Lawrence. She wanted Lawrence.

She tried flight to Santa Fe for some inconsequential purpose.

Lawrence took sick and went to bed. He didn't really believe in this "fight" at all. He didn't take it as seriously as Frieda or Mabel took it. "This being 'mad' with people isn't our real self functioning. It is something mysteriously imposed."

He hoped for something with Mabel, but she was in the process of rejecting herself. As he said later when he was free of her, "With your men you only want to resist them and overthrow them. Let's see who is the stronger."

But the book went on in its desultory fashion. Lawrence,

36

in bed with a cold, wrote to Mabel, "Now I want:

 1. How you felt when you drove to Taos.
 2. First days at Taos.
 3. First sight of the Pueblo."

Mabel filled pages of notes for him, poems, reminiscences. It is amazing that Mabel never realized her false position in relation to such a great man. "I wanted to seduce his spirit so that I could make him carry out certain things."

Sexually—? "I did not want particularly to touch him. There was no natural, physical pleasure in contact with him. He was too dry, not sensuous enough, and really not attractive to me physically.

"It was his soul I needed for my purpose, his soul, his will, his creative imagination.

"I wanted Lawrence to understand things for me. To take *my* experience, *my* material, *my* Taos and to formulate it all into a magnificent creation. *That* was what I wanted him for."

As for Lawrence—?

He was writing *Birds, Beasts and Flowers*. He was arranging for *England, My England* to be published. He was writing J. Middleton Murry about his wife Katherine Mansfield who had died. "The dead don't die," he consoled Murry. "They look on and help." He was writing Catherine Carswell, "*Kangaroo* is due in January. I seem to have a fair sale over here. *Women in Love* going now into 15,000."

And so this thing with Mabel was a little game. She thought of it in terms of a love affair. He temporized—at first charmingly, then irritably, finally violently. She didn't read him correctly. The subtle grace of his spirit which he offered her only tentatively—she was blind to. He with-

37

drew almost immediately when he realized the essence of her character. The situation was hopeless.

Mabel never knew how quickly she lost Lawrence nor the reason why. "You have rejected permanently the natural physical flow," he said to her, "you have rejected it all your life. Your *will*. The permanent insistence of your ego. You must learn to forget yourself."

And so he was through with her those first few weeks.

Mabel, of course, thought Lawrence's withdrawal was due to Frieda's opposition. "Frieda would never let him forget her." She "... burst a bomb-shell at him," complained Mabel. "At the end of an evening when he had not particularly noticed her, she would begin insulting him. He would almost dance with rage before her while she sat solid and composed, a glare in her green eyes, as she puffed her cigarette into his face.

" 'Take that dirty cigarette out of your mouth! And stop sticking out that fat belly of yours!' he yelled.

" 'You'd better stop that talk or I'll tell about *your* things,' taunted Frieda."

What is one to make of these obscene quarrels of the Lawrences? Exasperation on his part? A burning chest, a burning vanity? But no pride in governing the excesses of their emotions. A show for others? A despair in Lawrence, that he could not realize his dreams with *any* woman? A sort of intoxication with hate itself?

One doesn't know. Their vulgarity does not fit in with the beauty of his poetry—the greatness of his conception of life.

Was he outraged that *no* woman could accept the hypothetical role he gave her?

38

Frieda least of all. She was independent. Obtuse. She did not understand anything about Lawrence until he was dead. She defied him. She was outraged by anything new he said. She lay with him and he was perhaps impotent. And that belittled him in her eyes. Frieda was very animal. Lusty. No. Frieda could not agree to anything great Lawrence said. She fought his brilliancies with fury.

And Lawrence, though he was forced to be vulgar in turn, was really bored. He loved her but was bored with her childishness. Yet he loved her. Their tenderness with one another was supreme. And Frieda loved Lawrence—although she hated him deliciously.

So Mabel was really outside it all. Although Mabel's self-importance would not let her believe that.

Lawrence taught Mabel to scrub floors.

He taught her to dress differently. She wore cotton crepe gowns with wide sleeves and round embroidered necks. "These Mother Hubbards!" groaned Lawrence, throwing his eyes to the sky. "What is the idea of veiling the human form divine?"

"Well, if you had *my* form you'd veil it," protested Mabel. She was solidly built, was shy.

"No, no. A woman is a woman. A waistline is a waist line. Nice full skirts, with maybe a ribbon around the waist—and white stockings—that's the correct dress for a *woman*."

But he couldn't teach her to bake bread. She thumped and thumped the dough on the table while her maids stood around and tittered.

At tea time Lawrence came to sample it. It was very bad bread.

"Better luck next time," said Lawrence, and he threw his piece on the fire.

In turn Mabel taught Lawrence to ride horseback. He rode far forward humped over the animal's neck. The horse ran away with him.

Tony—the Indian—sat on his stallion and laughed.

Lawrence was furious. "That's all right, Tony." Lawrence cried. "Others can laugh too." They were never friends again.

Lawrence was fearless on a horse. Although he was uncomfortable he always rode with a free rein.

One cannot say Lawrence and Mabel were *not* in love. The first pages of the book he was doing about her were brilliant. Frieda said they were like nothing he had done before. "There is a kind of vitality and eternal youth in it," Frieda told Mabel.

But Mabel never saw the first chapter Lawrence did about her. The book was never finished.

The quarreling between the Lawrences and Mabel went on.

Lawrence came to Mabel across the alfalfa field with his irritation at Frieda. "I can't stand it over there," he said of his life with Frieda. He was shining, radiant, transfigured with rage.

Mabel mistook hatred of Frieda for love of Mabel.

Who knows what he felt for Mabel? He used her to perfect his rage over Frieda. Mabel was just a spectator in this drama. She thought she was the main actor.

40

They were all living at a high pitch of excitement. He was engaged with Frieda in a fight to the death. He beat her soft blonde flesh. Her eyes were red and swollen from weeping.

"I cannot stand it. He tears me to pieces. Last night he was so loving and tender with me, and this morning he hates me. He hit me—sometimes I believe he is mad. You don't know what it is like living with him. Sometimes I think I'll leave him."

Mabel momentarily sympathized with her. "Frieda, you must never leave him. You're the only woman he can live with. Besides, you know, he's not physically attractive to women. I don't think women want to touch him. . . ."

"Of course, they don't," said Frieda angrily. "He's dry. Well, sometimes I think I'll get out before it's too late."

Poor Lawrence. All women betrayed him. He wanted them to be the rich conception he had of them in his books. But these two women—? Frieda, a fury. Mabel, cold-hearted calculation. He couldn't work out his warm philosophy of love with either of these two women.

The Lawrences decided to leave Mabel's ranch and take a cabin in the mountains.

"But why, why?" cried Mabel in despair. She could not have him go now. He had lightened her life, made it thrilling.

"There is a destruction here," said Lawrence. "There is a green menace in the air. Oh, there is a witch's brew on this hill! And the Indians struggle against it—and I will fight it too. Yes, I value my own little bit of life and I will fight for it."

They were friends no more.

But Mabel would not let them go. That meant she would lose him. She, Mabel, had a ranch too in the mountains. Wouldn't they like to live on this old sheep ranch?

Lawrence talked it over with the Danes. The Danes—Knud Merrild and Kai Götzsche—were vagabonding artists of no importance, but companionable.

Merrild was a painter and a sculptor born in Denmark and had studied at the Royal Academy in Copenhagen. He came to New York in 1921 with his friend Götzsche. They met Lawrence in Taos and instantly became friends. They were to share the winter of 1922–1923 with Frieda and Lawrence on Del Monte Ranch. Merrild later became quite famous as a painter in Hollywood. Merrild is now dead but Götzsche still lives in Denmark. He is in his eighties.

"I should so like to get up into the mountains," said Lawrence wistfully.

"It *would* be wonderful up there," cried Frieda.

V

SO THE LAWRENCES AND THE DANES started for the ranch. But not before Lawrence had told Mabel what he thought of her.

"You in your fur cap!" said Lawrence. "You are like a great cat—with your green eyes. Well, I snap my fingers at you—like that!" Even if it was still her hospitality he was accepting high in the Rockies.

42

It was the latter part of November. The Danes sang happily as they trundled along in their 1918 Ford. Soon they were in difficulties. There was snow in the foothills and the car began to skid. The radiator boiled and the car stopped.

Lawrence sat in the back seat uttering his hatred of automobiles and machines in general.

The Danes got out and fussed with the motor. They cleaned the plugs. They cleaned the coil and filled the radiator. They cranked and cranked. But still the car would not start. Finally they asked Frieda to get out and help. Frieda pushed. The Danes pushed—it started! It went a short distance and then refused to take the next hill.

They all got out again. Merrild pushed. Lawrence pushed. But they couldn't make it go.

They abandoned the car and walked the last mile to the ranch.

What a sight that ranch was to the Lawrences on that bleak November afternoon. Two shabby shacks, some sheds. They were desolate, dismal, dirty. They had been abandoned years ago and were inhabited by pack rats, chipmunks and bats. The air was foul with odors of excrement.

But all around was the magnificence of the forest—spruce and fir and pine—and far far below them the golden gleaming desert.

They all set about clearing the smaller house. The larger house was impossible for the time being. They soon had a fire going in the old stove.

After supper the four of them sat close together around the stove in the tiny kitchen lit only by a candle.

Lawrence looked at the Danes seriously. "Frieda and I have decided to stay here for the winter and want you to be our guests," he said.

"Oh, it would be so nice if you could stay," said Frieda.

But Merrild demurred. "If we are up here all alone we shall be cut off from everything. The newness of the acquaintance will wear off. We would get on each other's nerves."

"Quite," said Lawrence. "But up here away from civilization, in the very heart of nature, we can start a sort of new life together—a life of our own. There is nothing else. The civilized world, believe me, has no life to offer."

Still the Danes did not know.

"The moon is still up," said Lawrence. "I suggest you go for a walk. You can talk more freely when you are alone."

The Danes went out alone in the grandeur of the night.

"I think it would be wonderful to stay up here for the winter," said Götzsche.

"So do I," said Merrild.

They went back to the cabin.

Frieda cried out jubilantly. "They are going to stay!"

"Good," said Lawrence.

"We will have to buy heavier underwear, sweaters—galoshes," said Merrild.

"I haven't much money myself," said Lawrence, "about a hundred and fifty dollars, but I think it will carry us through the winter. We will all share it together."

"We are going to have such a jolly time together!" said Frieda.

44

They blew out the candle and went to sleep: the Danes on the kitchen floor, the Lawrences on a mattress in the cold living room.

And so a new life started for the Lawrences 8500 feet up a mountain on Del Monte Ranch.

"We have an old live-room log cabin on this big wild ranch on the Rocky foothills," he wrote Catherine Carswell, on December 17, 1922. "The snow mountains behind —a vast landscape below, vast, desert, and then more mountains West, far off in Arizona, a sky line. Very beautiful. Trees all around—and snow. The coyotes come down howling at evening. We've got two young Danish artists in a tiny log cabin. I know now I don't want to live anywhere very long. But I belong to Europe. Though not to England. I think I should like to go to Russia in the summer."

He continued to write Mabel in his very real way, though he kept his distance.

We are settled in—very nice—Danes in their cabin. To-day we all four rode to the hot springs—Manby's—did me good to soak.

Life has been just a business of chopping wood, fixing doors, putting up shelves, eating and sleeping since we've been here.

No news from the outer world.

Let me have the bill for the honey and the shoes.

If we come to you for Christmas, I'll bring some mince meat. And I want to make Christmas puddings.

Saluti Buoni,

D.H.L.

45

Mabel rebuffed him. She could not have him as a guest at Christmas. "I cut him off—I threw him away—I left him."

Lawrence shrugged. He never responded to other people's hate of him. "I don't feel angry. But just that I want to be alone. Yrs. D. H. Lawrence."

"He threw me away did he?" thought Mabel. "Very well, we would be enemies now. I hated him and I was unhappy hating him."

She turned her tongue loose. She told funny stories about him. She emphasized all the weak things in him. He was easy to caricature. She wrote a parody about him and sent it to Walter Lippmann. She went about saying, "I had to get rid of the Lawrences."

John Evans, her son, told people, "Mother is tired of those Lawrences who sponge on her."

Tony went around saying Lawrence was a snake and poison and a sick man.

It was obvious from these pettinesses none of the people involved had any conception of Lawrence's greatness. That his life in Taos was only in passing, that the world would claim him, and that it didn't matter much *what* Tony thought of him, or that Mabel sought to banish him, hurt him.

At the same time there was something about Lawrence, his uneasiness, his hidden depreciation of you, that made people distrust him. "That's a *mal hombre*," said William Penhallow Henderson, a Santa Fe artist.

There was a fleeting malice about Lawrence. His demon perhaps. The same demon that permitted him to penetrate the depths of life could also be spiteful. His hostility was to

46

your mediocrity. He didn't present the consistent picture of a great man. He was often ill-natured, but always well-intentioned—eternally preoccupied with final meanings.

Mabel was no match for Lawrence's insights.

He too talked. He said Mabel was an evil, destructive, dominating will and that it would be the end of her. Lawrence said Mabel tried to take him up on her roof and make love to him.

Mabel fainted at hearing this—and remained lying on her bed for twenty-four hours with doctors working around her. Tony sat on the floor praying.

When Lawrence heard this, he said it was just defeat! That Mabel's will had been defeated for the first time and that it couldn't stand it. He was beginning to get the whole Mabel picture in perspective.

At the Christmas Eve Dances at the Pueblo they met in the smoke of the many fires and exchanged distant greetings.

Lawrence had won. He had found her out—her emptiness—and she was enraged. But the story would go on and on—into legend.

Lawrence's presence in the valley was the most important thing that winter. He was discussed everywhere and by everyone. Many false stories, many ridiculous stories. Taken together they did not approximate a great man. Everyone belittled him.

Margaret and I were very sad. There was no way of meeting Lawrence. Mabel had kept him to herself and now had lost him. We couldn't ride up into the mountains twenty miles in the snow and present ourselves. We waited.

47

Our life was full of ourselves—and Lawrence. We listened to the stories, his almost public quarrel with Mabel. But there was nothing to say. It wasn't a sympathetic picture of Lawrence. And it hurt us—we who loved him—even though we did not know him.

"It's Mabel," decided Margaret. She knew Mabel's treacherous ways.

Only one person in Taos beside us, admired Lawrence. Walter Ufer. Ufer worshipped Lawrence. Ufer was an abandoned, lonely, inarticulate man as all artists must of necessity be. "Dear old Lawrence," Ufer would say. "He is a man that I wish so much happiness. To have a man like that drop in Taos, and become my friend—!"

But Lawrence would have none of it. He despised Ufer. "A little man, and I *mean* a little man," he said to me once when I was talking to Lawrence on his ranch.

At that very moment Walter Ufer was receiving the highest medal of the Pennsylvania Academy, the oldest art institution in America. Ufer was among the most important artists in the country. But unimportant to Lawrence.

Thus, in a sense Lawrence misjudged Americans entirely. He took up with almost anyone—*made* them important by his attention—ordinary people like the Brett, Spud Johnson, and the Danes. If you were someone he didn't want to know you.

The winter was quite cold. It snowed and snowed and it was hard to keep warm. It was very bitter on the Lawrence ranch. Thirty below zero. Frieda says of that winter, "It was a real mountain winter. So sharp, knify cold, snow and ice, and the Danes and Lawrence had to chop lots of wood."

The Danes were easier to get along with than Mabel. They were very ordinary, Knud Merrild and Kai Götzsche. The Danes Lawrence described as "men to be at peace with." They did not try to impress him. That was the first requirement to retain the Lawrence friendship—do not try to play up to him.

The Danes were enough for Lawrence that winter. He could chop wood with them. He could walk in the deep snow. Sometimes they would trudge to the very peaks. Lobo Peak was his favorite. Between storms he and the Danes would try to scale it but they never quite made it. Between storms the weather was glorious. The air was clear and pure. The sun shone brightly over the whole Taos valley far below. It was indescribably beautiful.

"Look—! Look, how hopelessly empty it all is in the vastness of Death," Lawrence would say.

They would follow the footprints of animals in last night's new fall of snow. They would meet rabbits, squirrels, coyote, deer, bobcat and a lion—"her round bright face, bright as frost. Dark, keen, fine rays in the brilliant frost of her face. Beautiful dead eyes. *Hermoso es!*"

They would stand for moments in silence—Lawrence and the two Danes—in awe of the beautiful winter around them. It was a splendor, a magnificence never surpassed because Lawrence was viewing it.

But suddenly he would repudiate the beauty of it all there in the cold January afternoon. "But it is without soul, it has no spirit. It is cold and empty, the landscape of

49

the moon. It has no soul, America has no soul. And it will never have one. It is dead."

Each moment of life, each landscape, each hour of the day must be appraised poetically, leaving him strangely exhausted. He *cared* for the poetic truth of life too much, too deeply.

They never reached Lobo Peak.

Lawrence would lag farther and farther behind. He was lost far down the slope. He stopped and sat down on a stump. They had to go back to him.

He looked very tired. "I guess the altitude has got me."

And they started back—over the frozen crust of snow.

Frieda would have the meal ready for them. "Lorenzo, you look so tired! You mustn't strain yourself like that. You can't stand it."

"Oh, Frieda, why must you always tell me things like that. I'm all right."

After supper those cold winter nights, high in the snow-covered Rockies, the four of them, Frieda, Lawrence and the Danes, had a delightful, though often preposterous time. Since they were all from Europe, life was best when it was accompanied by music and song.

Lawrence had a flute with two missing keys. He let Merrild take it. Mary Ufer let Götzsche borrow her violin.

The Danes practiced furiously for two weeks then were ready to give a concert for the Lawrences. One bitter cold night in January they played Händel's Largo there in the little mortar-chinked cabin where Lawrence had exiled himself.

When they had finished they lowered their instruments.

"How perfectly awful!" said Lawrence.

50

But Frieda applauded generously. "Please do play some more."

Then they played a Danish folk melody. "Lette Bólge."

"How poetic," said Frieda.

"How dreadful," said Lawrence.

Lawrence had no appreciation of music. But Frieda played the piano well and had a good voice.

Lawrence hated to be left out of anything. So one evening he produced a comb and a piece of paper and played on that.

He couldn't keep time. The Danes tried to stifle him, and so he frantically played louder and louder. Soon he got up and tramped around the room and the Danes followed. Finally Frieda got two potlids from the kitchen which she banged together, and they all tramped round and round Lawrence's living room with its rough-hewn logs, its blackened fireplace, and tipped back rocking chair.

But while these riotous scenes were going on Lawrence was really preoccupied—not with Mabel, not with the Danes, not even with the grandeur of the Rockies to which he had lured himself—but rather with his exile from Europe.

"Truly I prefer Europe." Liberty—space—deadness. That was what America represented to him. "I belong to Europe." He repeated that over and over.

"It's good fun on this ranch—quite wild—Rocky Mountains—desert with Rio Grande Canyon away spreading below—great and really beautiful landscape—looking far, far West."

But in the meantime they must live the winter out in the mountains. The Danes were good company. Lawrence chopped wood and shoveled snow and climbed the trails with them. He appeared to take them into his confidence in those warm cosy winter nights with the bear and the coyote slinking around the cabin outside.

But Lawrence kept a certain impassable space around him—a don't-touch-me distance. He had a thoughtful reserve. He seemed very open when you met him. But he was merely taking you in, finding and handling your heart, weighing it—and then withdrawing. He was your friend. And yet he wasn't. A warm stranger. Aloof—some one apart.

Those were the days of bootleg liquor. Lawrence would go out into the bitter cold and get his medicine bottle full of corn whiskey which he kept cached in the little vegetable cellar beyond the porch. He would come back so happily to the supper table with this small brown bottle of raw whiskey and offer it to the Danes. It was terrible whiskey.

They would all take sips and get a little tipsy—and Lawrence would commence to talk.

Eventually he had to deliver himself of some profundity. His compelling philosophy of life could not be repressed in conversation whether he was cooking, washing and ironing his underwear or on horseback in the deep snow.

"Sex and Beauty are inseparable," he would suddenly proclaim.

"Beauty is an experience, nothing else; it is not an arrangement of features: straight nose, large eyes, etc. It is something felt, a glow or a communicated sense of fineness.

"Even the plainest person can look beautiful, can *be* beautiful."

Or he would rave hours long, "Now man cannot live

without a vision of himself. But still less can he live with a vision that is not true to his inner feeling.

"Christ crucified is untrue to the inner experience and feeling. . . .

"Satan, your silly temptations no longer tempt me. . . . I want life and the pure contact with life. Only life is lovely, and you, Mammon, prevent life."

There was a certain bitterness in Lawrence's truths, his triumph over darkness. He was erratic in his friendships but only because the people around him could never understand his tremendous new philosophy. People remembered his rage but not what he said.

There was something haunting about Lawrence—someone who had lived long, long ago. The Mediterranean of the Greeks and the Etruscans was in his blue eyes. He was the archaic spokesman for the past meaning of life on earth.

What struck you about Lawrence was his ordinariness, his naturalness. He was just a man. One who was confident and poised—but a man. He was not distinguished—his ruckled trousers, his oversized shirt, his heavy boots. We didn't care how we dressed in those days.

But when Lawrence talked he was a prophet. He included you in his inspiration. Before your very eyes you became part of his very creation of life in his high pitched voice as we sat on the wooden kitchen porch dangling our feet in unison. One was silenced before someone infinite in his inquiry into the meaning of life on earth.

The Danes were second-rate artists. They had many quarrels with Lawrence over art.

"Give me that brush, I want to paint that part of your

53

picture," and he would grab hold and try to wrest the brush from Merrild's hand.

And Merrild would have to engage in a bodily struggle to get back his brush. "If you *have* to paint pictures, paint your own," Merrild would say.

Lawrence did not like modern art. "Abstraction is a picture of nothing, and has no relation to life.

"Abstractionists are of the hideous machine industrialism and are only making a memorial to their spiritual impotence. The soul's disintegration.

"Life has been made unbearable and art has become the refuge of people living in fancy.

"As for your world of art and your world of reality you have to separate the two because you can't bear to know what you really are, so you say it's the world of art.

"The world of art is only the truth about the real world, but you are too far gone to see it. Isolating the soul, surrounding the heart with frozen air."

The dispute went on. Lawrence could easily outdistance the poor Danes with his brilliant insights. How he scintillated for them that winter up the cold cold mountain. They had a wonderful time talking.

Merrild would ask him: "What is God?"

He quickly answered, "I don't know what God is. But He is not simply a will. That is too simple. Too anthropomorphic. Because man wants his will and nothing but his will, he needn't say that God is the same will, magnified ad infinitum.

"To me there may be one God, but He is nameless and unknowable. For me, there are also many Gods, that come into me and leave me again.

54

"It is the multiplicity of Gods within us that make up the Holy Ghost."

Frieda would quarrel with every idea he had. She mentioned love.

Lawrence snorted. "Why must women talk about love. There isn't any such thing as love!"

"What about mother-love?"

"There isn't even such a thing."

This infuriated Frieda. "It's bosh, I tell you, bosh!"

Lawrence always enlarged petty quarrels into great philosophical ideas.

"The grinding of the old millstones of love and God is what ails us, there's no more grist between the stones. We've ground love very small.

"You can't lose yourself neither in women, nor humanity nor in God. You've always got yourself on your hands in the end.

"Say what you like, every idea is perishable: even the idea of God or love or Humanity—even the greatest idea has its day and perishes. Each formulated religion is in the end only a great idea. Once the idea is explicit, it is dead. Yet we must have ideas."

The winter ended and they were all still friends. In February Lawrence wrote to J. Middleton Murry, "We leave here in a fortnight. We are going down to Mexico City."

They all started packing.

Frieda gave Merrild a woolen sweater. Lawrence gave him a pair of blue Levi's he had worn. Lawrence also gave Merrild all the photographs of Mabel she had given him.

Lawrence was very serious now that they were breaking up. He had a fatherly concern for the Danes. They went to the corrals and patted the horses for the last time. Then they all got in the Danes' Model T Ford, Lawrence's tiny dog Pips in Lawrence's lap, and took the rutted snowy road to Taos.

Mabel was not there to see them off.

The Danes were the only ones to bid goodbye to the Lawrences that cold March morning in Taos in 1923.

Lawrence said of his six short months in Taos, "It was New Mexico that liberated me from the present era of civilization, the great era of material and mechanical development. . . .

"The moment I saw the brilliant proud morning sunshine high up over the deserts of Santa Fe something stood still in my soul, and I started to attend."

VI

MARGARET AND I WERE VERY SAD TO hear Lawrence had left Taos. There was a strange emptiness in the valley after he had gone.

What does one expect of a great man, such as Lawrence, in one's life?

Perhaps only contact. Reassurance that because of him

life is worthwhile. Lawrence was a presence in our lives even before we met him. Someone who stirred the highest things in us.

I was still in turmoil about my writing. The first winter before I met Lawrence I was confused. I thought "reality" must be documented. I did not realize that a song, a profound song of one's being, was reality too.

I could not write. I could only undergo the caprices of the mind that never ended—.

Margaret watched patiently. It was her life too—this ordeal of my writing.

That winter was very cold. There were many storms. The lonely valley was flooded with snow again and again. The emptiness of beauty—the sheer whiteness of life on earth—overwhelmed us.

The vast snow wilderness, the white, white mountains ever more distant until they became minute golden alps on the horizon filled us with simple, powerful thoughts.

The West in snow is unutterably beautiful. The implacable white peaks, the piñon-dotted foothills, the new moon low over the vast evening sky to the west. Flawless splendor of the scene that becomes also the splendor of one's imagination. One is never the same again after a winter in the West.

One marvels at the cold pure western light. The slow darkening of twilight, the strange exciting gloom that overspreads the desert. Suddenly the sierras become spectral presences, lying disordered at the edge of the snow-flooded valley—the whole mighty range lifeless now, diminished, disarranged in attitudes of the dead as the last phenomenon of evening appears—a sudden white light behind the peaks flaring spectacularly into the deep indigo of night.

Yes, that winter was wonderful. It brought us into direct contact with life. It filled us with meaning—sustained us.

Although we lived in a small mud house—it was the long night fading into the cold dawn, the white everlasting mountains rising, rising with the brilliant sunrise that increased our pitiful meaning beyond our comprehension. The tall golden landmarks burning in the first sun. The freshness, the newness of life each morning. The open wilderness of snow—the raw little mud village of Taos, the cold starlight, the last doubtful light of the old moon upon the final white world.

We were abandoned in this ultimate beauty. A sense of life's sublimity enlarged all our thoughts. That winter we were bold, fervid, powerful in our identity with life. Not our doing—rather the subtle dawns, the dangerous light coming gradually over the black snow-heavy mountains— touching the desert far far off. A low star lingering a last moment just over Abiquiu.

Yes, winter was exquisite. Life was exquisite. Love with Margaret was exquisite.

How eminently noble she was. Someone from the classic past who had come back to share my life during this short quick moment of history.

Swinburne Hale, Margaret's brother, came to the ranch that year.

Swinburne Hale and Frieda Lawrence were to meet in

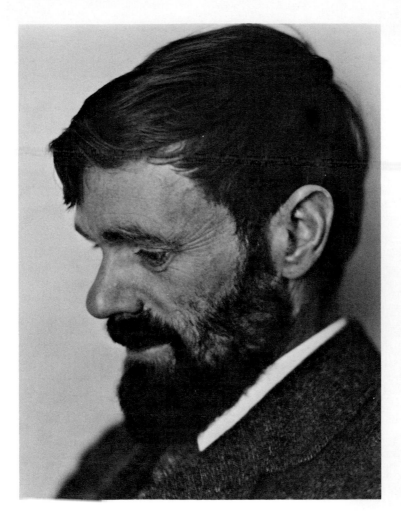

Lawrence by Edward Weston

Frieda Lawrence

his little log cabin in the sage and become fascinated with
one another. Their excitement when they were together
was to enrage Lawrence.

Swinburne was very tall, very handsome, very rich—
almost a millionaire, an Adonis who swaggered. He had had
many women, very beautiful, very avaricious girls of sixteen, women of forty who were attracted to his handsomeness, his wealth.

He was dazed by his life. He talked incessantly, with a
Harvard accent, a little stupidly, a little pathetically. His
New England Puritanism made him feel guilty about life.
Ashamed.

Swinburne Hale was to go utterly insane.

And he looked at you quizzically to see if it were so.

He had had a brilliant career at Harvard, in law in New
York, and during the war, in Washington. He was one of
the coming poets of America.

Still there was that ever increasing daze to his thoughts.
The dark mockery of his other self that told him he would
never achieve success. He could write like Shelley. But his
dark side laughed and laughed at him—amused that he
should ever hope for anything.

Yet he would write poetry in the desert. The dark laughter of his other self almost disappeared that year, but for
his New England conscience. How do you kill a conscience? You don't. It kills you.

Swinburne Hale came quite humbly to Margaret and
asked her for asylum. He had had a breakdown. He was in
anguish. Could he live with her?

Of course, said Margaret. There was an old log cabin on
the other side of the ranch in the sage. He could live in that.

I saw how much she loved him—was concerned with his

59

coming downfall. But Swinburne was weak. He knew he was going insane. What does one do in the meantime?

Women and horses. Horses seemed to be a symbol—(his mother?)—to Swinburne. He had a score tramping round and round his log cabin in the snow. He petted them, groomed them, fed them oats from the palm of his hand, saddled them, unsaddled them all day long.

Yes, he was inspired by the West. Soon he would start a long poem about the desert.

The log cabin he lived in was so nice—so far away in the snow. Inside on the bed lay a naked young girl—waiting.

"We must be patient," said Margaret after she had taken in the situation of her brother, his women, and his coming doom.

Margaret and I continued to live in poverty in contrast to the profligate way Swinburne and his paramours lived across the sage in the snow.

Poverty was a self-imposed reality. We loved it so much we felt unreal without it.

I found it difficult to believe Margaret and Swinburne were brother and sister. They spoke so formally of Mamá and Papá and of their childhood in Rome. But they had nothing in common. Swinburne, urgeless, now that he knew he was to be insane.

Was it true—this coming insanity?

Harvard had said he was to be the poet of the century.

But the Imagists had arrived—Amy Lowell, H.D., Richard Aldington, Ezra Pound—the iconoclasts of two millenniums of prosody.

Swinburne Hale, Witter Bynner, Van Wyck Brooks—
all friends at Harvard . . . were to go down.

All fine men steeped in the greatness of tradition. Made
less, however, left behind by the Imagist movement, that
was destined to trigger the Literary Renaissance of the
twentieth century.

But Swinburne Hale, writhing with his New England
Puritanism, writhing with the shame of his million dollars,
could still be enchanted by the beauty of the desert.

He started a long poem:

> The gray edge of life hangs round me—
> Like mountains about the rim of the desert. . . .
> I am the desert,
> Arid,
> Beautiful to no purpose.
> The mountains call me,
> Exquisite in their grayness pointed to saffron,
> Fringed with purple in the sunset,
> Beckoning me always
> Out of the desert.
>
> Beloved,
> Beloved in the desert,
> Woman lying upon my breast
> Shielding me from the stars,
> Desert cloud of a woman,
> Light upon my breast against the sky—
> Do I love you or the desert?
> Are you, too, the desert,
> Arid,
> Barren?
>
> Is it better not to love
> Here in the desert?

But his despair increased. His mind, his guilt gave him no rest. The desert enchanted him to no purpose. It was wonderful to be lost. His heart longed for the coming darkness. Sanity became a burden, an inconvenience. He did not want his sanity reestablished ever again. His instincts now were—death. Death was seducing him.

He had irrational moments brought on by long drinking bouts with himself or his woman—whoever she happened to be. While drunk he made marginal annotations in Chatterton, and between hiccoughs he edited the Bible. He read Traherne and shot out the windows of his little log cabin all night long.

We did not dare go near him for days at a time. He was undergoing his life very badly. It is always a risk to face one's own meaning. Swinburne could not.

But, of course, there was the darkness creeping over him, mocking him, summoning him to the greater darkness—Death.

> Aye, the night is lonely! And the days are long!
> Sullen-hearted is the heart that lies alone. . . .
>
> Who is that, waits outside?—
> Where the dark spreads wide,
> Just beyond the window's light?—
> Who is that, dimly guessed,
> After lovers go to rest,
> Standing, waiting in the night?

This was the man to whom Frieda Lawrence was to be attracted that spring.

VII

LAWRENCE HAD GONE TO MEXICO. He always moved on when an experience was without further possibilities.

I think Mabel intrigued Lawrence, puzzled him, angered him and finally left him cold. She didn't read any of her lines correctly and he had coached her so carefully. Pleaded with her to follow him, Orpheus, into Paradise. But she could not.

So he simply left. Lawrence's indifference could be utter and final. He would, however, be drawn to the ranch and the high far-off view until the end of his days.

But Mabel—there was nothing there. So he went to Mexico.

In Mexico he was instantly impressed. "I like Mexico. The Indians are attractive. There is a good natural feeling—a great carelessness."

Lawrence was looking for something elemental in Mexico. And Mexico *was* elemental. Lawrence was elemental too—his rages really came from nowhere. People took offense. But he could not help his hatreds. They were upheavals in his very soul.

Lawrence was preoccupied with the elemental in civilization—in poetic terms. The Mediterranean held him spellbound to the end of his days. But the old, lost wonderful civilizations of the past still sang in Lawrence's lyric spirit.

It was the elemental he craved. The elemental meaning of man moved him most and he traveled and traveled the world over hunting the elemental meaning of life, rejecting what he saw everywhere because it was *not* valid, *not* elemental. Modern Europe, India, Australia, Mabel's America, never realizing that the elemental he sought was a powerful mirage in himself projected back into the lovely lost past. Had his dreams ever been? How violently, how lyrically he lived them. He confused the fantasia of his own thoughts with the *now* of the world, the *now* he could not accept. There was something grander, grander— the deep bell sound of *his* eternity he carried with him wherever he went.

And that grandeur he didn't find in India, in Australia, in America—and he was enraged. He quarreled with reality; nothing in it corresponded with the deep elemental dream he was pursuing. What a passion he had for his dream. It was a yearning for a beautiful world of illusion. Yet the illusion, he knew, was the *real* world. It was elemental and seeable only to him. He became violent when anyone violated its least truth to him. Could they not see?

But how can you see another man's dream? You were bound to make a mistake. You could not utter three words without violating Lawrence's secret of life. And he told you. His hatred came out of nowhere. You had in your small talk, your small opinions violated the absolute truth of life on earth. And Lawrence would fly into a rage. What, what had you said to bring down his wrath? But he had *felt* a truth and you had only *said* a truth.

64

Truth was something almost religious with him. But to you truth was just a matter of opinion. And so he let you have it—with what harsh violence only someone who has faced Lawrence will ever know.

I do not think there was a single friend of Lawrence who escaped his wrath. It was because of the indescribable living thing Lawrence conceived life to be. And all men he met were full of ideas and dead. Men were patterns of death to Lawrence—of their own death. And he hated death, and he hated death talking in ideas. And he slapped you instantly across the mouth with the stupidity of what you said.

No one, not even Frieda, realized the deep elemental conception of life that was ever present in Lawrence—the larger scheme of things he was forever occupied with. Frieda didn't know what he was thinking—ever. Her antagonism finally became a philosophy of her own, a very challenging one. Still it was negatively inspired by Lawrence.

Frieda challenged you to be real and strong. She challenged Lawrence, but he only jeered at her. He was working at something too grand for her to comprehend. So they spat at each other, these two fine people. Still they had to live together.

Frieda was brave, but bravery was not enough to understand something so secret, so new as Lawrence's message that was going to take over the world eventually.

It was the changing relationship of human beings that

Lawrence was interested in—the rejuvenescence that came with valid contact.

Lawrence hated England because it failed to be as great as he thought it should be. And Europe he hated. "Europe is dead, dead." It too failed him. Failed his imaginative concept. Only the Mediterranean held him to the very end. The long gone wine-dark sea of the past—*that* held him.

The past really can't betray you if you worship it in such sublime measures as Lawrence did. The Etruscans: they were his ideal because they gave themselves to life—not to conquering as the Romans, nor to the limited concepts of the mind as did Aristotle and Plato. Fate, he believed, had paralyzed the Greeks' imagination.

Lawrence was an inspired scholar of ancient history. It was so real to him, this lovely dream, that Lawrence as he talked made you believe it was the secret of the world. Such was his power.

But Mexico—!

Here was an actual country that was still elemental, that had the secret of life. If a country could testify to the truth of life it was Mexico.

He loved the frail distances from the train, the dim-seeing mountains sharp-edged with menace, the silence, aboriginal and empty. Silence as of life withheld. And always the day seemed to be pausing and unfolding again to the greater mystery.

Yes, Mexico. He could do a novel in this elementary country that he could never have written in the United States.

He wanted the savage truth of man. He was savage too. Alive. His depths were alive. And he hated anyone who was not alive.

He walked and walked in Mexico City. He was intense in his observations. His indifference disguised his fascination.

The crowds of white-clothed people fascinated him. They were somber. They had smooth alive skins. Haughty, dangerous, as they sauntered barefoot across the Zocalo. He saw their unchanging eyes. They lived without hope. Yet they were gay—careless. He watched and watched them—a dowdily dressed Englishman with a red beard.

Yes, his novel was forming now—running away with him as such things always did. He was angry he could not get to work. These subdued, savage people in white coats and white baggy trousers would be his characters.

Impassioned with the past Lawrence walked the modern city. He studied the twenty-five-ton calendar stone of the Aztecs. He pored over Terry's Mexico. He thought, thought, thought of the past, of Montezuma's thousands savagely holding off the handful of Spaniards of Cortez.

At last his plot was shaping. His message was a beautiful obsession. Mexico! His vision illumined him. It was pure and it was lovely—an enchantment—as he roamed the streets alone. He longed for life and creation— to be flung into the transcendence of creation-death.

These people so fierce, so tender, so soft, boundless and gentle, were living something greater than the truth of the present. They had *life*—and it gleamed in them with a fourth-dimensional quality. Yet they understood death in a living way. They were creative in their souls about death.

This he gathered from the barefooted white-trousered hordes crossing the Zocalo. They were broken, hopeless, lost—yet they acknowledged the wonder of life, responded to it to the utmost.

Wherever he met them on the narrow streets they were intolerable presences. They had unchanging eyes. They were subdued. They gave themselves to the uncertainty of life—to something deep, beyond knowledge, and it made them gay, careless.

All this he observed the first days he strolled alone in Mexico City. On the Insurgentes, on the Reforma, in Chapultepec Park, in the Bellas Artes.

Here was a people he admired. A people who lived with the quivering uncertainty of non-knowledge, non-power— with a pure fierce passion of essentiality *beyond* purpose. They had achieved real feeling—a thing almost impossible for modern man.

In those first days Lawrence loved the Mexicans, made them into a magnificent epic. He was in a religious state about them—a great awareness to their least meaning.

Is it any wonder he didn't meet Spud Johnson and Witter Bynner at the ramshackle railroad station as they had planned, instead left them to shift for themselves?

When he finally bumped into Spud in a downtown street Lawrence had of necessity to desert his inner voices and become his querulous ordinary self.

Spud was the only living man who did not annoy Lawrence. This was principally because Spud never said anything, never thought anything. Spud did not upset

68

Lawrence in the least. Spud was a sweet, faintly poetic soul. He had no part in Lawrence's hatreds. He did not answer Lawrence.

Other people made the mistake of contesting Lawrence's ideas. Spud listened. He was an admirable companion. He did not talk back. He said nothing. Spud accepted Lawrence, and Lawrence accepted Spud. They got along admirably.

Lawrence didn't want his ideas contested. He just wanted to be delivered of them. He didn't want them challenged. Frieda fought every new idea Lawrence ever had. Spud never did.

Together Spud and Lawrence roamed the streets of Mexico City.

They visited the big market. Such a babel and hubbub of unwashed wild people sitting with their big bare dusty feet in the street before their wares.

There were heaps of roses, heaps of hibiscus, beautiful blankets, very nice crude pottery, three-day-old calves, bright blue and scarlet birds fluttering on a man's shoulders. And awful things to eat.

"Fried locust beetles," said Lawrence.

Spud's thin white aesthete's face looked disgusted.

"Seventy percent of these people are real savages," said Lawrence idling on.

Spud said nothing.

Mexico enchanted Lawrence these first few days with Spud. He loved the dark-faced men in cotton clothes and big hats. "How silent they are," he said to Spud. "A sort of mass silence."

"And those white clothes," marveled Lawrence. "And

the dark faces. And their great white calico trousers flopping about their ankles as they walk."

Frieda would have answered—but not Spud. Spud was perfect for Lawrence's purposes. He never disturbed Lawrence's dream.

It was not long before Spud and Lawrence knew everything about Mexico City in their quiet way.

In the side streets behind the Cathedral among the poor they found the crowds living in great confusion. "They have so many children," said Spud.

"Well, they don't care," explained Lawrence. "They don't care about anything. They don't care about sex. They don't care about women. They don't care about making money. They don't care about making anything. They don't care. They just don't care."

Again Frieda would have shouted her doubts. Spud said nothing.

People were swarming about them. "It's a living confusion," said Lawrence. "Life must be a bit of an adventure. They do everything at crazy hours—their brass bands practice at two in the morning in the street—life must be a variable. It's fun."

But the streets were so awful they could hardly make their way through the littered alleyways. "See how they throw their shoulders back. How proudly they hold their heads. Their black hair gleams like wild rich feathers."

Why when he was with Frieda did he have to defend his most beautiful thoughts so violently? And why did Frieda challenge the most beautiful center of her man?

70

Frieda could not talk until he had first shaped an insight. Then she would attack it. And he would rage. He was very unattractive when he raged. But didn't his rages always follow some beauty of insight—rejected? Frieda hated the beauty of Lawrence's insights. She attacked them —but from a mediocre point of view. She was always right—or so she convinced herself—and the beauties of Lawrence's mind being born, he found hard to defend. Lawrence always came off second-best.

"I like their sudden charming smile," said Lawrence. "Let's go back to the hotel. The Queen Bee will be worried."

Yes, he loved Frieda. She destroyed him every time he attempted to say something beautiful. But he did not mind.

When Bynner came to Mexico City Lawrence became truculent, ordinary.

Bynner was a distinguished man—expansive, articulate, urbane. He was very large and self-confident of his peculiarities. He was very darkly handsome and rich enough to have his own way.

Bynner was very famous in academic America—welcome in all the great universities for convocations. He had a surprising cultural drive, a big man with a slight muse. He made a great deal of his minor poetry. His mediocrity was fragile, graceful, evasive. He overwhelmed you with his vast, obtuse knowledge. It was out-of-date and he was frightened. Anything Bynner said was true in 1905. But the world was moving rapidly in literature and art in the

71

1920s—it was an earth-shaking Renaissance: Rilke, Eliot, Joyce, Lawrence, Picasso, Kafka.

Bynner was to go down, be left behind with his mid-Victorian excellences.

The two men fought constantly.

Lawrence was outraged by Bynner's academic mummery. "Leave off fine learning!" he advised Bynner.

Bynner, baffled by this strange Gothic spirit—a species of human being never, never to be encountered in literature, wrote of Lawrence, "He is one of the uncanniest human beings imaginable. Did I say human? I am coming to the conclusion that he was misborn a man.... From my point of view there has seldom been a writer less fitted to discuss human affairs."

Bynner really thought Lawrence a beast.

Lawrence quarreled with Bynner's lack of essence. When Lawrence became outraged he became petty. He created scenes. People remembered only the scenes that embarrassed them—rather than the great philosophical truth Lawrence had spoken.

With the coming of Bynner everything Lawrence had loved in Mexico became something to hate. One moment he saw the good in Mexico—and then suddenly all his insights were hate.

Mexico City changed in his eyes overnight. He became afraid of its repulsiveness. Mexico City had an underlying ugliness, a sort of squalid evil. And he was afraid of it. He saw everything differently now. The men were loutish. They even stood making water against walls. The women were fat mamas, greasy, grey with an overflow of face powder—clown faces—distasteful.

He was shocked at a bullfight and left in disgust. He turned on Spud and Bynner for staying to the bitter end. "You Americans would run to any street accident to see blood."

He hated Bynner, but Bynner was not really Bynner to Lawrence—he was an *American*. And an American tolerated anything, even a thing which revolted him. He would call it life.

But life to Lawrence—? "...is pure being where I am absolved from desire and made perfect. This is where I am like a rose, where I balance for a space in pure understanding. The timeless quality of being...."

And so Lawrence always disagreed with a mediocre interpretation of life. Life consisted in achieving a *pure* relationship between ourselves and the living universe around us. If you violated his great secret feeling for life by responding with conventional cant, he would fly at you in a rage.

He refused to be present at the May Day celebration in the Zocalo.

Half a million Mexicans were milling about the great plaza—the same plaza where Montezuma's priests had plucked out the hearts of thousands.

The workers were everywhere—waving red flags with a stripe of black running crosswise—Death. The Mexicans always included Death in their celebrations.

73

All the shops were closed. There were no street cars. There was a bit of red ribbon in everyone's lapel. Spud and Bynner bought some red bunting for Frieda's parasol.

Everyone was in the Zocalo that morning—Communists, Obreros, Trade Unionists, Anarchists, Syndicalists. "We have suffered long enough. Bourgeois, shave your heads and get ready for the guillotine." Icemen, seamstresses, bartenders, bullfighters, grave diggers. But no Lawrence.

Spud and Bynner decided to join a band of plotters and hoist a red banner with hammer and sickle on the Cathedral's flagpole. And ring the great bells.

"What fun you'll have!" said Frieda. "Could I go with you?"

"No, Mrs. Lawrence," said one of the plotters. "We don't know who else will be up there and we might have a scrap."

"What fun!" cried Frieda. "Yes, have a good scrap and beat them. I'll be watching."

Spud and Bynner raced for the Cathedral and climbed to the belfry where with hundreds of others they helped ring the huge old bells. But on the way down they were confronted by five stern-faced men who raised their arms and pointed revolvers at them.

After hours of hiding on the lichen-tiled roof they found their way back to Frieda in the square below.

"And did you have great fun?" she asked eagerly.

"No!" said Spud.

"Oh, I had fun!" she cried. "I loved the parade. And then the Russian flag and all the people looking up and shaking their fists at you. And the soldiers! Why did Lorenzo have to miss it!"

74

But when they told Lawrence of the exciting events in the Zocalo he shook his head solemnly. "It's sheer folly to take part in any of these movements. Leave it to the rascals who understand it and profit by it. Have nothing to do with mankind in the mass, with any political surge. Leave it aside. Let them do what they like in their political world. Reject it. Go about your own business."

The perverse almost vicious hatred of Mexico now persisted.

In Orizabo he would not even leave the railroad station. "We are not staying here, Frieda. We are leaving. The place is evil. I won't go to the Hotel. I won't go anywhere. The place is evil, the whole air is evil. The air creeps with it!" and he screamed at the porters to go away.

The sense of evil—? Did his fears miscreate a poetic horror he believed was true? Where did the fear come from? A sudden alchemy of his genius turned beauty into hate.

Often Lawrence hated brilliantly. He could not control his insights. The coming of Bynner might account for his scoffing—at Mexico?

Bynner was urbane. An imperturbable man in horn-rims. Very famous in America—a poet, a millionaire. He said all the wrong things to Lawrence. Bynner, although a highly cultured man, had no personal depths. He was social, democratic, successful. Bynner suffered only a personal tragedy —he did not suffer the *meaning* of life itself.

They couldn't agree. Lawrence insulted Bynner constantly. It was Lawrence's way of destroying a dead philosophy.

75

Bynner fought back—posed the grandeur of the classics against the inchoate beauties of Lawrence's new religion on earth.

Bynner lost.

Bynner was only a philosophical guinea pig to Lawrence, a sounding board for Lawrence's rush of ideas. As was Mabel. And perhaps even Frieda.

This then was Lawrence—a man involved in a tremendous drama of shaping by indirections, by inconsistencies, by poetic prophecy a great new meaning of life.

And those little people he quarreled with, roamed the back streets of Mexico City with, climbed the Pyramids of the Sun and the Moon with—or even his love he clung to nakedly in the heart of the night—how foolish *they* were to think for even a moment they were important in his transcending fantasy that was attempting to redeem life on earth—lost, lost through the stupidities of mankind these countless millenniums.

And Lawrence *did* redeem the world in some grand way.

But even though Bynner was empty, Lawrence wanted him. Even though he deprecated Spud, even though Frieda was stupid—he wanted them all in his life.

He could not live without people. Much as people's emptiness irked him he could not do without them in his life.

For one thing he was afraid.

Lawrence's fear is a strange thing.

Mexico was bandit ridden. He followed the reports of the killings on the highways closely. He bolted the doors and windows cautiously. He always slept with a peon outside his door.

One does not know where this fear came from. In boyhood he called out in his sleep. He thought someone was trying to kill him.

Mexico was in a state of revolution. Lawrence's fear was the uneasiness of a highly sensitive nature. The restless searching for an outer protagonist to actualize his inner anxiety of creation.

The fear was there. Awake, as well as in dreams. Fear of what? Aren't fears atavistic?

Lawrence's fears were memories of the race's past. He lived in the eternity of man. Each day all man's history was present in the poetry of Lawrence's mind. The day might be ordinary for other people, but not for Lawrence. He was delightfully adrift in *all* of the past. Lawrence worshipped the great *total* meaning of man. Centuries and centuries of remembrance exhilarated him—of Homer, of Job, of Jesus, of the Jews, the Greeks, the Etruscans— mere suggestions of ancient life flared in him constantly as he dickered for a bit of colored pottery in the market among the crowds of Mexicans.

The past recurred over and over again as a lovely litany in Lawrence, in the poetic sunshine of Lawrence's mind. And the dangers, the fears also of the past. The wonderful battles of Troy, Actium, Thermopylae, Carthage, the destruction of Carthage by the Romans. Fear. Death. It was all a monotonous fear-dream of man's life on earth.

History—human crimes and misfortunes. It wasn't just the moment, but all man's life on earth that Lawrence was thinking of. The killing and killing of history—man's fear, man's killing and killing in consequence, to quiet his fears —killing, killing—man's meaning—?

Here in Mexico to Lawrence's beautifully inflamed imagination it seemed so. Man, since Abel, killed. Thus releasing himself from the urgency of life.

And at night he had only his imagination: the strange wonderful thing history was: Death and Resurrection. The life-flow neglected, lost by modern man. A thousand lost meanings of history overwhelmed him in the Mexican night—the beautiful history of man. Life! Sometimes completely rejected as by the Romans, at other times sensitively experienced, obeyed—the Etruscans. At night his imagination was at large in the beautiful realms of history—far far back. Man's presence in the world was beautiful—exempt from the dependency upon anything but life, life. In Lawrence was the remembered greatness of man, back, back to the beginning of time.

But in the night was also fear. Man's failure. Fear of life. Since Lawrence was a sort of Christ who suffered not our sins but our mishaps, our failures, our unfulfillment—with life—through fear—he too was filled with fear at night. A haunting fear of history's failure to be more than pictures of history's crimes. Life was not a crime. Life was not a tragedy. It was not outward things the Egyptians, the Romans struggled for and ended atrophied, diminished, aborted. Until their failure became an enormous fear and they killed and killed.

Yes, the fear of history was Lawrence's each night. It is a fantastic concept? But anyone who has looked into Lawrence's blue, blue eyes knew they were preoccupied with the past, that his thoughts were everlastingly dwindling into a historical vanishing point when man had worshipped Life and not his alienation from it, not his delectable substitutes, his materiality.

Lawrence's fear was one inherited from the past, the uneasiness of a tormented imagination.

At breakfast one morning he said to Bynner and Frieda. "I was awakened in the night by the sound of breaking glass. The moon was across my door. The small pane by the lock had been broken and a hand came through."

Frieda looked at Bynner. "I heard Lawrence jump in the room, a great thump on the floor, a noise in his throat, and then he was in my bed, his head against my shoulders, saying, 'They've come!'

" 'What, where?' I asked.

" 'My door,' he answered.

"And I was out of bed and his door was not bolted, and there was no one in his room, no one in the house, no one in the garden, only the moonlight."

"It's not good, Bynner," said Lawrence gravely. "We must leave."

"Are you sure you had your door locked?" asked Bynner.

"I always lock it. I saw the hand unbolt it, the moonlight on the fingers, and there was a knife in the hand.

"We must leave this place, Bynner," repeated Lawrence.

So *The Plumed Serpent* was already being written in the middle of the frightened night.

His quarrels with Frieda increased. They became his characteristic relation with her. He resented her in public. "You sniffing bitch, stop your smoking."

"And why should I?" Frieda replied.

"I won't have it. Take that cigarette out of your mouth," he said with anger.

"I will not."

In a fury Lawrence leaped to his feet and swung his arm, full at Frieda's face. But she was too quick for him, she dodged the mighty swing and Lawrence missed his aim.

Frieda ran into the kitchen. From the doorway she sneered at him. "You brute, you bully. Pah! as if I cared! You think that nothing but goodness and virtue and wonderfulness come out of you. You don't know how small and ugly you are, you petty conceited creature. You're not big enough not grateful enough to do anything real. I give you my energy and my life and you treat me as a charwoman. Acknowledge me first if you have any gratitude, before you can be any good."

Frieda took her case to Bynner. "Sometimes I think he's crazy," she said.

It was always tumultuous around Lawrence—his frenzies, his arrogances. But this was the most serious time of their life. She was about to leave him. Neither could resist the excitement, the intoxication, of their quarrels.

They moved to Chapala with Bynner and Johnson.

The Lawrences took a house at Number 4 Zaragosa— "pleasant," he wrote, "near the lake. Our own little garden: the first corner after the Villa Carmen, house next the dark trees. We can bathe from the house."

To J. Middleton Murry he wrote, "I wanted to do a novel here. I could never begin in Mexico City. But I have begun here in Chapala. It's a big lake, 20 miles across: queer. I hope my novel will go all right."

He started to write in earnest now. He sat each morning under a willow tree overlooking the lake and wrote. That is why *The Plumed Serpent* is so full of the spirit of the lake.

But his story now—all fear, all terror, all beauty—was ready to be told. "Mexico!" he cried. "Mexico is another Ireland. It is not an easy country to understand. You wanted to flee it. The country pulled you down.

"To pull one down. It was what the country wanted to do all the time, with a slow reptilian insistence, to pull one down. To prevent the spirit from soaring. To take away the free, soaring sense of liberty.

"Mexico is like an old egg that the bird of Time laid long ago, and she has been sitting on it for centuries, till it looks foul in the nest of the world. But still it's a good egg—Mexico's.

"And politics and all the social religion is like washing the outside of the egg to make it clean. But I want to get inside the egg, right to the middle, to start it growing again."

He gave himself to the riddle of Mexico as he sat under the willow tree at the end of Zaragosa Street—staring at the lake.

Ah, the lake—so still and filmy as to be almost invisible. Everywhere the shores rose up pale and cruelly dry.... And on the little hills the dark statues of organ cactus poised in nothingness.

"...unreal waters, far beyond which rose the stiff resistance of mountains ... far off in the dry air.

"No sound on the morning save the faint touching of water. Silence, an aboriginal silence, as of life withheld. The vacuity of a Mexican morning.

"And the great lymphatic expanse of water, like a sea trembling, trembling, trembling to a far distance to the mountains of substantial nothingness."

Mexico!

But the people too.

The Market: "On all the pavements round the plaza squatted the Indians with their wares, pyramids of green watermelons, arrays of rough earthenware, hats in piles, pairs of sandals side by side, a great array of fruit, a spread of collar studs and knickknacks called *novedades,* little trays of sweets. And people arriving all the time out of the wild country, with laden asses.

"When dark fell the vendors lighted their tin torch-lamps and the flames wavered and streamed as dark-faced men squatted on the ground in their white clothes and big hats, waiting to sell.

"The food stalls were brilliantly lighted. Rows of men sat at the plank boards drinking soup and eating hot food with their fingers. The milkman rode in on horseback, his two big cans of milk slung before him, and he made his way slowly through the people to the food stalls. The peons drift slowly around. Guitars were sounding, half secretly. . . . A motor car worked its way in from the city, choked with people, girls, young men, city papas, children in a pile.

"The rich press of life, above the flare of torches upon the ground! The throng of white clad, big hatted men circulating slowly, the women with dark rebozas slipping

82

silently. Dark trees overhead. The doorway of the hotel bright with electricity. Girls in organdy frocks, white, cherry-red, blue from the city. Groups of singers singing inwardly. And all the noise subdued, suppressed.

"The sense of strange, heavy suppression, the dead black vapor of negation in the souls of the peons—that perhaps was hate. . . ."

So Lawrence wrote of Mexico.

VIII

THE QUARRELING WITH FRIEDA WENT on and on. Even though he was writing perhaps his greatest novel he carried on this tormented, anguished fight with Frieda. In a sense he was a little like Job quarreling with God over his destiny.

Lawrence's destiny was to be born free of the dishonest misconceptions of mankind.

As with Job, Lawrence's anguish was growth. Growth and reconciliation with his own greatness. But he knew his growing enlightenment as anguish. Every moment of Lawrence's life was anguish—and Frieda's too, in consequence. He was being born into a new concept of life on earth and it was all torment. And Frieda must suffer as well.

Frieda understood. Lawrence understood. Their quarrels were inconsequential. The more vicious they became, the more they indicated the agony of Lawrence being born

83

into something new. Job. "Though I speak I am not assuaged. Behold I cry out of wrong, but I am not heard."

In public they created impossible scenes.

At a tea in Mrs. Stone's house in Chapala, Lawrence suddenly attacked Frieda. "Frieda, don't be stupid. I should slap you for that!"

Sometimes Frieda struck back. "I can't be so dumb when you quote me all the time in your books."

Lawrence's tantrums were now reaching their peak. For Bynner, they overshadowed Lawrence's great profundity.

"The longer I think about him the cleverer and shallower he seems, a thoroughly specious person."

Bynner considered himself the patron of the new poets, the Imagist group in America. Lawrence condemned them. He begrudged everyone the little talent they had. Of Pound, Lawrence said, "A mountebank." Of Amy Lowell and her Imagist anthology, Lawrence said, "It's all nonsense." Of Somerset Maugham he said, "Disagreeable. A narrow-gutted 'artist' with a stutter." He hated Hardy, Henry James, Dostoievski, Proust, Joyce. And Mabel Dodge Luhan.

He raged and raged while profound visions were passing through his mind as he sat writing under the willow tree by the lake.

Why?

"It's fear, the ultimate fear of death, that makes men mad," he decided.

Frieda loved him, understood his love for her below his hate. When they were alone there was love. And she could suffer his outbursts in private. She knew that his irritability came from illness. He called her a nincompoop because she could do nothing. And she agreed to her uselessness.

Yet he knew how closely she watched his health. He knew in spite of all his ugly characterizing of her, she was the only one who satisfied him.

They were in love in a strange way—deep deep down in their hearts. But in public he made her absurd and ashamed. He said that no decent woman in England would have anything to do with her.

She didn't know what to answer. To reply would bring about a scene. So she sat and stared.

"Sometimes I wonder if any other woman would live with him," Frieda said to Bynner.

She puffed on her cigarette. "I sometimes wonder if I myself can live with him."

Then, "I am caught."

Love made her helpless. Their love was a battle, but it was a great love.

Lawrence finished the first draft of *The Plumed Serpent* under the willow tree.

They decided to leave Mexico and go to England.

To Knud Merrild he wrote on June 27, 1923, "We shall leave next Monday for Mexico City—and probably shall be in New York by July 15th. Don't expect to stay more than a month. Then to England. I know I am European. I may as well go back and try it once more."

Idella Purnell tells of their leave-taking. "When they

left Chapala I accompanied them to the station in a boat, round trip paid by Lawrence. When we got to the station, Frieda unabashedly blew her nose several times, saying I *like* Chapala, I *like* Chapala! But Lawrence was glad to go."

In New York a furious battle broke out between the Lawrences. They exchanged fierce angers on the pier. They ranted at each other.

He wrote to Bynner, "Frieda sails on Saturday for Southampton. I'm not going. Where am I going? Ask me? Perhaps to Los Angeles, and then to the islands, if I could find a sailing ship. . . . I've booked Frieda's passage and she's setting off alone, quite perky."

To Knud Merrild he wrote, August 7, 1923, "When Frieda is gone, I shall come to Los Angeles. We might spend the winter in Palm Springs. Or we might go again to Mexico. If there is nothing else to do, we might take a donkey and go packing among the mountains."

On August 30 the Danes went to the station in Los Angeles to fetch Lawrence in their Model T.

He was a sad man. He was not himself. Without Frieda he was restless and in a gloomy mood.

The Danes put him in a hotel room. He was lost. He spent most of his time wandering along the beach or wharf.

He was alone, mindless, meaningless by the sea. All his greatness, his fame—without Frieda—had come to naught.

A vacancy overcame him. He had no soul, he had no heart, he was utterly alone. He walked with his hands in his pockets along the sea. He drifted into indifference. All the old life—his greatness—fell away from him. And there was only the vacancy of California without Frieda. Everything that had meant anything to him was gone.

The landscape? He cared not a thing about the landscape. Love? He was absolved from love, as if by a great pardon. Humanity? There was none. Thought? Falling like a stone into the sea. "What have I cared about, what have I cared for? There is nothing to care about. Absolved from all."

Was this then the great end of his genius—this utter hopelessness, however beautifully expressed in his dark hole, a rooming house on Grand Avenue in downtown Los Angeles?

The Danes were barely making ends meet doing odd jobs in Hollywood.

Lawrence was determined they should all go to sea. "I am a bit tired of the solid world!" he said. He would hire out as a cook—and the two Danes as sailors.

While the Danes were at work, Lawrence was out chasing ships and seeking hire in Los Angeles harbor. But without success. No ship's captain wanted a strange thin man with a red beard for a cook.

Since his plan to go to the South Seas was thwarted, Lawrence typically took to anathematizing the life on the Pacific in beautiful poetry:

"Those islands in the middle of the Pacific are the most unbearable places on earth.

"The heart of the Pacific seems like a vast vacuum in which mirage-like continues the life of myriads of ages back. It is a phantom-persistence of human beings who should have died, by our chronology in the Stone Age . . . the glamorous South Seas.

"The Pacific Ocean holds the dream of immemorial centuries. It is the great blue twilight of the vastest of all evenings; perhaps of the most wonderful of all dawns. Who knows?

"It must once have been a vast basin of soft, lotus-warm civilization, the Pacific. Never was such a huge man-day swung down into slow disintegration as here. And now the waters are blue and ghostly with the end of immemorial peoples. And phantom-like the islands rise out of it, illusions of the glamorous Stone Age.

"Samoa, Tahiti, Rarotonga, Nukuhiva, the very names are a sleep and a forgetting. The sleep-forgotten past magnificence of human history.

"There on the island, where the golden-green great palm trees chinked in the sun and the elegant reed houses let the sea breeze through, and people went naked and laughed a great deal and put flowers in their hair, great red hibiscus flowers and frangipani. There they are, these South Sea Islanders, beautiful big men with their golden limbs and their laughing, graceful laziness. . . .

"But we can't go back. . . . The South Sea Islander is centuries and centuries behind us in the life struggle, the consciousness-struggle, the struggle of the soul into fullness. There is his woman, with her knotted hair and her dark inchoate, slightly sardonic eyes. I like her, she is nice. But I would never want to touch her. I could not go back on myself so far. Back to their uncreate condition. She has soft, warm flesh, like warm mud. Nearer the reptile, the Saurian Age. *Noli me tangere.*

88

"We can't go back. We can't go back to the savages—not a stride."

So everything produced poetry in Lawrence—even an upset in his plans to go to sea.

He was horribly depressed in Los Angeles. "Why have I cared? I don't care. How strange it is here, to be soulless and alone."

That was the perpetual litany in his mind.

Frieda? Back to Frieda? No, no, not England ever again. England had repudiated him. Frieda had deserted him. The entire world was black. The past all gone. What have I cared about, what have I cared for?

There is nothing to care about.

The Danes took him to a public dance hall on the beach. He loathed the music and detested the tail-wagging dancing of the girls. He sat at a table and made sarcastic remarks.

One of the girls cried, "Hello, Santa Claus," as she danced by him waving her hand at Lawrence.

Lawrence grinned.

The Danes took Lawrence to the Hollywood Bowl. He didn't like the music. He sneered again and made jokes, annoying everyone around him.

No. Lawrence hated Los Angeles. He was a queer duck to everyone he met. He was restless to get away—somewhere.

Mexico?

He didn't want to go alone. He wanted the Danes to

come along. Götzsche was willing, but Merrild was un-willing. He knew it would be a failure.

"It is folly," said Merrild to his friend Götzsche, "to go down into the back country of Mexico and live among Mexican Indians and half-breeds, facing revolutionaries with knife and revolver in my belt. No."

"I feel fortunate," said Götzsche, "to be able to go to Mexico with Lawrence no matter how it turns out and I am willing to spend my last penny with him."

And so Lawrence said goodbye to Merrild. "We can wait for you and prepare," said Lawrence. "We have to be a few men with honor and fearlessness and make a life together. There is nothing else, believe me."

Lawrence wrote to J. Middleton Murry on September 24, 1923 from Los Angeles.

"Dear Jack: I am setting off tomorrow with a Danish friend down the West Coast of Mexico for a place to live. I hope I shall find it. If I do you must come."

But the trip into Mexico was a nightmare.

"Here I am wandering slowly and hotly with Götzsche down this West Coast," he wrote to Witter Bynner October 5.

"The West is much wilder, emptier, more hopeless than Chapala. It makes one feel the door is shut on one. There is a blazing sun, a vast hot sky, big lonely inhuman hills, and mountains, a flat blazing littoral with a few palms, some-times a dark blue sea which is not quite of this earth— then little towns that seem to be slipping down an abyss— and the door of life shut on it all, only the sun burning, the clouds of birds passing, the zopilotes [buzzards] like flies, the lost lovely palm trees, the deep dust of the roads, the donkeys moving in a gold-dust cloud. There seems a sentence of extinction written all over it."

He was suddenly soulless and alone again. It was his darkest hour—a death-hour Götzsche did not understand. "It is evident to me that inside he is fighting himself, what to do, because as an author, he likes best to stay here and build a new colony in this country, a new simple, ideal life, but as a man he likes to go back to England and culture."

Lawrence wrote to Merrild: "Götzsche is getting very red in the face—with this fierce sun. He looks at these broken, lost hopeless little towns with silent disgust.

"We went to a big, wild, cattle hacienda. They are strange, desolate, brutal places: beautiful enough, but weird and beautiful. I doubt if we could bear it."

Götzsche was having a hard time. "Lawrence is a queer snail and impossible to understand. He seems to be absolutely nuts at times.

"He overestimates himself. He thinks he can show by his feelings what people think and do.

"He makes everything much more complicated and artificial than it is in reality."

They continued their journey from Tepic by muleback.

"Nine hours by mule back!" wrote Götzsche. "So our behinds and knees were plenty sore when we arrived in Ixtlan. . . . There was no hotel so we slept in a shack on the floor with some Mexicans rolled in their serapes, coughing, spitting, and snoring all night.

"Early the next morning at 5:30 we had to get on again, new mules, new guide, but no new seat or knees. Without breakfast we had six hours on mule back to the next station Etzatlan.

"I cannot help being amused by L. He is always so concerned about the spirit of the place that he isn't aware that it is he himself, his own mood that determines his impressions of the moment, or the landscape.

"I think he is at times insane."

But poor Lawrence was in mental agony. Without Frieda he was nothing. The trip down the west coast of Mexico with Götzsche was the greatest single testimony to Frieda's meaning in his life.

"Back to Frieda," he thought. "Frieda? Another bird like himself. If only she didn't speak, talk, feel. The weary habit of talking and having feelings. Why do I wrestle with my soul. I have no soul.

"Frieda and he? It was time they both agreed that nothing has any meaning. Meaning is a dead letter when man has no soul. . . . Who dares to be soulless finds a new dimension of life.

". . . the meaninglessness of meanings, and the reality of timelessness. Do you hear the clock tick? The clock means nothing with its ticking. And nothing is so meaningless as meaning."

This was his mood—a great philosophical despair—without Frieda.

They reached Guadalajara. Lawrence was disappointed.

Frieda had been here with him in the spring. Now it was fall and Frieda was in England.

They stayed with Idella Purnell and her father in Guadalajara.

"Poor Miss Purnell, who is poetry-mad and talks verse
with Lawrence," sympathized Götzsche, "gets some very
hard thumps from him. I am avoiding Lawrence as much
as possible at present, because considering all things, he is
really insane. . . ."

People in London were writing to Lawrence, begging
him to come back and saying that England is beginning to
be the leading culture again. Frieda wrote him that it was
the best country in the world and he must come.

But Lawrence was obdurate. To Götzsche he said, "I am
sure I will *die* if I have to see England again." He looked
really sick and pale and his head hung way down on his
chest. Götzsche did not know what to do. Lawrence *was*
insane. Götzsche did not realize Lawrence was insane with
sadness.

The next day after receiving another letter from Frieda,
Lawrence came to Götzsche and said, "It is just as well to
go to Europe, don't you think? One might just as well, I
feel I don't care any more. I just go."

So they sailed from Vera Cruz November 22, 1923, for
England—and Frieda.

England—!
Immediately there was a circle of friends to reassure him.
J. Middleton Murry, shy, nervous, a small man, a friend-
enemy of Lawrence throughout his life. Lawrence considered Murry to be England's greatest literary critic.

93

Murry was the husband of Katherine Mansfield, the short story writer.

Koteliansky was short, broad shouldered, powerful with a fierce black look. Samuel Solomonovich Koteliansky was a radical escaped from the Czarist's secret police.

Mark Gertler—Katherine Mansfield's lover—a young poet, a painter, a recluse, a dreamer, who in the end was to take his own life.

Catherine Carswell, mortal enemy of Murry, was to be Lawrence's most reliable biographer.

Gilbert Cannan, a famous novelist eventually to be destroyed by megalomania.

And the Brett. The Honorable Dorothy Brett was a member of London's Bohemia. She was the daughter of Viscount Esher and the sister of the wife of the rajah of Sarawak. She scoffed at being an aristocrat. She was one of the first women in England to bob her hair, to wear trousers. She painted very ethereally, was shy, deaf, and terrified of meeting Lawrence. Yet the Brett was the only convert Lawrence ever made to his Utopia in America.

It was the Brett he is interested in now. Not Frieda.

They all waited for Lawrence at the Café Royal in an ornate over-gilded red-plushed room.

Lawrence stepped into the crowded room, slim, neat, with his overcoat folded over his arm, looking at them proudly.

"Where is the Brett? I want to meet her."

The Brett turned round.

Lawrence came quickly forward. "So this is Brett." He was eager and alert to meet her. She sat on his left at the long table.

Mrs. Cannan, James Barrie's former wife, in a huge black

hat, sat on his right. Koteliansky, Catherine Carswell, Gertler, Frieda and Murry. All dead now—except the Brett.

Brett put her hearing box on the table beside Lawrence. He looked at it and laughed quizzically.

"It's quite impossible to make love into such a box," he remarked ribaldly.

The Brett was shy, attentive, silent. And Lawrence began in his delicate, sensitive way to woo her. "Would you be afraid to come to Taormina with me, Brett? Or shall it be New Mexico? But will you come or would you be afraid?"

The Brett, nervous, shy, overwhelmed, murmured, "I will go anywhere with you." She was silent, sensitive, deaf—her essence attractive to Lawrence. Was this the beginning of a new love?

Frieda watched narrowly. Frieda knew everything, and already she did not like the Brett.

They all drank round the table, and Lawrence made a speech inviting everyone to go with him to New Mexico to make a new life. "Would you be afraid to come with me?" he asked, looking down at the Brett.

She took up her hearing box and listened intently. "No, I would not be afraid," she said when she understood his words.

Lawrence turned to Murry.

"And you, Jack—? Will you go to America with me?"

"I should do it out of a purely personal affection for you," smiled Murry.

"No!" shouted Lawrence. "There must be nothing personal about it."

Murry got to his feet too. "I love you, Lorenzo, but I

won't promise not to betray you! You always deny what you actually are. You refuse to acknowledge the Lawrence that really exists."

"I'm sorry . . . I'm sorry," said Lawrence, teetering now. Port was not his drink.

Suddenly Koteliansky began smashing all the wine glasses and shouting, "No woman here or anywhere else can possibly understand the greatness of Lawrence!"

Murry kissed Lawrence fervently. The women were silent. Koteliansky made another speech. The glasses were flung over their shoulders, splintering on the floor. Lawrence became dazed, leaned forward and vomited. Brett took his hand and stroked his forehead.

He is speechless, helpless. Koteliansky and Murry carried him downstairs to a taxi.

Lawrence pursued Brett now. Every day he ran to her little house in Pond Street. He hated the house, hated her furniture, hated the whole thing, but he came, nevertheless, to woo her.

They sat opposite each other and made flowers in clay and painted them. Lawrence must always be doing something, painting doors for Mabel, painting clay for the Brett.

Very delicately he probed into Brett's life. They were quite silent because she is deaf. They sat there intensely aware of each other, modeling flowers.

One cold day Lawrence and Murry climbed the steep narrow steps to the Brett's studio. He sat in the chair Katherine Mansfield used to sit in.

The Brett was scared when she showed Lawrence her canvases.

Lawrence looked at them and exclaimed: "They are dead, like all the paintings now; there is no life in them. They are dead, dead! All these still lifes—no life in the painting."

Brett felt the power in him—the pent-up, storming power. She explained what she felt about light, "double lighting," she called it.

Murry asked, "But what does she mean?"

Lawrence was impatient, "I know what she means." Then to the Brett. "Go on."

But he was not happy in London.

Dear Bynner—here I am—London—gloom—yellow air—bad cold—bed—old house—Morris wall paper—visitors—English voices—tea in old cups—poor D.H.L. perfectly miserable, as if he was in his tomb. . . . I wish I was in Santa Fe at this moment.

De profundis

D.H.L.

He longed for New Mexico. He took the Brett to a London cinema to see *The Covered Wagon*. He was intense with excitement and she was moved by his love of the West. He sat next to the Brett in the dark and watched *The Covered Wagon* as if he were a part of it himself. "How like it is. How like it is," he exclaimed. The West, the West—what a power it had over Lawrence.

He hummed very softly to the Brett the theme song of the movie, "Oh, oh Susanna, don't you sigh for me, for I'm waiting here in Oregon with my banjo on my knee."

97

Yes, he and the Brett were excited—in love.

But the excitement, the irritation of London made him restless. London irritated him, people irritated him. Most of all Frieda irritated him.

Murry, Koteliansky, Gertler, the Brett, Frieda and Lawrence were always together in Lawrence's flat.

Lawrence talked constantly.

Suddenly Frieda began attacking him, then denouncing him, finally accusing him of wanting to make a God of himself.

Lawrence's temper rose. In broad dialect he denounced her.

Suddenly he seized the poker and started breaking the cups and saucers. "Beware Frieda! If ever you talk to me like that again it will not be tea things I smash, but your head. Oh, yes, I will kill you. So beware!" And he smashed the teapot with the poker.

Murry did not go with them to America. But he saw them off—Frieda, Lawrence, the Brett—at the station. He was cold and unrelated. He leaned through the train window. "I shall follow you soon."

Lawrence's lip curled impatiently. "If you want to go to America *bien*. Go without making me responsible. Let us clear away all nonsense. I don't *need* you. That is true. I need nobody. You know I don't care a single straw what you think of me. Realize that once and for all. I don't care what you think of me, I don't even care what you say of me, I don't even care what you do against me, as a writer. Your articles in the Adelphi always annoy me. Leave off having any emotions. You don't have any genuine ones, except a certain anger. I tell you if you want to go to America as an unemotional man making an adventure, *bien allons!* If you want to twist yourself into more knots don't go with me. That's all. I've never had much patience, and I've none now."

Murry was silent.

Aboard the *Aquitania*— "too big," he wrote. "Like being in a town. But I like to feel myself travelling."

He stood next to the Brett in the stern. "I am always a bit sad at leaving England and yet I am always glad to be gone."

And they stood watching—the two of them—watching England sink into the sea.

IX

THAT WINTER LONG AGO OUR LIFE was mostly horses, the utter beauty of the valley. Its seven impassable canyons of snow. The crumbling adobe town of Taos. The wind, the sun, the solitary butte of Abiquiu. The rose sunsets on the stark white peaks of the surrounding mountains —and our love.

Ours was a certain heroism of isolation. A daring to have

our own emotions, our own thoughts. We never thought of it as daring—but I do now. We were just living life truly—one with the other—the bleak white peaks, the snow-laden sage, the low volcanic surge of the lava flows on the yellow horizons our only witnesses. Yes, it was heroism. Emotional heroism to express life as we thought right.

There was nothing else but our love.

Still, a delicate vein of conscience ran through my life, and Margaret's in consequence: Write. Write!

I was experiencing the beauty of life, of Margaret. How could you write if you were already fulfilled?

Nothing really mattered that winter but that the horses must be taken to water. And we must ride every afternoon —into the absolving grace of the desert. And we must get water from the well—and look at the sunset while we chopped wood. Are we out of bacon? Molly is lame. Isn't Joyce too extravagant in the way he scatters literary allusions through his work? Shall we have French toast for supper? I'll melt the honey on the stove. I think Lawrence is greater.

"I wish the wind would stop," said Margaret.

It blew and blew. The snow fell every night and whitened the mountains above 8000 feet. The sharp spires of the winter peaks surged higher and higher into the timeless blue sky.

We watched the lighting every afternoon on the slopes, the vast shadows of the great rocks and the baffling perspective of eternity to the west where the new moon nigh her setting was guarded by a single bright star.

Oh, the West! We submitted to its greatness, its power.

It was past comprehension—this magnificent state, which came from the violent beauty around us. We were small, vulnerable—powerless to be anything but real under such mighty circumstances. And we were happy there was something great—so very great beyond us.

In winter one became aware again of the Indians.

They reclaimed the valley as their own. Winter was the Indians'. They reappeared quietly, naturally, everywhere on their little shaggy horses. The land was theirs. They were sensitive to its beauty, its magic. They were susceptible to the glory of life in the valley.

They revered the land, the snow, the might of the mountains—life. Wherever they went they were vivid and powerful—yet shy. They had an old, old fathomless secret and they wanted it to be undiscovered. They wanted their secret to remain forever. Their depths were theirs and theirs alone. They had a pre-historic alienness that had at first bothered me. Now I saw that the Indians were beautiful—their somber smooth skins, their instinct to grace.

An Indian was all silence. A wonderful stillness. His stillness communicated with you. They said nothing, nothing, yet a tremendous thing was passing between you. Their faces were changeless, vivid with changelessness. Their eyes brilliant silences. Everything about an Indian is open—still and silent and fearless. And the stillness is unbearably true.

It was Margaret who taught me that the Indians had a great sweep of life within them. The huge nature of things that they can never forget, that ruled them in a strange unthinking majesty.

But winter was hard on the Indians. Things were very bad at the Pueblo. No food. The old men said they had to endure. Things would be better next summer. And to endure. Think, think intensely and the cold of the winter would go. It *must* go because the central will of the Pueblo desired it. Endure, endure. Be joyous. The cold of the winter must go. Do not go about much. Do not move things. Attend the dances and keep silent while the men were in the kiva praying. *Be* the summer, the warmth, the joyousness, the bountifulness of the Next Year. Do not hurry in your thoughts, sink into everything-that-is and know that generations and generations of the Dead had survived that way also.

Winter was real to the Indians, full of beauty and fear and hope.

The old men prayed and prayed. The spring, the summer, would be good. Bountiful. Great stacks of hay—the corn ears the largest ever. There would be water, water—and the beans would ripen early. It would not be long, a few months now, and they would have plenty. In the meantime they must dance and dance. The strictest attention must be paid to ritual.

Chief after chief got up in the kivas, was fumigated, asperged and then talked and talked of the wonderful summer coming. Outside the snow came and came in great tides up the mountains. Even the coyotes, their friends, were slinking into town.

There were few beans left in the Pueblo, it was true, but want had been greater in the past. They must endure. The Dead had endured. Had starved many times with zeal. And they had survived. Hunger was not bad. It was something that could be endured. They must pray and pray—and this thing would come to pass. Do not buy the foolish things the whites try to sell you. Be thrifty. Be benevolent. Forever joyous.

Endure.

Above all do not feel hatred, bitterness toward the white oppressor.

Remain deathless within.

And the whole Pueblo washed its hair ceremoniously in the icy water of the river and went back to the kiva to pray and pray "For corn, for wheat, for melons, for onions, for chili, for apples, for peaches, for soda pop, for clothes, for shoes, for a long life."

Every night the young fellows went over to the kiva and smoked and danced and cut up.

> Hai yu   Hai yu   Hai yu   wat si
> Naaaa ya   Hai ni yu

All pretty hungry, so they were pretty wild. But the living thing was there too. They were all naked and dancing haughtily, the utter final living thing in all of them as they danced, danced their indifference to hunger, to their poverty.

The old men sat round the circular wall chanting, chanting into the wonderful depths of the world. It was an old song that went back and back to the Beginning.

After a while the young bucks got excited and started to dance the Ghost Dance. Danced and danced it desperately—exhausting their last energies, wiping out their last connection with this life until they became the ultimate living thing they all were in this rhythmic madness:

```
Ya   ha   e   hi   ya
Ya   ha   e   ya
He   ya   eyo   e - e - e
He   e   yo   e - yo
He   i   yo   e - yo
E   yo   i   ya   he   yo
E   yo   i   y   he   e   yo
```

About two o'clock everybody was tired. They felt better. Tired dancing. Tired singing. Better go to bed. Better stretch out. Good night, fellows. So they all drift out. Throw their flannel blankets over their sweating shoulders and drift away. Lots of nothing to do tomorrow. Got to go now. Goodbye!

They go up the ladders and across the snowy roofs and down into their fire-hot kitchens to their wives.

In winter the Pueblo generally ran out of salt.

The old men said they would all have to go on a Salt Pilgrimage—past Santa Fe. It was a very long pilgrimage to "onyage," The Place of the Salt, in the snow. But it was the only thing to do. Everybody was out of salt.

Salt was a sacred item. The winter was hard but one must master one's life. One must endure and master defeat —therefore one must go.

And so all the young men of the Pueblo started out on the Salt Pilgrimage in the snow.

They sported and laughed on their horses, sang and mimicked things, and talked to their wives in their thoughts. They were joyous, joyous, as they started across the snowy sage. They trotted and they loafed and they galloped, the snow clods flying behind them.

The moon was pretty big now. The snow-moon looking down, down on the snow-world. The soft vast silence was theirs. The snow, the snow. The wind, the moon, the snow. And they laughed and made their horses kick and kick in the snow and gallop off into the moonlight.

They were all lost now, straying all over the windy desert, singing and singing far off to each other in the snow. Oh, the snow-white night, the snow-white moon. They galloped as one into the bigness of the night—the snow-light of the winter, the last light, the first light, of the world. Cold and comforting. The final Magnificence— the Great Nothing. The utter, final, absolute manless beauty of the universe.

It was not long before they reached The Place of the Salt and they were happy. They prayed to Old Woman Salt to give them some salt and she did. Not far in the brightness of winter, scarce two hundred miles. They were back in the Pueblo in a week with plenty of salt, the kind they must use.

"What did you think of? What did you think of?" asked their wives anxiously.

"Oh, I thought of *p'o* [the moon]," said their men.

"What else?"

"I thought of *sip'ophe* [the underworld]."

"No, you did not. What else?"

"I thought of *'opa* [everything that is]." The men thought most of that on their ride in the snow.

"You did not think of *her?*"

"Sure I thought of her."

"Do you love her?"

"How can I tell. I have not met her yet."

"Do not meet her—ever," pleaded the wife.

"Ha ha wah ha!" laughed her man.

This was Taos in winter fifty years ago.

X

Late one sharp spring afternoon, Walter Ufer drove up to the ranch in his dusty Buick.

Was that snow in the stark valley? No, the wild plums were in bloom. The cottonwoods were tentatively a soft green. But winter was not over, we knew.

Margaret and I went out into the patio as we always did when a car arrived in those days. It was such a rarity—a car.

I remember most how relentlessly the wind blew from the sage desert across the mesa.

One by one, and very unwillingly, three figures got out of the rear seat of Walter Ufer's touring car.

"Margaret," said Walter, "This is D. H. Lawrence."

"Hello," said Margaret.

Lawrence grinned or gleamed whatever non-commital expression he was forever using. I saw him look at Margaret intensely. But he said nothing. He had a very heavy beard, and his cowboy hat was huge. He scrutinized everything about him and said nothing, nothing.

"Margaret," said Walter again, "this is D. H. Lawrence."

Lawrence was amused. I saw he thought little of Ufer, but he was amused. He withdrew. Let the situation develop itself. Walter had arranged it. Lawrence would have nothing to do with it. I saw his blue eyes narrow and look at the approaching spring in the valley below us.

Someone in a large misshappen velvet coat and a small hat and a wind-red face came forward now and extended her hand. "I'm Frieda," she said.

She was very forthright, with a certain animal *savoir-faire*. If her eyes were on me, her whole being was with Lawrence as he stood there in the windy patio, aloof from all of us.

"I'm Joseph Foster," I said. I could not bear to lose one moment of Lawrence.

"Yes, Walter told us." She hissed her words. It was she who made the situation tense. She spoke always to Lawrence, and Lawrence shrugged it off.

"And this is the Brett," she said to me, to Lawrence.

He was amused with the efforts of others. Around him one was always ill at ease.

"How do you do?" I said to the young Englishwoman.

She was young, pretty, reserved. She said nothing, utterly, utterly nothing, but looked at me with strange inquiring eyes. She held a little brass horn under my mouth —and her eyes asked and asked—but what was she asking?

I did not know what to do with the brass horn. I'd never seen one before. I couldn't say anything. I became embarrassed, and seeing this she took the horn away again courteously.

Lawrence, his back to us, was talking to Margaret. But

107

he had seen the exchange between the Brett and me and he was amused.

"Walter has told us about you and Margaret," said Frieda. "How you live to yourselves. And as you like. Isn't it wonderful! To be free of people—yourselves. Lawrence! this is where they live," taking in the old adobe house, the greening field of alfalfa beyond us and the far far off blue mesa that was the flat-topped mountain of Abiquiu.

Lawrence flung her an angry look and I realized there was a secret language of hate between them. The Brett listened and listened with her horn—never quite catching on to what was being said. Did she talk, I wondered? But we were all embarrassed that day. Lawrence was so sensitive, so forbidding.

Lawrence and Margaret talked quietly. He kept his hands clasped behind his back and shrugged a little forward.

Conversation with Lawrence was a strange experience. He thought with his eyes and then said things quietly. He was quiet and powerful talking to Margaret that day long ago.

Ufer was talking now in the windy patio. "I wanted you to meet D. H. Lawrence, Margaret." He admired Lawrence, but he was absurd in his eagerness. Lawrence made him absurd. He had a contempt for Ufer. He hated Ufer.

The Brett had approached me again. "Do you ride?" And she placed the brass horn under my mouth again and waited for my reply.

"Oh—yes!" I said, sounding almost English myself in imitation.

When her eyes had understood what I had said into her horn she took it away again. "Jolly!" she said. And I saw her looking at the pale ocher desert beyond. I did not then know she was a painter.

I couldn't quite, quite get the rhythm of their English speech. Their elliptical sentences, the undercurrent of things understood, all the strange nuances of their conversations. I realized there were alien sensibilities involved between the Brett, Lawrence and Frieda that I did not quite understand. Frieda, in spite of her heavy accent, was very English, forthright, always aware of Lawrence, ready to contradict him.

"Margaret," said Walter Ufer, "I want him to meet your brother, Swinburne. Margaret's brother is a poet. He graduated from Harvard."

Frieda looked anxiously at Lawrence. He was annoyed now. He did not want to meet *any* more people. No telling which way his anger would strike. "Lorenzo," said Frieda. "Margaret's brother is a poet. He lives across the fields. Shall we go over and see him?"

They said something angrily with their eyes. We must all wait until this silent battle was over. It lasted a dramatic moment. Frieda had won. It was agreed we were to go across the fields to Swinburne Hale's log cabin in the sage.

Margaret and Frieda and the Brett went ahead. Walter Ufer, still excited with the event, walked backwards before them. "I have been invited to send to the Rome International—expenses paid," boasted Walter.

"So?" said Frieda.

Lawrence was walking at my side—looking at me. He was always gentle with me. "What do you do?" he asked.

"Oh—" I did not know what to say. I did not dare say

109

I wrote, although years later I wish I had. What *did* I do? Loved Margaret. I couldn't say that.

He waited patiently for my reply. "Oh," he said at last. "One has only to live in New Mexico—as one's excuse for being. It's such fun." He looked at me another moment and then he withdrew. I was too young for a complete experience with him. He saw that.

He looked about him naturally. He did not want to keep up with the others. "It's nice out here," he said quietly, really taking in the mountains in a deeper, more final way than I was capable of. "There is something pristine, unbroken, unbreakable."

I wondered at the strange identity he had with the nature of things. The instant way he verbalized beauty in some philosophical scheme of regret. All his life Lawrence regretted that the beauty of life could not triumph over man.

When we got to Swinburne's cabin it was twilight. There was a pale new moon on the cadmium-red horizon. All around us the mountains were darkening. Lawrence looked at the scene thoughtfully. His contemplation was typical of him—not his rages.

There were horses around the back door, and Lawrence waited while I drove them away.

"Margaret's brother likes horses," I apologized.

"Ah," said Lawrence. But he was still looking at the pale mountains—and the moon low in the deep orange sunset.

Inside there was a fire blazing in the fireplace. Frieda and Margaret and the Brett sat on the sofa—or bed—their faces glowing. Ufer crouched on the floor before them. He was telling Frieda some impossible story. Frieda, as always, forced her interest. Her eyes shone with Walter's clumsy story telling.

The Brett shrank far back on the bed. She kept her horn hidden. She did not want any of Walter Ufer because she knew Lawrence did not like him. The Brett's connection with Lawrence was excruciatingly sensitive but had less meaning than Frieda's. The three of them were still estranged from all of us. They were English, and their private drama went on and on wherever they went.

Swinburne Hale, Margaret's brother, stood tall and handsome in the firelit room, his bald head among the rafters. It was almost a trapper's cabin. There were coyote skins spread on the wall, a rifle, a bear trap, some teacups hanging from nails in the logs, a line of books—poetry, novels, a Montgomery Ward catalogue—a woven horse-hair lariat. A stage setting that really didn't suit Swinburne Hale, Harvard University '05.

"Good evening," he said to Lawrence. His dark flannel shirt was open at the throat, and he wore a silk handkerchief, cowboy style.

He was blond, open, a boy. A boy of forty who wrote verse and drank bootleg whiskey. And was waiting death in this small log cabin in the desert.

Lawrence did not really acknowledge Swinburne Hale. An opinion of him formed immediately in Lawrence's tired face—one of scorn.

"Won't you be seated?" asked Swinburne.

But Lawrence never liked to sit down. He stood with his back to the fire—the flames lighting up his clasped hands behind him. He seemed about to be leaving. He would not let any meaning form of this visit. He seemed to strike the life from all of us.

The Brett placed her brass horn under one mouth after another, as if to encourage us to speak. When no words came she put the horn away again and shrank back.

Yes, the occasion was meaningless. Lawrence meant to keep it so.

Suddenly Swinburne spoke: "I would rather have written the first thirteen pages of *The Rainbow* than anything else in English literature."

"Pity you didn't," sneered Lawrence. And he turned his back on Swinburne and communicated something to the Brett in that silent way the English have.

Frieda caught the whole play. She admired Swinburne's handsomeness. He was tall, blond, English in bearing. Yes, she was taken with Swinburne and he was playing up to her. Lawrence had sensed this instantly when he entered the room—and spat his hatred, his jealousy.

Ufer could not understand. The situation escaped him. He squatted before Frieda, back to the firelight, his pince-nez glinting as he tried to recapture her interest. "I will most likely get a few murals to paint for the State Capitol of Missouri—"

"Lawrence!" interrupted Frieda. "Isn't it nice the way Swinburne lives—here alone in a log house? He has fifteen horses. And he writes poetry."

Yes, she was taken with Swinburne, so handsome, so presentable. Not all the bother connected with a genius.

Lawrence walked around the room—disconnected himself from the situation. We sat before the fire and waited for him to give meaning to the moment, but he would have none of it. He wanted to be rid of all of us. Frieda too. Yet he and Frieda maintained this intense conflict in silence. They hated, they hated. She was taken with Swinburne. And Lawrence's looks were black.

"I have a horse Azul," said Frieda to Swinburne.

"I have only mares," confessed Swinburne.

Frieda and Swinburne were getting along famously. He had the devil in him and Frieda was egging him on.

The Brett looked from face to face. She could not make out Americans. She wanted to use her horn but she was too shy to point it at anyone. After all Frieda and Lawrence were carrying on privately. Lawrence raged and strayed about the room, and Brett was concerned for him.

Frieda looked at Swinburne admiringly. "And where were you born?" asked Frieda. That she must know.

"Oh—our folks came from New Hampshire. Three of our direct ancestors signed the Declaration of Independence."

Margaret was uncomfortable that he boasted of their lineage.

"Lawrence!" shouted Frieda. "These are real Americans —Swinburne and Margaret."

"There are no real Americans," snarled Lawrence, at the door now.

Was he going to leave? No. I realized this was their relationship in public. They fought at a distance. She really played up to his hatreds. She wasn't interested in Swinburne at all— just in nettling Lawrence.

The Brett sat back farther on the bed. *She* knew Lawrence wasn't going to run away. They were just warming up to the fight—Frieda and Lawrence. The Brett

adored Lawrence—quivered deliciously when he spat his
hate.

Ufer now, in his naïve way, turned to Margaret.

"Margaret, what do you think of D. H. Lawrence?"

"I'm very glad he came to see us," said Margaret.

"To have a man like Lawrence in Taos!" boasted Ufer.
He looked at Lawrence across the room. Lawrence could
not make up his mind to leave the room or not.

"And you are a glorious woman!" confided Ufer to
Frieda.

Frieda's eyes clouded. There was no way to compliment
either Frieda or Lawrence. She looked at Swinburne. He
was so handsome. He, rather than Lawrence in her life?
She let her being flow across to Swinburne a moment,
excited him with her admiration, but her eye too was fur-
tively on Lawrence.

I did not know what to do. Everything was at cross-
purposes. Margaret looked at me. She knew I was disappointed that such a petty thing was happening—not something great. If Lawrence was there something great ought
to happen. But it didn't. It was all discord and it was
Lawrence's doing.

I started to talk on some philosophical subject. I do not
remember what it was about, it was so long ago. Margaret
listened, Frieda listened, Ufer listened, and Brett leaned
forward with her horn.

I talked and talked as I did in those days. It was something I had just learned in the University. I talked very
proudly to the people on the sofa. Lawrence made me
talk. He had that effect on people, to make them extend
themselves, ingratiate themselves with him.

Lawrence stood by the door and listened. He could be

very still when he listened—and took you in. He still wore his big Stetson hat in the house as though he were only there for a moment and never meant to stay.

After I had talked quite a while I stopped. There was a silence. Everyone looked at Lawrence. Finally he spoke in that high whining voice. "What are you saying? You aren't saying anything."

And he came over to the fire and looked down into the flames indifferently.

It was an insulting rebuff. I had made a fool of myself.

Frieda turned and said to Margaret in her booming voice, "Lawrence and the Brett are building a porch to our kitchen."

"How nice," said Margaret.

The Brett leaned forward.

"It's hard work," she said, in her shy English voice. Her eyes popped in astonishment as she passed her horn around to us for our comments.

Lawrence gave her a look and she took back her horn quietly.

I felt very ashamed that I had displeased Lawrence with my talking. No, I had not said anything, it was true. That way of talking was all nonsense, university nonsense. Lawrence had made me see that. In an instant he had made me see that my way of thinking was nonsense. How could a man do that to you—change the whole meaning of your life in a few seconds of time? But Lawrence did.

"And how do you get your food at the ranch?" asked Margaret.

Lawrence looked at her quickly. "We ride every day to the Hawks for milk. And then Mabel brings us our stores now and then."

"We are always exhausted after Mabel has gone," flared Frieda.

"Pity," said Lawrence sarcastically.

Swinburne went to an old bureau below the bear trap and got out several necklaces and silver belts, and some straw wallets filled with rings. They were crude handmade rings of hammered silver. The bracelets had many crooked blue stones. They had once been worn by Navajo Indians and their swarthy war-painted wives behind them in the saddle as they galloped across the red desert of Arizona. Swinburne was very proud of his collection. It had taken months of traveling and dickering at out-of-the-way trading posts in Navajoland.

Swinburne took them to Frieda. He dropped a dozen turquoise rings in Frieda's lap and laid out large silver concha belts and squash blossom necklaces on the bed beside her.

"Lawrence!" she cried. Lawrence came unwillingly to the edge of the bed and looked at the silver jewelry. "Look Lawrence!" she cried, holding up a necklace.

But Lawrence was not impressed. Frieda's eyes sparkled in the firelight.

Swinburne opened another straw wallet and dumped another dozen rings in Frieda's lap.

"Lawrence!" she cried. She made his name ring.

He said nothing. He could not be a part of her joy. She was overdoing it—forcing her enthusiasm.

We all watched her happiness. Lawrence would not be moved.

"Isn't that a handsome one!" she said, trying one on. Quite a simple one with a plain blue turquoise.

116

"Would you like it?" asked Swinburne.

Frieda looked at Lawrence in utter fear. She knew he would be angry. Yes, he was angry. "Lawrence! he wants me to have it."

"You don't want the ring—and you know it." They fought with their eyes—with their souls.

"But yes!" cried Frieda. And she held up her hand again to the firelight. "It's beautiful."

Lawrence came forward and got out his wallet. "How much is the ring?"

We were all shocked. It was obvious that Swinburne intended it as a gift. Lawrence knew that as a gift it would serve as a pledge to friendship.

"No! How much is it?" cried Lawrence, annoyed. He had opened his wallet and was feeling for his money.

"I don't really remember. Nothing very much."

Lawrence got out five dollars and handed it to Swinburne.

Swinburne did not take it.

Lawrence, angrily, threw the bill on the bed.

"Lawrence!" cautioned Frieda.

He turned again and looked at the fire. We were all embarrassed. All the jewelry around Frieda on the bed now meant nothing. It had lost its glamour.

Swinburne put all the rings back into their straw wallets. Frieda looked very chastened. Swinburne took up the belts and necklaces. But he did not touch the five dollars.

It was an impossible moment. Lawrence was drunk with rage. He turned quickly and went to the low door of the cabin out into the sage. Where could he possibly go in the darkness?

Frieda was talking as though nothing had happened. "We are staying at Mabel's until Saturday."

"Do you like her?" asked Margaret.

"Well, there's been a fight between us, you know. But we're trying again. Clarence Thompson is here and he and Lawrence walk to the Post Office. They brought back a bottle of moonshine. Terrible stuff. The Brett got drunk–"

"What's that?" said the Brett when she heard her name.

"You, Brett, you got drunk!" said Frieda directly into Brett's horn.

The Brett thought about that a long while. "Very drunk. I fell down," she confessed shamelessly, then she sat back again.

"We dance to the gramophone in the studio," said Frieda.

I got up quietly and went to the door. Outside I found Lawrence leaning against the wall of the cabin looking at the lingering yellow of the sunset. The vast yellow mood of the evening sky.

I stood by Lawrence and he accepted my presence naturally. We did not say anything. He seemed to be looking at the new moon still there in the transparent yellow sky.

"I have a telescope," I said.

"Oh, do you?" he said quite interested.

"Shall I go to the other house and get it?"

"Yes, fetch it and we'll look at the moon."

I left him standing alone, leaning against the log cabin. I ran across the evening fields and got the long black telescope and came back.

He took it from me and pointed it at the moon.

"You have to adjust the eyepiece a little," I said.

"Yes, of course. Ah, there," and he gazed in wonder

through the long black scope silently. After a while he handed it to me. "Have a look," he said.

I looked at the moon a long while with Lawrence. Whatever he was thinking he did not say. Events in life were but tangent to an enormous other-universe of Lawrence that flourished only after the insignificance of the moment was over. Everything that Lawrence experienced at the time became something larger, more significant later.

"Shall we ask the Brett to come?" he said.

We went to the door and looked inside. They were still talking, but the Brett from where she sat on the bed was instantly aware of Lawrence.

"Come, Brett, and have a look at the moon." He showed her the telescope.

The Brett looked frightened.

"Come on, Brett. Look at the moon through the telescope."

She shook her head vehemently. Lawrence understood and did not press her. We went back again outside.

"The Brett is superstitious." He laughed in his queer high animal laugh—the last light on his pale face. He looked a long time at the moon and then said, "Strange." He was very moved.

The others were all coming out of the log cabin now. Frieda, the Brett, Swinburne, Margaret, Ufer.

"Lawrence, we're going." Frieda called.

Lawrence said nothing, but waited. He disapproved of the whole world as soon as Frieda appeared. She was his inspiration yet he hated her. It was one of those strange mysteries. I saw he was almost in a rage now that Frieda was there.

"Mabel will be angry," said Frieda in her loud voice. How it violated the silence all around us. "She does not want us to see anyone but her."

The Brett passed her horn from person to person to catch our replies. But what could anyone say? Mabel was Mabel.

Frieda now boomed again. She knew Lawrence would not say goodbye. "Thank you, thank you," she said to Swinburne. "I like your jewelry. I like your house. I like the way you live—alone. Thank you for the ring." The five dollars was still on the bed untouched.

"Come on, Frieda," said Lawrence. "It's late. Mabel will be angry. We've been away so long."

We all walked across the fields in silence. At the car we all stood uncomfortably.

"Now you've seen D. H. Lawrence, Margaret," said Walter Ufer foolishly.

Lawrence gave a sort of whinny.

"Goodbye, goodbye, goodbye," said Frieda grandly. "Thank you, thank you, thank you," climbing into the car heavily. And then the Brett.

Lawrence sat moodily next to Ufer in the front seat. He had not said goodbye to anyone. He nodded his head to me. I stepped over to the car.

"Come up some time to the ranch—you and Margaret," he said quietly.

"And Swinburne too!" shouted Frieda.

"Good night, Margaret," said Walter Ufer.

We stepped back and the car lurched down the hill.

Once inside our ranch kitchen Margaret lit the kerosene lamp and I made a fire in the wood stove.

"He's not the way I expected at all," I said.

"Oh, you can't tell what he's like," said Margaret. She got eggs from the brown crock. She gave me the bacon to slice.

"I know, but when you think of *Twilight in Italy*—he's not the same man."

"He's the same man," said Margaret, lifting the lid of the stove. I saw she had been moved. "He's not always creating, you know. He's just a man sometimes."

"Well, I was disappointed. And all that thing—between him and Frieda. Is it necessary?"

"Apparently." She was frying the eggs now. She was thoughtful. Yes, she had been very moved.

"Well, I can understand *The Rainbow*. But I can't think of him as writing it."

"He's only himself when he writes," she explained. "When he isn't writing—he's convalescing. Just as an actor is someone else when he's not on the stage."

We talked for hours about Lawrence's books.

"They're all so different," said Margaret.

"Norman Douglas says he doesn't know how to write —that he's redundant."

"Oh, no. It's poetic iteration. He shapes his subject with his feelings. He works and works on a subject until he molds it into being—that's his style. He knows how to write. Douglas doesn't know how to *feel*. Douglas *thinks* his way through a book professionally. Nothing new. Lawrence is new."

"Yes—new," I agreed.

"There was life before there was art. And Lawrence has gone back to life. People don't like that—life—don't recognize it."

"Yes, yes. It really isn't literature, is it?"

121

"He doesn't care for literature. Something deeper—elemental. Ancient. Lost. And he has rediscovered it. Given himself to it—this great lost meaning of life. You must use his books merely as a guide *back* to life—"

"He is so passionate," I said.

"Yes. He has a vision."

I thought of that. He had absented himself from the small talk of the evening. He resented anything but the *deep* thing of life. He was very quiet as he looked at the moon through the telescope. Yes, his vision was always upon him. He was plagued with a vision.

"What did he talk to you about?" I asked.

"Oh, that he found Taos calming—and perhaps Taos was the place and that one must make friends with one's destiny."

"Do you think he ever will?"

"Well, I think he lives with his destiny—however tormented. I like him," she said simply.

XI

IT DID NOT TAKE LONG FOR MABEL to hear that Lawrence had been to see us. She asked us to come see her immediately.

"Now what?" I asked.

"Oh, she can't bear not to be the one who arranges things."

"Do you want to go?" I didn't.

Dorothy Eugenie Brett

above: Mabel Dodge Luhan
below: Tony Luhan, Sara Higgins

"I like Tony," she said evasively.

We saddled our horses and rode into town. As we took the steep hill up to Mabel's a thousand pigeons swirled over us.

"It's beautiful here," said Margaret, looking at Mabel's three-story sun porch and the golden rooster weather vane.

We rode between the houses and looked out over the sage Indian land and the low hills beyond. We went through the big gates into the patio.

Mabel and Tony were waiting for us. Mabel was very tense, dressed as usual in flowing blue chiffon. Did she feel as angry as she looked? What was her real self? This anger—was it for us? How had she been thwarted merely because Lawrence had called on us?

We tied our horses under the cottonwoods and Mabel watched us angrily. Tony was very tender—real. He knew Mabel was angry, but he did not know what Mabel was angry about.

"How are you, Mabel?" said Margaret. Margaret was handsome and striking after she had been riding.

Mabel was very angry and did not even reply. She turned to me. "What did you say to him?"

"I—? Who?"

"Lawrence. Frieda said you talked and talked."

"Oh, I didn't say anything. Just nonsense."

"Frieda said you had something new. What is it?"

I had never seen Mabel this way before. I was very embarrassed.

We stood there in the patio. Had we been summoned to the queen to give an account of ourselves?

Margaret walked to the flagstone portal and Mabel had

in consequence to do the same. We all sat down on the wooden bancos and there was a silence.

"What was it you told Lawrence?" She pressed me for an answer.

"He didn't say anything much, Mabel. He just talked. It was an embarrassing moment—and so he talked."

"Frieda said you had something new," insisted Mabel.

"No."

"Did Lawrence listen?" She wanted every moment of Lawrence's life to be hers.

"Tony," said Margaret. "Is the land back of here all Indian land?"

"Someday not," said Tony.

"But why?"

"You'll take," he said, laughing. "You" being the white race.

"Just what did you say to Lawrence?" insisted Mabel. But even as she asked she distrusted my answer. She distrusted everyone. She was never quite real because she was always angry.

I felt very strange. She made me feel strange because she was not real. She was always *assuming* feelings of irritation and impatience. She wasn't real with most people she met.

Sara Higgins saw her as real. And perhaps Ralph Meyers, Taos' most sensitive painter. With Lawrence—? Well, she *wanted* Lawrence desperately. And so she wasn't real with him either. She couldn't be real.

She tried to make me feel uncomfortable. She wanted to overcome me, belittle me. My mind wandered a million miles away. I forgot what she had asked me. I felt guilty.

124

Her anger with me was so meaningless. "I do not know," I answered at random.

"Of course, you know!" And she made it a situation now. I tried so hard to remember what I had said to Lawrence—but he had said it was nonsense. And I saw now it was nonsense, university sophistry, nonsense. Lawrence had that power to make you *see*. I felt like Saul on the road to Damascus. Lawrence had in three almighty words set me right.

But Mabel—? She was bored. Life was always dying out in her and she was afraid of death. She was angry with her own death and projected her anger on others. Everyone, everyone must pay for her fear of death—of being no one. In her fear of being no one, how magnetic she was. What a strange power she exerted on everyone. Yet her power was a desperation with her own vacancy.

People were attracted to her hostility. They collected around her. They talked and talked, ingratiating themselves with her. They felt more important for having known her.

She loved her power yet everything was forever dying within her, and she was afraid that life would give out unless she filled it with people—*none* of whom she ever understood.

Yes, she was a remarkable woman. And the center of her life was Lawrence—whom she had lost.

What could I tell her of the few moments Lawrence had spent at our ranch?

Nothing.

"I think we ought to go," said Margaret. She realized Mabel was intent upon humiliating me.

"Well, then you didn't talk to him?" insisted Mabel.

"Oh, yes—we talked," I admitted guiltily.

"But don't you remember what you said?"

"We looked through the telescope together."

"Telescope!" She could not take it in. "Whatever has *that* got to do with it?"

"Goodbye, Mabel," said Margaret.

I arose uneasily. Mabel was very angry. I hadn't told her anything. What could I possibly tell her? You can't describe the mood of an evening. The evening with Lawrence at our ranch was an everlasting mood I didn't want to share with anyone.

"I hate your silence—it does not mean anything," and she got up from the banco and went into the house.

"Goodbye, Tony," said Margaret.

"Goodbye, Margaret. Don't get mad. Come back."

"We shall, Tony."

Suddenly spring vanished into a three-day blizzard.

"We'll have to put off going to the Lawrence's," said Margaret.

Outside I was dazzled by the whiteness. There was snow everywhere. The fruit trees that had blossomed prematurely were all frozen. All the houses were blasted white —the trees, the fence posts. The roads were gone. The little Jerusalem-like village across the way was a lost city buried under snow.

The mountains were white ruling presences after the storm. Sharp, cold, triumphant. Their cathedral peaks rose and rose in the storm-blue sky.

126

I could not move, my wonder was so great. There was a final truth to this white world of the desert. The tall, white mesas, the snow-heavy sage, the strong winter wind had greater veracity than I had. I was all doubt—and they were accurate statements of themselves. Almost too immaculate a symbol of what life could be. Whiteness. Truth. The actual life of the valley was submerged below the beauty of the cosmos. Yes, beauty had conquered in its dazzling right.

Margaret was standing in the doorway of the kitchen when I came back from the corrals. "Well—" she said.

"It's—it's overwhelming."

"You'll get used to it. Will you get me some water?" She handed me two pails.

"I am to accept all this, then, as ordinary?"

"Well, it's past comprehension, is all. It is a day out of Genesis."

I took the pails and stood a moment and looked at the vast arctic scene. I suppose I must forget that white winter day fifty years ago, turn from the ecstasy that was ours. One that had taken full possession of us—was exhausting us with its infinite meanings.

I looked again at the whiteness, the slumberous snow mountains to the east. The cold, still summits—their long sculptured ranks sloping down to the wide horizon of nothingness of the cobalt-blue north.

Swinburne kept to his cabin across the snowy sage and did not bother us. He was alone, he had no woman. He drank bootleg whiskey and wrote snatches of poems and shot out the kerosene lamp with his old-fashioned .38 at night when he was drunk.

Some of his poems were almost beautiful:

> The world is dead tonight
> My candlelight
> That flickers whitely through the room
> Cannot illume
> The far departure of her funeral.

The uneasiness, the awkwardness in his poems is his premonition—of insanity. How can you compose if death is lingering at the door?

He bought more and more black horses. Perhaps they were a symbol of love—the thing that he had never had from any of his women. He would tramp about in the white snow with an oat bag, the thick furry creatures nuzzling him. Then he would go back to his room and write another weak poem and drink himself into oblivion.

He was very handsome as he stood at our door in a blizzard one Sunday afternoon. "Will you go for a ride?" he pleaded with me.

"A ride?" I exclaimed. I saw the storm raging over his great shoulders, but he had two beautiful saddle horses behind him.

I looked at Margaret. Her eyes pleaded with me to go with him because he was her brother and he was going insane. And so I said, "Yes." I put on my red woolen socks and my high-laced boots, two ragged sweaters, and my sheepskin and my army hat and black velvet ear muffs. I went out into the snowy patio where the horses snorted white cloudy blasts and I mounted the heavy black gelding.

128

We raced toward the blizzard in the mountains into the open wilderness of the storm. There was no road, just the white blizzard wasting into many fantastic forms. He urged his horse toward the desolate foothills where the green desert bushes disappeared before our very eyes. He seemed to be casting his life away joyously in the wild storm.

Our horses were up to their bellies in the drifts, but he still wanted to go on, on, cast himself away on such a day. He was fleeing, fleeing his own death, madness first and then death. Yes, he could outwit it—up and up the storming mountain. His mare stumbled and he laughed. What a diabolical, joyous laugh. He was throwing his life away and it was glorious. The peaks were desolate above us. The whole valley below us lay abandoned to the storm.

Our horses stopped. We could go no farther. And Swinburne laughed, his great crooked smile. No, he couldn't throw himself away today. I saw a certain peace overtake him, a resignation to his destiny.

"Shall we go on?" he asked.

"It's straight up from here," I demurred. I was icy cold—and I did not have madness, as he had, to drive me on.

"Fanny could make it," he boasted. He was proud of his horse.

"I'm sure she could. But Margaret will be worried."

He said nothing for a moment. He let his mare paw the snow. Then he said almost absently: "Yes, back."

Swinburne was a brave man—but unnerved. There was a certain splendor his handsome gestures made toward life, but he was defenceless against the coming night of his mind.

On the way down the mountain through the twilight storm we said nothing. We were both thinking of Margaret.

She was in the doorway as we tied up our horses. "Did you have a good ride?" She was beautiful in her concern.

"I almost lost Joe up a mountain," roared Swinburne.

He ducked his big bald head to enter the low adobe kitchen.

Margaret was tall too. They were alike—two classic medallions from ancient Greece.

"Will you have some tea?" She was concerned for him —for his agony. But his agony he passed off as a joke.

He flung himself into the swing seat and watched her as would a lover. He admired her strong woman's body busy about the stove. He loved her, his sister, in his decent way, although oppressed with some desire for *release* from decency. "What would Mamá and Papá say to our sitting in a mud house in a blizzard in New Mexico?"

"They are very fine people," defended Margaret. Her face was grave. And I saw the whole history of their youth —pagans born into a Puritanical New England family.

"When are we going up to the Lawrences?" he asked.

We knew he was thinking of Frieda.

"Heavens! There's no road. Not until it gets warm," said Margaret.

"He is a queer duck," said Swinburne, "offering five dollars for a ring I'd given her."

"He is proud," said Margaret.

After tea he rose. He towered in the low peasant kitchen. "I suppose my cabin is somewhere over there," he said. He didn't want to leave us.

"Would you like a lantern?" asked Margaret.

"If you have one?"

Margaret went into the pantry and got the old blue lantern with the thick lens. She lit it carefully and gave it to him.

He looked at it with amusement. "Good-night," he said very formally.

"Good-night, Bob," she said, and I knew she was steadying her voice.

We watched him make his way across the snow-swept field in the night.

Summer came at last. The sun swept over the mountains each morning and lighted the desert a far-off pink. We saw the valley below us, the black figures in the green fields, the early shadows on the Sangre de Cristos, the lovely light of dawn—a vision but a vision of a forgotten creation —the bed of a great sea dried up unthinkable ages ago, leaving an austere, dry silence of red and redder shores from which the water had sunk slowly aeons ago, leaving only the orange dust of Paleolithic times to awe us.

One July morning we decided to go up to the Lawrence Ranch.

The valley was very wild in those days and the roads were mere rutted trails. Almost impassable.

Swinburne had a brand new Cadillac touring car. It was red and had huge spoked wheels. It weighed two and a half tons and cost $7000.

131

We did not know if the flimsy aspen bridges across the many streams would hold the big car, but Swinburne wanted to go. He wanted to see Frieda again.

Swinburne was very happy. There was almost—almost—a meaning to life again for him. Frieda had liked him, his tall easy going handsomeness. And Swinburne longed to have women like him. He was lost, lost, his time was coming—insanity, death, but his eagerness for life was still there and Frieda was an exciting woman. Yes, he wanted to see her again. "Let's try it!" he said, grasping the huge wooden steering wheel.

We took the road north along the mountains. We didn't quite know where we were. We went down many narrow trails in the sage desert and over rickety narrow bridges. We were constantly getting lost up lonely roads that went nowhere. We went along slowly, the dust trailing behind us. Twenty miles an hour was fast in those days. An hour later we crept to the rim of the Hondo Canyon. It was a deep gorge. Far below was the green filament of the Hondo River. There was no road down.

Swinburne drove the big car along the edge. Finally we found a narrow wagon trail that dropped sharply into the canyon itself.

"Heavens!" said Margaret.

Swinburne put the big car in gear and we started down the narrow steep road—down, down until we were on the wild shores of the Hondo River.

"There's no bridge!" said Swinburne when we reached the water.

"You have to ford," said Margaret.

The river was very high, a rushing current. Would we

founder? Swinburne did not want to get his big car stuck in the river.

"Very well," said Swinburne. "I'll try it."

We entered the water slowly. The stream was quite swift. Would we make it? The water came up over the running board. Swinburne shifted gears again, and slowly we pulled out of the water onto the sandy bank. We saw a lonely sandy road winding up into the pines.

"Let's take that road," said Swinburne. "It must go somewhere."

Very slowly we chuggged up the sandy road in the hot afternoon. The woods smelled of resin. There were huge pines on either side. The road turned and turned. There was no road. We did barely five miles an hour.

It was peaceful in the dusk of the pines. Hot. Dry. Waterless. A wasted place that was beautiful. The hot resin smells of the pine forest. We were going up, up. Occasionally there were aerial vistas—endless distances below us. The earth's curve defining the far-off volcanic horizon. And then snatches of the snow peaks through the trees—so high, so high. We were suffocating with the hot smell of resin. There was something lonely and unconquered about the delicate powerful woods around us.

All this abandoned beauty on the way to the Lawrence Ranch.

The engine of the big car was boiling. We would never make it. We looked far down in the giddy heat to lower and lower mountains, deeper and deeper washes spreading westward, beautiful flashes of the plain reaching us now and then. We could see the white bergs set on the far horizon. The multitude of black crater hills in the near foreground. We were high, high in the hot forest, but even higher were the tall peaks, ragged, empty, hostile. Voiceless.

We came to a cattle run. The trees on either side of us were blazed with ax marks.

"To show where the road is in winter," explained Margaret. "The snows are very deep."

"Look!" cried Swinburne.

Three small log houses under the pines. The Lawrence Ranch.

There was no one to greet us.

I am a little disappointed. We stand near the big red car—Margaret, Swinburne and I.

There are only three white mortar-chinked cabins under the huge pine trees. One of the cabins is so small it is little more than a shed—the Brett's.

And there is the larger cabin with the famous porch where later Lawrence and I would talk. There is a handmade table with lunch things still scattered about. Jelly, bread, butter and three chili-stained bowls rimmed with flies. There are three straight-back chairs. A dented washbasin. A lantern on the post. A half bucket of water—and a white cat.

The door to the kitchen is wide open.

No one.

"I thought they'd be here," said Swinburne.

"They're here," said Margaret.

Opposite the porch is a conical adobe oven with blackened opening where Lawrence bakes bread. A little wooden paddle with a long handle neatly standing against it.

Above the whole ranch, out the very kitchen door

towers a huge pine. It shelters the summer life on the little wooden porch.

How still it is up the wooded hillside. The whole ranch is really chipped right out of the mountain. One hundred sixty acres that shoots straight down among the pines. The ranch clings to the side of the mountain—high, high up— 8500 feet—and there is the wind again soughing in the pines.

I looked down through the pines at the strange undulating wilderness of the desert submerged in blue light. The horizon transpiring into the far blue desert—into the blue sky.

What a place to live!

Someone is in the doorway of the kitchen—Frieda, angry, a cigarette dangling from her lips. Yes, she is angry. But quickly she recovers herself and smiles. "Hello! Hello! So you came!" she cried, seeing us all, yet seeing only Swinburne. "Look!" holding up her large hand. "Your ring!"

She wore a gingham dress, a very long gingham dress. Her hair was mussed—had she been napping? But she was smoking. And her eyes sparkled warmly at the thought we had come to see her—at the thought of Swinburne.

"Come up, come up on the porch—out of the heat. It's too hot—even in the mountains." Her anger was dying down now. Slowly her goodwill asserted itself.

"We got lost," said Swinburne. He was very tall on the porch. He and Frieda—looking at each other frankly.

"Yes. Yes. Of course. Everyone gets lost. It's such a terrible road. But then isn't it beautiful when you get here?"

"Very beautiful," said Margaret.

"I want only to lie in the hammock and look through the trees—at the desert below. To wonder perhaps. It is very beautiful to wonder—satisfying."

Her anger was gone now. A certain glorious mood was upon her. Without Lawrence she was calm and happy. There lingered only a sadness in her blue eyes—Lawrence's fierceness toward her, to which she would not, would not give in. She seemed very strong today—herself.

"And did your car boil?" She laughed.

"Yes," said Swinburne, admiring her openly. They were greatly taken with each other.

"Mabel's car boils. Even Mabel's. That's one thing she cannot control!" in a jeering tone.

Mabel's presence was there momentarily.

But I was thinking only of Lawrence. Each clumsy charming detail of the crude carpentry, the porch, the doors, the picket fence. How gaily he painted and sawed and nailed this quaint little ranch together.

"We'll have tea," said Frieda.

Yes, she was happy we had come. It was a release from the terrible battle between her and Lawrence that went on and on. A battle she must see to the very end.

"Shall I help you?" said Swinburne, so obviously taken with her. And Frieda accepting him graciously, enjoying the possibilities.

Margaret and I sat on the porch while Swinburne and Frieda talked in the kitchen. Her voice resounded. She was fearless—never giving an inch—even to Lawrence's greatness.

"It's so high," I said to Margaret.

136

"Yes, almost 9000."

We both wanted Lawrence to come. Was he absenting himself purposely?

"You suppose he's around?" I asked.

It was peaceful under the pines. Margaret had no anxieties. She lived the beauty of the moment.

"I am so thrilled you write poetry," boomed Frieda's voice in the kitchen. "It is the only thing that matters. To break through—do what you *have* to do."

Margaret and I listened to her throaty German-English. This advice to Swinburne who was so sadly coming apart —going to his death?

She was in the doorway now, beaming at us. The tea things steaming on a tray. "Now we'll have tea!" gathering in Margaret and me in her joyous eyes. "Joe, will you go and get Lawrence. The Brett too. They're cleaning the spring—"

"But where are they?" I ask.

"Just down in the hollow—you'll know. You'll hear Lawrence shouting to the Brett."

I got up from the chair on the porch and went through the trees toward the hollow. Yes, it must be this way. Ah, the stillness. Nothing, nothing has ever been here before —just this tree silence. It is overpowering. And there is the wind soughing slowly, surely through the highest pines. I lose myself, my meaning, as I picked my way to the ridge and look down into the small arroyo choked with trees.

And there is Lawrence and the Brett struggling with a rusty pipe in the hillside, trying to twist it out together.

He wears a blue shirt and white corduroys stuffed into

137

his black rubber irrigating boots. "There! There!" he said. He is impatient with the Brett as they try to twist out the rusty pipe.

The Brett is quite another person than the one I first met on our ranch. She wears an orange blouse, riding breeches and high-laced boots; in the top of one gleams the handle of a knife.

She is no use wrenching the pipe loose. He is irritated with her, really angry. And at each word of anger the Brett lowers her ear trumpet to Lawrence's mouth to catch his words.

I look a moment in silence. He's really just an ordinary person struggling with a pipe—but no, there is something more about him, an intensity—a knowingness—a strange depth of meaning he can give the moment. He works— naturally, gracefully if a little self-consciously—but that was the Brett's fault. The Brett would make anyone awkward. Her willingness, and her clumsy devotion irritated him that day long ago in the shady canyon.

"Ah!" he said when he saw me. He quickly went out to me. He is so sensitive to me standing there above them on the ridge.

"It's no good, Brett. You know we can't get it out today," he said. Irritation is his connection with her, and she rather loves it. She listens with her brass trumpet long after he has spoken.

He turned back to me smiling. "We're cleaning out the spring. The water has been tasting funny lately."

The Brett has listened and listened and then she says to me, "We're digging up the pipe. Yes?" And she holds the horn out to me to reply.

138

But I am aware only of Lawrence, and he knows that. He knows I am thinking too much about him. All his books, all his greatness, his fame. And he is very sorry for me, for he is just a man standing there in the shady canyon in a blue shirt and dirty corduroys and black rubber boots and touseled hair. Just Lawrence—smiling faintly.

"We'll give it over today, Brett," he said turning to her. She listened intently to his words, then put her ear trumpet down on the ground.

They both knelt at the pool and washed their hands. Lawrence beardy, frail, pale—yet powerful. Brett, the young woman, her silence embarrassing to her and to us. I look again at the knife stuck in her boot top. Why? She is so shy. How could she possibly use it?—even in an emergency? Oh, it's symbolic, of course.

Lawrence dried his hands on his corduroys. There was a bright light in his eyes. A queer questioning look. Perhaps he was challenging me to come alive. He led the way back through the low firs up the little hill and then toward the clearing where Frieda, Margaret and Swinburne were sitting on the porch talking in the late afternoon sunshine.

Frieda and Swinburne were getting along famously. Frieda was agreeing joyously to Swinburne who had a handsome devilish smile on his face. But she was a bit wild-eyed. She knew Lawrence was coming and there would be a fight.

Lawrence went up to Margaret courteously, said something simple. Yes, he was taken with her—her serenity, her fineness. He admired Margaret. Then he turned to Frieda. "Susan has eaten the potatoes."

Frieda's eyes flashed furiously. It would be a wonderful

fight. And instantly, forgetting her warm relation with Swinburne, she denounced Lawrence. "I knew. I knew. You and the Brett cannot take care of that cow. And now my potatoes!"

"Damn your potatoes," said Lawrence, sitting down on the stoop. He did not acknowledge Swinburne, turned his back on him in spite.

Swinburne was amused. He admired Lawrence. What Lawrence did was all right. But the petty scene made Lawrence look very bad to us all.

I saw he was really not in the drama which he himself had created. His eyes were dreaming far off. At the golden desert far below us. He absented himself from the conversation over tea on the porch. He didn't like Swinburne.

"Lawrence!" cried Frieda. "Swinburne will give me a book of his poetry. Isn't that nice!"

"Child's talk," he snorted.

He looked over his shoulder and said to me, "We'll have a thunder storm." The sky was black over the peaks. "Come and have a look at my adobes. We'll cover them."

Brett rose, but a look from Lawrence made her sit down again. She watched his moods closely.

Lawrence and I went down the way a bit, across the steep alfalfa field to a place where a few pathetic adobes are drying by the ditch. What cracked, crooked, curled-up adobes they were.

"They're not much," he confessed. "But I'm to make a chimney."

We took some black roofing paper and covered the twisted brick. They were very badly made adobes, but he had made them.

The air was heavy and disturbed with the coming storm.

140

There was a certain harmony between us. He did not talk as we carefully covered his mud bricks. He looked again at the black storm on the peaks. "It'll come," he said.

I am very silent. There are so many things I want to say. There is something quick and understanding about him—waiting for me to speak. But the moment passes. What can I say?

He looked again at the far scene below us in the slanting sunshine. "There is something in looking out on a new landscape all together." He always started with the landscape—looked and looked at it—and gradually became profound about man, the universe. New Mexico was the greatest experience he ever had. Yet was he not homesick for England? Restless, disappointed, hurt with his exile?

I cannot tell. I only know that there were depths and depths in Lawrence that sustained him. His quarreling never seemed to matter to me. Nor do I think it did to him. He raged at Frieda while he triumphed in a beautiful reverie of his own.

Lawrence and I walked back slowly. He did not want to return to the porch and the things being said around the tea table. The whole sky was black now and the mountains colossal white monuments against it.

As we strolled across the field I realized how alert he was to the scene, as startled with life as a deer, as curious. It was nice to be with him, you were alive to everything through him. He was a spirit—so ordinary, yet a spirit passing by—alert, almost frantic with the meanings of the moment.

No, I was unequal to his depths. And he was sorry. He looked at me queerly. As he walked he would have liked our walk to be gay.

He was happiest picking flowers—and reacting with delicious fear to the black storm tumbling down the mountain. It was such fun that darkening moment of the storm coming down the mountains. He walked lightly with the thought of the storm. He loved life and the things around him. His blue eyes thought and thought of the wonder of the coming storm.

"We'll catch it if we don't run!" And he started out quickly before me. He kept his head down and ran up the field, I following. I knew he was experiencing the beauty of the storm. It was a big thing to him—the storm.

When we got back to the porch there were huge drops pelting us. It was black under the pine tree. And I saw all the white faces anxiously waiting for us.

"Did you have to go and get wet!" cried Frieda, concerned.

"Rubbish!" said Lawrence.

He looked at me concerned. Yes, he felt responsible for me. I was fifteen years younger. Yet he was worried about my getting wet. He had liked me, something had passed—but I was too young. It had been a living moment—running with him across the alfalfa field. An extreme experience of nature for him—and hence for me. We had said so little but its effect on my life was to be final. He had that power over one—to alert one to the final meanings.

But now he was in a rage with Frieda! She and Swinburne!

"Get inside, get inside—you fools!"

"But Lawrence—!" cried Frieda.

"Get inside. Get inside. The storm will have everything that's out."

142

We all crowded into the kitchen. It was very neat. The stove, the table, the curtains, the shelves. Frieda's kitchen. But Lawrence had taught her to keep house.

Again the room, the people, the drama of our anxious personalities became instantly significant because Lawrence was there. He made us all genuine. He was exasperated, angry, God knows why. But the angry moment was real.

He made us all sit down and wait. The moment must be exactly as he wished it. Just so. Margaret and Frieda and the Brett at the table. Swinburne and I at the stove. Lawrence detached from all of us—but directing the moment with his anger. Yet it was fun. He made it wonderful waiting for the storm to break.

There was a terrible explosion of thunder quite near. The Brett cowers. She looks at Lawrence and cowers. The thunder reverberates in canyon after canyon.

"It's good to have a storm," said Lawrence. "It's real, Brett. It's real."

The Brett is too frightened to look up. Frieda smokes casually. Swinburne is smoking too with grand gestures.

"And do you like thunder?" asks Frieda.

"Very much," said Swinburne. "But what happens to the road?"

"Yes," said Lawrence, understanding that we have to drive back. He's very sympathetic. Perhaps he likes Swinburne after all.

We hear the thunder farther and farther down the slopes. The storm had passed.

We all go out onto the porch. The yard, the slope is devastated by the storm.

"Look, Brett," said Lawrence. "Look at the marvellous

color of your mountains. Look at the storm sweeping across the desert. The sand is rising to meet the rain."

They seem to be wondering together at the passage of the storm. Frieda is left out again.

Margaret, Swinburne, and I ran for the car.

"Goodbye, goodbye!" cried Frieda. "Take care! Take care." She stood there shouting on the porch. "Better luck next time."

When we get in the car, we find Lawrence white faced beside us. "The first three miles will be bad. Quite bad. The rocks will have covered the road, you know. Do drive carefully. I'm sorry we had a storm. You'll make it. I'm sure. Goodbye. Come again."

All his temper was gone. What a good host he was at last.

But we didn't make it. The road was impossible. The huge Cadillac went through a bridge. We had to abandon it and walk miles in the dark.

XII

WE SAW A GREAT DEAL OF LAWRENCE that summer.

We were eager to be near him. His greatness overwhelmed me when we went about his ranch together. Often he was not great—but merely drying the milk pail or petting his kitten. He was tender with animals, his being transfused with theirs—with every living thing—and he was another self. He was another self too when he looked at the white clouds over the 12,000-foot peaks. And still another self when he was near a tree.

But when he looked at you he was his deepest, finest self. He *knew*. And you bowed down to his sentience. It was true and everlasting—a love he bestowed on your being. And you wanted his knowledge of you because it was inviolate.

Swinburne did not go up to the Lawrence Ranch again.

Swinburne could not quite follow through with his attraction to Frieda. He had a new woman, very beautiful, very calculating, a girl of seventeen—and he tried to lose himself in her, ward off the catastrophe of his life a while longer with a riotous, almost indecent love in the log cabin across the sage.

But soon the girl became terrified and fled in the night.

Margaret and I did not quite understand that he was dying, savagely extinguishing his spirit with drink and women. We did not realize how difficult it is for a broken psyche to survive its own shame. For Swinburne was ashamed, ashamed, ashamed. He was overburdened with his failure to live his life as his New England parents desired. He was diseased with his parents' goodness, and his regret mortally wounded him. There was the cancer of his parents' goodness within him—and he was ashamed.

I do not know how Frieda felt. She always asked after him—somewhat eagerly. He had not come again and she was rather sad.

How much did she care? Frieda was so spontaneous, life leaped across from her to everyone she met. She had that rare ability to admire without being taken in. Her blue eyes thought and laughed and encouraged life in you. Her skepticism was buried deep deep within her but it was there though it never dampened her spontaneous good will.

Frieda's mind, her convictions were different from Lawrence's. If she expressed them in Lawrence's presence it was at the risk of derision. She had to fight for every idea she expressed. It was his habit to jeer at her in public. In private, I imagine they did not hate, but loved.

After Lawrence's death her statements became more valid without his interruptions. I do not believe she ever said anything that was not, even obscurely, related to Lawrence's great conception of life. We shall never know how much was her original insight and how much was Lawrence's genius. Although they always appeared at odds they were one. Certainly after his death, her entire urge was to defend, to eulogize, to love him. I think her interpretations of his genius are the most clarifying, the finest of their kind, in literature.

Often Margaret and I would ride up to the Lawrence Ranch on horses. Or we would go in someone's car.

The forest was lovely on either side of the steep road. The resin perfume of the pines overwhelmed us.

Even today, fifty years later, a strange feeling overtakes me. We are going to the Lawrences! But Lawrence is dead, and so is Frieda, and so is Margaret and Swinburne.

And Spud. Only the pine-resin smell remains—evokes that summer—and it all becomes timeless in my heart.

I remember one afternoon Margaret and I arrived at the Lawrences' steep clearing in Ruth Swaine's Buick. We had boiled and boiled on the way and waited almost an hour for the motor to cool. We were all exhausted from pushing the car. But the enchantment of going to the Lawrences was there for all of us. The altitude makes us all a little eerie. Again there is no one to greet us. It is an empty stage.

The big pines all around seem to exude a drowsy perfume. What a hot indolent moment in the afternoon to arrive. There is a dramatic apathy everywhere. We are all insensible with the heavy mountain heat. No one.

But yes! Frieda is on the porch before a washtub, washing white clothes. She's in a straw hat. Her face is red with the heat; a cigarette as always droops from her mouth.

"How nice!" she cried. "Did you have trouble?"

"We boiled," said Margaret. "We waited in the woods. They are so lovely. Frieda, this is Ruth Swaine."

"How do you do. I am washing. Lawrence taught me. In Italy he taught me. He said I must learn." She seemed to live the events of her life with Lawrence over and over.

There was never a moment—even years after his death—when the intense drama of Lawrence was not in her frightened, brave eyes. Everything she said, the least remark, related to Lawrence.

She lifted the big sheet from the washtub now and wrung it out very naturally.

"Come up, come up on the porch—out of the heat. It's July. But at night it gets cold. Lawrence dreads the snow already—the big one that comes in December. We'll go south again. Lawrence wants to finish his novel. I so like it here. But Lawrence is restless. And do you live in Taos?" she said to Ruth Swaine.

"In a big tent on Margaret's ranch. My husband is an architect. We're from Dallas—."

"Ah," said Frieda, taking the tiny woman in. "It's so nice to live in a tent. Not a house. Lawrence and I once slept in barns on our walking trip across the mountains in the Tyrol. We had fearful good times on that trip—on foot, with shoulder bags. Yes, we slept in haylofts. We made tea and our meals by the rivers. We crossed the mountains. Lawrence found a lovely little chapel, quite forsaken. And Lawrence lit the candles and looked at all the *ex voto* pictures—so strange. It was the pass—we were at the top. We slept that night in a hayloft in an Alpine meadow. It was icy and clear. I undressed and lay in the sun. We found Alpine roses and Edelweiss. Sometimes we drank with the mountain peasants and danced a little. We were happy. And how we loved each other. Lawrence was writing *Twilight in Italy*," and she looked at us brightly for our approval—?

Was she confessing? No, it was her life with Lawrence and she lived it and lived it.

Behind Frieda was Spud, thin, remote, hostile. He was annoyed because we had come. His silence disturbed me for years. He was young and white and beautiful in his resentful way. Never, never responding. Always allowing his silence to give the impression of profundity. What he thought even Lawrence didn't know.

148

Spud was the enigma of Taos. Even a greater enigma than Mabel. He was an important witness of every drama that occurred in Taos, and yet one wonders if he was actually present at any of them.

Lawrence felt an affection for him, used him to fill in the cast of characters Lawrence always needed around him. He practiced literary scales on Spud. He once wrote him: "Dear old Horse, you'd never be azure or turquoise here in London. Oh, London is awful: so dark, so damp, so yellow grey, so mouldering piece meal. With crowds of people going about in a mouldering, damp, half-visible sort of way. . . . Horse, Horse be as hobby as you like but let me get on your back and ride away again to New Mexico. I don't care how frozen it is, how grey the desert, how cold the air, in Taos, in Lobo, in Santa Fe. It isn't choking, it is bright day at day time, and bright dark night at night. . . . Oh Horse, Horse, Horse. . . ."

Spud never seemed to annoy Lawrence even with his harmless remarks. "Listen to the Spoodle," Lawrence would say. "How happy he is in the little he knows!"

But Spud and I—? That was another matter. We were both Americans and could see through one another. I could never engage him in discussion. He would merely yawn. He was sleek, beautiful, a cupbearer to the gods. Everyone liked Spud—and he was annoyed that I didn't.

Years later, after Lawrence was dead, we greeted each other quietly when we met. Even between enemies there is a warmth that memory brings. I saw him one evening before he died, a little old man crouching against the wall of his house, taking a last look at the sunset.

Spud did not acknowledge me as I went up on the hot porch. His acerbity seemed affected. Although he kept his face impassive, I wondered, wondered even then as I do today, what unfinished worlds there were in Spud's sad eyes.

We sat on chairs as Frieda finished washing her white clothes.

"Lawrence will be here," she said. She knew it was Lawrence we had come twenty miles to see. "He and the Brett went down to Rachel's for the milk. And they will bring the mail. Lawrence hates the mail. Letters are empty he says, dull as dishwater and of no use to anybody. But I notice he writes a dozen a day himself." Her eyes flashed. She entertains us as we wait for Lawrence.

Spud immolates himself against the wall. He wants us to go.

There are voices—riders coming across the alfalfa field beyond the white picket fence. I recognized Lawrence urging his dappled grey forward. Even though he is nearly home he is still urging his horse. He must be first, he must be first.

Behind him are two Americans, a man on a white horse and a slight girl on a sorrel mare. Last of all the Brett— stolidly humped over the horn of the saddle. She clutches the reins in one hand and her brass horn in the other.

Frieda exchanged looks with Spud. "The Gilletts," she said. "They are very nice."

We wait while they all ride over to the white picket fence, dismount and tie up their horses.

Lawrence comes up slowly to the porch. His beard was heavy, unkempt. He wears a blue shirt and ruckled corduroys stuffed into his enormous misshapen boots.

Does he or does he not acknowledge us? There's a

twinkle in his eye—a devil. First he must make war with Frieda, establish their enmity almost lovingly before he can say a word to us. He has one white letter he hands to Frieda, a huge letter. "Mabel is coming for us—" rolling his eyes heavenwards. "Or rather Tony and Clarence."

"Clarence!" hissed Frieda.

Spud remained immobile. Does he hear? Does he understand?

"And where's the rest of the mail?" asked Frieda.

"He blew his nose on it," says the Brett. And she listens for what we have to say to that. She passes her horn from person to person for our offering as would a vestryman in a church.

We are all very uncomfortable now. Lawrence does not see fit to enliven us. He is very pale. Perhaps he has one of his headaches. The Brett looks at him consolingly. Frieda hates her.

No, it's not going to come off as it did the time before. A certain desuetude, even with Lawrence present, overtakes us. None of us can say anything. It is very embarrassing.

I look at the girl now Bobby Gillett—young, urgent—a little wild? She wears Western riding breeches, a white shirt, a yellow kerchief around her throat. Black bobbed hair. What a big painted mouth she has—a voluptuous little creature. But shrewd, knowing, dangerously alive. Her husband, tall, pale, genial—of no consequence.

We all wait for Lawrence and Lawrence isn't going to make the scene come alive. He looks and looks at Frieda. They would like to fight awhile—but there are so many guests.

We are all frozen in place on a stage—the huge pointed mountains behind us. It is Frieda and Lawrence's play. If he decides to animate us, he will. The Brett waits. Spud waits from habit. The Gilletts wait. Margaret and I wait. Frieda is talking to him angrily—but only with her eyes. He relishes their fight in silence.

He was just a man today and it wasn't right for us to stay and see his ordinariness. He was very pale. He spat into his handkerchief.

"And what are we to do at Mabel's?" shouted Frieda. "We don't get along. You wanted to kill her when the Danes were here. And riding that time she wanted to hit you with a stick. Yes!"

Lawrence turned to Ted Gillett. "I'll come when we get back from Taos. We'll make that bake oven. It's only that you've got to have triangular bricks. It's difficult. We'll do a little each day. I bake twenty loaves at a time —in half an hour," gesturing to his own Indian oven at the edge of the porch.

Bobby laughed. "Well, then we'll see you, Lorenzo?" She was boyish, urgent to experience life, a very attractive American girl.

She and Ted turned to go.

"Goodbye. Goodbye!" cried Frieda. "We'll be down at Mabel's for a while. Tell Rachel and Bill to save us some buttermilk. We'll be back. It won't last long there at Mabel's. Lawrence will get mad. You'll see."

"Goodbye, Frieda," called Bobby, going to her horse at the fence. "Don't let Mabel get you down!" She was so at ease with Lawrence. "Goodbye, Spud. Keep your pecker up." Bobby could be quite shocking.

152

Spud wrinkled his nose at her as they rode away.

Lawrence was so ordinary that day. He did not care to be his usual gleaming self. He had this fight going on with Frieda, and Mabel for tomorrow. Why should he light up for me? He refused the relation the magic of his being. He didn't want to be great today. Just a man.

"Would you like to see the tree the lightning struck?" he asked in his high thin voice.

"Yes!" I said.

We left the others on the porch and went down to the big pine tree.

"After you left the other afternoon the storm returned. And it was struck and struck," pointing to the white scar that made its way round and round the thick black bark and down into the ground.

"The tree fairly bounced."

"Vibrated?" I said.

"No, *bounced*," he insisted.

We looked at the tree a long while. He was suddenly sensitive toward me. The huge wounded reality of the tree made him sensitive to everything alive. He saw me for a sudden quick moment. And I saw a thought pass slowly through his blue eyes. He accepted me at that moment. His being had touched mine—even if mine, however eager, was too young still to know his.

"Will it die?" he said.

"They generally do," I said.

"Pity," he answered.

However, the huge pine, Lawrence's tree, is still there today.

"Shall we go back?" he said quietly. He had shown me

the tree, but the instinctive thing had also happened between us. I had received from him some sort of quicken-
ing. He confirmed the fact that I lived. Everyone he met
he tried to quicken. That was what his rages were all about
—when he failed to quicken those he talked to he grew
angry.

Spud turned and went into the kitchen when he saw us
coming. Frieda did not give herself that day. She sat on
the porch ponderously with Margaret and exchanged
politenesses, her eyes darting accusingly at Lawrence. It
pleased Lawrence that she was hurt. But we had no clue
to the play. It was a silent dialogue we could not understand.

The Brett had got out a very large electric box and was
fiddling with it. It was a hearing aid that Marconi himself
had designed for her. Lawrence killed her with a look and
she quietly turned it off and put it away.

They were all waiting for us to go. But even our moment of leaving, Lawrence somehow made important. You
were always in a very intense situation with Lawrence. The
moment was more than the moment. Lawrence heightened
the simplest occasion. But not intentionally. He was merely
there—and a tree was more than a tree, a storm more than
a storm. The words you said casually suddenly stood out
as though you had said them on a stage. Nothing could be
incidental if Lawrence was listening. His presence was
enough to dramatize the moment.

I think much of the antagonism to Lawrence was due to
the fact that most people saw him only as a man. But he
touched life and sought to have *them* touch life, and he
became enraged; most people were stones. He had a living

154

Lawrence's tomb, Lawrence Ranch, New Mexico

Lawrence by Jo Davidson

imagination—and those he met were already dead. And he hammered himself to pieces again and again over the dead because he really could not believe in death.

We said a very awkward goodbye. It was still hot and bright under the pines.

"Goodbye, Margaret. Goodbye," said Frieda, relieved we were going. "And thank Swinburne for the ring. I wear it."

Lawrence's eyes narrowed. But Frieda didn't care.

"I shall, Frieda," said Margaret. "Goodbye."

We went to the car.

Lawrence stood at the car door. He said nothing. But he was saying goodbye to Margaret. It was a gracious mood of farewell. Then he turned to me in the back seat. A half smile came over his pale face. "You think too much, my lad," he said.

XIII

LAWRENCE SPENT A GREAT DEAL of time at Mabel's that summer.

One wonders why he returned and returned to Mabel. They had parted bitterly the previous fall. But Lawrence was everlastingly making peace with his enemies.

"Let's try and be really sensible when we meet again —and laugh and send most things to the devil. None of the strain of insistence. Why insist?" he had written Mabel.

Then there was the graciousness of the huge estate, the

many houses, the beautiful location on the very edge of Indian land. The wealth, the leisure, the exclusiveness appealed to Lawrence.

And Mabel—? He was drawn to her. She was a new Mabel. She affected submissiveness.

Soon they were taking horseback rides together in the sage. They rode knee to knee. And Mabel tried her new role out on him. She trembled. Her limbs turned to water. "I am not the same as I was," she murmured, ashamed.

But it just wasn't right—he and Mabel. The false note of calculation was there. He knew, and he dashed off ahead of her. He was truly reckless on a horse. He did not look very well on a horse.

But Mabel had him again at her house. She had added numerous guests to fill out the cast:

Jaime de Angulo, a fantastic figure in Spanish *alpargatas* (rope-soled slippers) and beret—quite mad, with a hodgepodge insight into life. De Angulo liked to show off by doing headstands on a horse.

Clarence Thompson—gentle, effeminate, weighted down with Indian silver—a delicate face but an inner black ruin.

Ida Rauh, an actress, a sculptress in horn-rims and a black mop of hair. She immediately started a head of Lawrence in clay. Lawrence will not sit for her—and so she runs after him at intervals to have a look at his head.

Spud Johnson.

And the Brett.

Mabel disliked the Brett instantly. She found her oldish, pretty, childish—arrogant, English. Was this Lawrence's new love? wondered Mabel. They met hostilely.

The Brett failed to penetrate Mabel's evil designs. She

thought of Mabel as having poise and self-assurance. She liked Mabel. But the Brett had no insight. She was ever-lastingly shy, frightened, incapable of judging anyone. Her deafness inhibited her. She was never quite there. She was almost a servant to Lawrence. Her strangeness was em-barrassing—to herself and others.

Mabel was irritated with the Brett. Why did Lawrence prefer the Brett's love to Mabel's?

One morning on horseback she asked him. "What *is* it about the Brett you like?"

"I don't know," said Lawrence. "Somehow I feel she has something of a touchstone about her—that shows things up. . . . I can't explain."

What could such an odd collection of characters do together?

Charades.

It was Lawrence's passion—to make people act out silly dramas.

How brilliant, how very funny Lawrence is as an actor. He keeps up a patter of talking and everyone is convulsed with laughter. The Brett is a tiger in Mabel's fur coat, she pounces suddenly at Lawrence, growling. Lawrence jumps back. His hat falls off. (He always wore that big ten-gallon hat even in the house.) He looks scared to death. Ida, act-ing with him, is helpless from laughing. It was so funny they couldn't finish.

Then Lawrence would design an entirely new charade.

Lawrence was uneasy in Taos. He longed to be up on the ranch. There he could be himself—without tension.

All these strange people—Mabel and de Angulo and Ida Rauh and Spud. Why had he ever left England? For this?

He loved the ranch. He could look far down across the desert, and the June morning shining.

They were whitewashing the kitchen. And puttying the windows, and chinking the log cabins. Building a chimney. Shingling the Brett's roof. Making more adobes—thirty-four. Listening to the "squirrel-enlivened night." And writing *Pan in America*.

It is pleasant on the ranch without Mabel. The Brett and Lawrence make furniture for Lawrence's room. They saw and chop and hammer—and make a very awkward heavy bedstead. They call Frieda to come and help them drag it into Lawrence's room. It looks quite nice with Lawrence's red blanket laid over it.

They were happy on the ranch.

They decorate the kitchen. They decorate the living room. How the three of them delighted in spattering naïve designs on everything within reach. Even today you can see Lawrence's snakes and Phoenixes and sun-flowers and Eves everywhere on the ranch.

Lawrence felt better. The writing was going marvelously. He went off into the woods each morning and came back each noon with a large sheaf of manuscript.

He is full of his new story to be known as *St. Mawr*, the story about a stallion who burns with the mystery of life.

He sits down to lunch with Frieda and the Brett and reads the pages he has just written under the tree. The lunch grows cold. Lawrence's eyes are twinkling with amusement. He laughs so much over what he has written that he has to stop.

158

Lawrence read very vividly, changing his voice to suit every character. Frieda and the Brett sit entranced. Finally he gives what he has written to the Brett. "How are you getting on with the typing?"

"Very well," said the Brett.

"Why, oh why can't you spell the same way I do, when it is in front of your nose!" wailed Lawrence.

"Why not, indeed?" replied the Brett.

After supper he always lectures the Brett. "All the Gods, Brett, have blue eyes."

"I am sure there are Gods present," said Frieda, looking sarcastically at Lawrence's blue eyes.

"To bring the Gods, you must call them to you," replied Lawrence reverently.

But he writes and writes, very rapidly under the trees. He has a headache. He has a cold. He cannot go for the milk one evening. He sits up late reading in the kitchen. He coughs incessantly. "Damn these coughs and sore throats! Why doesn't someone else get them instead of me?"

Some days he merely lies in the hammock. Withdrawn.

Then another short story. He writes them so easily.

The Brett is painting a very long narrow picture of the desert.

Lawrence talks of the fierceness of the land, of its savagery. He is very intense and rather sad.

Then Mabel arrives in the Garden of Eden with Clarence.

Clarence—charming, boyish, vain in all his silver rings

and bracelets, his huge turquoise belts—was inflamed with Lawrence.

They must all come to Taos, Mabel insists. She and Clarence will come tomorrow and fetch them.

Frieda does not like it. Lawrence turns the corners of his mouth down.

"We've been very busy," he demurs.

"It will be a nice weekend," said Mabel. "And we'll be all alone."

"All alone—?"

"Well, there's Clarence and Mrs. Sprague—and Jaime. I don't know what to do with him. And there'll be Ida and Spud."

Lawrence is deciding, shall he or shall he not go to Taos with Mabel.

"I rather like Ida," said Lawrence. "I think the Spoodle is really nice—in the last issue. He's lost—but nice."

"What a perfect day," declared Frieda. She looks frightened. Mabel has won.

"Yes," said Lawrence. "We'll come."

So the nonsense started all over again.

The charades, the rides in the sage, the evenings of Majong, the quarreling, the petty jealousy, Mabel's indomitable drive to have Lawrence from Frieda.

There was a new emotional strain to the gatherings. Clarence.

Clarence was dazzled by Lawrence's power. He longed for Lawrence in his strange effeminate way. He was tall and blond and vainly arrogant. He wore a dark red velvet

160

tunic with full sleeves—trimmed with Navajo silver buttons. It belonged in the court of the Medici. Nevertheless, it made Clarence even more effeminate.

Lawrence was taken with Clarence. They went riding in the sage together—Lawrence and Clarence. The women didn't like it. Lawrence spent the whole weekend talking to Clarence.

De Angulo was there too. He talked about Indian philology, the collective subconscious and brain surgery—and at the most inopportune moments he would tear off his shirt in the dining room and strut up and down showing what fine muscles he had.

Lawrence was mortified. "He's not quite all right," insisted Lawrence. "Next time he'll rip off his trousers, I wouldn't wonder."

In the evening they danced, played charades, or quarreled.

Lawrence's hair needs cutting.

Mabel would like her hair cut too—by Lawrence.

The Brett is made the barber.

Lawrence sits on a chair in the middle of Mabel's big studio with a towel round his shoulders and a bowl over his head.

Brett snips gingerly, running the comb through Lawrence's hair lovingly.

"Don't pull so!" Lawrence looks at her with irritation.

"It's a bit jagged," murmurs the Brett. "You don't mind, do you?"

Lawrence's suspicions are aroused. "Fetch me a mirror, someone," he commands. He looks at himself in astonishment.

"For heaven's sake!" he cried, alarmed. "Get a man to cut my hair. You've given me a debutante bob. I want a man's haircut."

De Angulo arrives, his own hair touseled, and makes quick work of it. Lawrence looks thin and lean after it.

Now it is Mabel's turn. She longs to have Lawrence cut her hair.

"I'll do it," offers the Brett. "I always snipped Katherine Mansfield's hair for her."

Lawrence hovered around and told the Brett how to cut Mabel's hair.

Brett slashed and slashed at Mabel's hair.

"Oh, that hurts!" exclaims Mabel.

"Yes, you *are* rough," said Lawrence.

Mabel turns her head suddenly, and the Brett cuts the end of Mabel's ear off. The blood ran. "Why you cut my ear off!" exclaimed Mabel.

Lawrence looked very pale and gave Mabel his handkerchief.

Frieda and Lawrence and the Brett—refreshed after an interlude of nonsense—all go back to the ranch.

The porch is still not quite finished. Lawrence and the Brett go down to the woods, with axes. "When I am in a temper, I like to go out into these quiet woods and chop down a tree: it quiets the nerves. Do you feel like that too?"

"Yes," replies the Brett. "I do."

"I'll chop this one down," and he begins to chop a tall straight pine. "Look out, Brett!" The tree creaks, sways, and falls over with a crash.

Lawrence looks at it proudly. They both trim off the branches. "Let's see if we can lift it."

They lift it with great effort and stagger through the woods up to the house.

Frieda, over the washtub, cries out.

"We'll have to saw it," Lawrence tells her. "You can sit on it as you are the heaviest."

Frieda doesn't like that remark at all, but she sits firmly in the middle of the log while the Brett and Lawrence saw it.

It was a very innocent life there among the trees that summer—Lawrence, Frieda and the Brett.

XIV

ONE MORNING LAWRENCE SPITS A bright splash of blood. Frieda is frightened. But the Brett pretends not to have seen.

After lunch, looking white and ill, Lawrence goes to bed and stays there sleeping most of the day. The following day he is still in bed. And in the afternoon he spits blood again.

Frieda sends a message to Bill Hawk. She asks him if he will not drive down to the Hondo and telephone for the doctor.

Lawrence is in a wild fury. "What do you *mean?* Why have you sent for a doctor!" He is sitting up in bed tense with rage. "How dare you!" And he hurls an iron egg ring at Frieda's head.

"You *know* I dislike doctors. I *won't* see him— I *won't!*" His voice is shrill. "I'll go out and hide in the sage brush until he goes. I'll teach you!"

Frieda is bewildered. "But Lorenzo, I was worried about you. If it's nothing, we'll all be relieved; and if it's serious, the doctor can help."

He was suddenly quiet now. He lay looking out through the open door—angry, helpless.

It grew dark.

Brett stood behind the big tree, watching the lights of a car far below coming across the desert.

The lamp is lighted in Lawrence's room now. He is sitting up in bed, wrapped in a shawl, miserable, shamed.

The light of the car in the desert far below disappears in an arroyo, reappears a short while, then disappears again. An hour later the light shines faintly through the trees across the alfalfa field.

Finally an old touring car comes to a halt before the picket fence.

Dr. Martin. He is gruff, crusty—a horse and buggy doctor of the '80s. "Well," he said. "Who threw all those rocks in the road? Living up here! Are you crazy? Mabel said he was somebody! Getting me out at this hour. Can't he have a hemorrhage at a decent hour? Say! you're the Brett. Mabel said you wore a knife. What for? Let me tell you about these Indians. Take Tony. Mabel thinks—"

"He's in the other room, Doctor," said Frieda.

The door is open. The light makes a deep socketed skull of Lawrence's face. He sits up bravely.

164

Doctor Martin lunges into the room with his little black satchel. He's a canny old man—a talker, a fighter, but his eyes are shrewdly on Lawrence.

"Say, you've got a beard. Too much trouble. Are you some kind of a writer? Mabel says you're somebody. Mabel got the best of you yet? You know you can't win with Mabel. All that money. And her own way always. Tony don't know, but Mabel's got the best of Tony already. Better off an Indian. . . . Say! have you got a temperature?"

Lawrence looked amused.

Doctor Martin shook down his dirty thermometer with his arthritic old hand and thrust it between Lawrence's pale lips.

"And he spat blood, Doctor," said Frieda.

Lawrence looked up at her, betrayed.

"Well, what did you want to do that for?" said the tired old man. "Let's look at that chest."

Lawrence, still with the thermometer in his mouth, let Doctor Martin fumble with the buttons of his undershirt. He patiently permitted the panting, puffing, tobacco-smelling old man to listen to his white chest with the stethoscope.

Finally Doc Martin was through listening to Lawrence's tired white chest. He started reaching in all his pockets, a strange look of dismay on his brown-blotched old face. "My pipe," he said. "Must have left it somewhere last night. Every time I get a pipe broke in I walk away and forget it."

He took the thermometer from Lawrence's mouth. Looked at it for a long time. "I don't know why I'm so crazy about that pipe. But when they're asking five dollars for a Kay Woodie they aren't asking a cent too much. Whooo! it's cold up here in the mountains. Even in summer. You think Mabel'll ever stop building houses? She don't have to build houses. She get's crazier every day—doing this, doing that, doing nothing. Thinking up stuff—Mabel. Everybody knows Mabel. Just Mabel don't know Mabel." He got up slowly and shambled his enormous old body over to the door. "Keep him in bed," he said to Frieda.

"What, Doctor?"

"Keep him in bed."

"Will he be all right?"

"Well, who is all right in this world—except Mabel. I said, 'Mabel, you don't have to build any more houses. You go skipping and skipping around—like a jackrabbit with fleas. Life ain't that complicated. Spend money, yes—but don't work so hard spending it.' "

"And it's the bronchials, Doctor?"

"Sure. Sure—and a lot of other things. But let it be the bronchials. Say, I can remember when Tony was just a young buck—with no future."

"The lungs are strong, Doctor?"

"Just keep him in bed. Whooo!" he said going out into the starry night. "You people sure are far away. A million miles away. You aren't hiding out, are you—?" looking at Lawrence mischievously.

Lawrence was smiling. The tension was gone.

Old Doc Martin passed Spud and the Brett waiting anxiously on the porch.

"Whooo, it's zero up here. Say, Spud! Where is that road now? Was there a road—?"

166

"Just go around the alfalfa field, Doctor Martin," said Spud. "And then down. It'll only take two hours."

"You're all right, Spud. It's just Mabel—she'd demoralize Hercules." And the old car started toward the moonlight desert far below.

The Brett and Spud went into the room.

A sort of ease and repose had spread over Lawrence. He is smiling.

Frieda is smiling too. "It's all right. Nothing wrong. The lungs are strong. It's just a touch of bronchial trouble— the tubes are sore. I am making him a mustard plaster."

Lawrence smiled at the Brett and Spud.

He is very weak. He lies in bed and looks out the doorway at the far pink desert through the pines.

Spud and the Brett are trying to bake bread in the Indian oven outside his door. They chop wood together and start building a fire in the adobe oven.

He is impatient with them. They are so inept. He gets out of bed in his bare feet and comes to the door wrapped in a blanket.

"Let me put the wood in," he insists.

"No, Lawrence," cried the Brett.

"It's got to be exactly in the center."

"You'll get a sweat. Go back to bed. Spud, help me."

They shoo him back to bed in his little house.

He lies there, angry at his helplessness. They are not doing it right. "It's hot enough now. Take the fire out. Take the fire out!"

Spud and the Brett are uneasy. They rake out the coals.

"Now the dough! Now the dough!"

Carefully they put in the dozen loaves in the center of the hot oven and look at him inquiringly on the bed.

"The stone, the stone before the hole, you fools! The oven will get cold!"

They scurry about for him sick there on the bed.

In half an hour the bread is baked, and they take him a hot loaf to his bedside.

He sniffs and taps it professionally. "Not so bad," he laughs.

He gets better. But still he must lie in bed. The bright morning is streaming across the floor of his cabin. He is pondering "The Woman Who Rode Away."

The Brett catches a hummingbird and takes it to him. "Hold out your hand."

"What is it?"

"Hold out your hand." And she places the bird in his large sensitive hands.

A look of amazement comes into his face, almost a religious ecstasy as he feels the tiny fluff of bird. Suddenly with a laugh, he tossed it into the air. The bird hums away through the door and out into the forest.

He is up and around again. He does the chores. Rides down to the Hawks for milk each day and races the Brett back. They are happy—Frieda, Lawrence, the Brett.

But Mabel has another plan. The Snake Dance. She wanted to take him to the Snake Dance in Arizona—four hundred miles away—across the most impossible roads in America.

168

"It seemed to me," reasoned Mabel, "that if Lawrence could emancipate himself from that limitation of the known, the grip of the manifest fact and folly of mankind, he, of all men alive, could perceive the peculiar vestiges of another mode of life that had miraculously survived [in the Southwest]." She was still directing his destiny from her sun porch on the third story of her ranch.

But Lawrence did not know if he wanted to go to the Snake Dance. It was too far. There was also the problem of the Brett. Mabel didn't want her to come along. She had to be left behind.

Then there was Lawrence's throat—terribly sore. "Bring a good gargle for my throat: it hurts like billy-o! this evening."

Not a very auspicious beginning for a trek across the Great American Desert the first week in August, 1924 for Frieda, Lawrence, Mabel, and Tony in Mabel's little touring car.

Lawrence was uncomfortable in the big Harvey House for dinner in Albuquerque. He began to ridicule American food. There was a hostile atmosphere around him. He threw looks of hatred everywhere.

They pushed on into the warm desert night through Navajoland. There were red buttes jutting far forward in the darkness.

"The lonely stars," said Lawrence. "Would you like to be a star?" he asked Mabel.

"No," she said. "I would rather be just what I am: the space between the stars."

Again she had failed. It was a love gesture on Lawrence's part. She had no sensitivity of response—ever.

They traveled far into the night to a small ruined town in Arizona.

Hopiland!

Margaret and I have been there again and again. There is no experience like it.

I remember the crimson, the carmine sands, dune-ing the desert in a final compositional silence—a last emblazoned mode of life. And the sky was atmosphered in azure dust—sometimes cerulean, at others the perfect cobalt, though at night it was always a living black on which the coyotes scrawled their pitiful warnings from canyon to haunted canyon.

It did not rain. It never rains. We counted the ruined kivas of Pueblo Bonito, where the Indians had lived and died, and buried their dead, doubled knees to chin, in painted baskets ten centuries before. And we pieced together the lost designs of shards and laughed at the lilac lizards on the rocks and Margaret wondered at the brown cliffs, the brown ruins, the golden greasewood blooming. We were lost, lost in the rare red air, I thought forever, while we contemplated a lonely surge of stone scathed by the world's last sun, its ragged shadows strewn toward eternity.

Hano, Walpi, Shipaulovi, Sichomovi, Shungopovi, Mishongnovi, Oraibi, Hotevilla, Bakabi, Moenkopi are the ruined cities of stone, cliffed high above the intoning silence. The desert does not satisfy, nor does love. Dust into dust—but spirit into spirit as well. It is madness to deprive oneself of what the red wastes are offering.

One dawn we went up through the purple rocks and

walked through the stone streets of Walpi and listened to an old man calling off the names of the nine villages, his white eyes rotting in his old skull—the nine mesas, which the sea, receding, had left as rocky islands high above the unflowering red floor of the desert below us. And we stayed all day high in the ruins of Walpi until day and night were fused into the white twilight on the sea of rocks below—the horizon littered distantly with minute mesas exhausting themselves in the sun's last scarlet.

But Lawrence did not really like the desert. "One wonders what one came for. The Hopi country is hideous," he wrote to Spud Johnson. "Death-grey mesas sticking up like broken pieces of ancient grey bread.

"Three thousand people.... There were Americans of all sorts, wild west and tame west, American women in pants, an extraordinary assortment of female breeches: at least two women in skirts, relics of the last era. There were Navajo women in full skirts and velvet bodices: there were Hopi women in bright shawls: various half breeds: and all the men to match.

"And what had they all come to see—come so far, over so weary a way? Men with snakes in their mouths, like a circus? Nice clean snakes, all washed and cold-creamed by the priests (so-called). Like pale wet silk stockings. Snakes with little bird-like heads, that bit nobody, but looked more harmless than doves? And funny men with blackened faces and whitened jaws, like a corpse band?

"Just a show! The Southwest is the great playground of the white American. The desert isn't good for anything else."

So Lawrence wasn't going to write an epic about the Indian for Mabel.

On the way home from the Dance they were not happy. They set up two camps among the pines on the Continental Divide. Lawrence and Frieda in one. Mabel and Tony in another. They hardly spoke. Mabel was cross.

Lawrence had an earache. His throat was raw.

There was a deadly silence.

Lawrence wanted the coffee made weak. Mabel wanted it made strong. There was only one coffee pot.

Back in the De Vargas Hotel in Santa Fe, Lawrence handed Mabel several sheets he had written about the Snake Dance. She thought it dreary, with no vision, no insight—unworthy of being dedicated to her.

Mabel knew now that Lawrence was her enemy—would reveal her to herself. Lawrence could see into the very center of your being. His blue eyes would tell you silently what you meant—and that *was* what you meant.

Mabel did not want to know what she meant. Lawrence would not let her live. He had actually overcome her. With some strange power he told her that she and her American woman's will were an abomination. His very nearness became hateful to her. She was shaken, stricken. In a panic, she hastened to Dr. Brill, her psychiatrist in New York, to save her from Lawrence's insight into her.

Good old Brill, sitting in his office, laughing at mysteries, with a quick name for any subtle dilemma. "Well, Mabel," he said, "You've got to work for your living."

But Lawrence had more profound advice, "Try above all things to be still and to contain yourself.

"You always want to rush into action. Realize that a certain stillness is the most perfect form of action, like a

172

seed can wait. One's action ought to come out of an achieved stillness—not be a mere rushing on."

But Mabel did not understand.

Mabel gave a big party that summer. She invited everyone in Taos.

She wanted to show Lawrence that she had a life of her own, that she was important too. He was a frail failure of a man. She could not be bothered. Her life would go on. She would release herself. She was more powerful without him. She would *live*.

But she was living for Lawrence, all her life she sought Lawrence's approval. But Lawrence never approved anything about Mabel from the very first week. He saw through her.

So she gave up Lawrence. He was incapable of friendship. His core was treacherous. She told him so. And it was no use, no use at all to believe in him, in his friendship, or even his actuality.

And Lawrence simply replied, "... it will be hard for you to get over your disintegrative reaction toward people ... as you say, you went that way long ago.

"We shall be going down to Mexico in October. My chest and throat stay sore, I want to go South."

You could not get the best of Lawrence—he saw the truth of one. He had the secret of life of others.

It was dark when Margaret and I arrived at Mabel's party that evening. The patio was full of riding horses, buggies, buckboards, and several dusty touring cars. It was one of Mabel's big parties—the whole town. All the artists, all the Indians, all the Mexicans, all the trades people—the druggist, the lumberman, the doctor, the undertaker, the sheriff, the dentist. Everyone, everyone, was at Mabel's that night.

It was wonderful coming to Mabel's parties. Mabel was the Queen of Taos. The quixotic queen, it is true. But Mabel was royalty. She was the nerve center of town. If someone belittled Mabel you can be certain they had not been invited. To be in Mabel's circle was everyone's ambition.

The Indian dancers were arriving all around us. They filtered into the huge moonlit patio on their short shaggy mustangs. Mabel always invited the whole pueblo. They came in tens and twenties, singing their strange songs in the moonlight as they rode into the white woman's corral.

He   yo   he   yo   Aaaa   Ah   yo

I heard them giggle as they tied their many horses to the hitching rails. It was strange to hear Indians laughing, laughing in the moonlight as they made fast their piebald ponies in Mabel's corral.

"Margarita. Margarita!" they all sang to Margaret.

"Oh, Juan! Oh, Alberto!" she cried.

"He   yo   he   yo!" they chanted sweetly as one.

We moved along with the crowd of laughing Indians to the front door.

They all went into the brilliantly lighted drawing room —a horde of smiling, smiling savages, delighted with their role as guests. They walked lightly in their bright green moccasins, smiling their bland effeminate smiles, flinging their long black pigtails over their strong men's shoulders.

174

Mabel was waiting for them—in an Empress Josephine white gown. She was always a little strange in her dress—not out of style, but with a style of her own. But that night she was beautiful, and strong, and sure of herself.

Tony—in a beautiful white shirt, a blue chief's blanket over his huge shoulders, his glistening black braids hanging down his chest—stood at her side.

"Where we go?" asked the handsomest, tallest Indian.

"Go?" said Mabel. She was always a little obtuse or affected it. A queen may, if it pleases her, not understand.

I was spellbound by the grandeur of the Indian maleness, this bright troupe of smiling, smiling gentlemen in their red and green blankets.

"We have to dress," said the tall Indian, and he raised a little hamper of clothes in which sleigh bells jangled and eagle feathers glistened and war paint stank deliciously.

And all the other fine-faced Indians raised their little bundles of war clothes too and laughed and laughed affectionately.

"Oh, yes, yes," said Mabel. "Go into the pink bedroom. Take them, Tony."

"Thank you, thank you," and all the brown-skinned Indians started to sing and dance a Round Dance toward the bedroom.

"Well, Margaret—" said Mabel, ignoring me disapprovingly.

Margaret smiled. "You look very lovely this evening, Mabel." It was true.

Mabel turned to me haughtily. "Will you empty the ashtrays," she said to me, turning and moving off in the crowd.

I was furious.

"Come on," said Margaret, taking my arm. "She is that way. Let's go and talk to people."

We went into another brightly lit room, even larger than the first. You could not move, there were so many people.

We saw Leon Gaspard, destined to be Taos' greatest artist, near the punch bowl. I heard him laugh his merry, amused, foreign laugh.

"Just like in Rosshia—no?" he was saying to several people around him.

Everything was just like in Russia to Leon.

"Vonderful, vonderful color is a crowd of people when dronk and happy. I could paint people happy all my life. Once I am at the Imperial Ballet and the Czar is there watching in white uniform and gold frogs. You must stand through the whole performance. Afterwards caviar, cheese, sardine and liquor. People, people, people, dancing and dronk. And this now the same—Rosshia."

"You old fool," said his wife Evelyn, morose, hostile, at his side. "What's this got to do with Russia? You're crazy."

Everyone laughed, everyone loved Leon who painted the brilliant pageantry of Asiatic Russia from memory— Turkestan, Outer Mongolia—in firecracker reds and magentas—its fakirs, its fairs, its beautiful slant-eyed women, its shaggy Mongolian horses, its golden mosques.

"Once Renoir had a show in Paris. I hung it—."

"He's drunk," said Evelyn. "Now he'll tell nothing but stories—."

Margaret drew me toward the punch bowl and took a large silver ladle and filled two glasses for us with pink champagne.

176

More and more people came in from the patio. There was still no music, the Indians were still not ready to dance.

A huge woman was at my side suddenly, in black lace. She ruffled out all her black shining feathers. "Do you know who I am?" she shouted at me.

"No, I'm sorry, I don't."

"I'm Mary Austin."

"Oh," mildly.

She was furious. I saw how taken she was with her own fame. Later I was to realize she had written *Land of Little Rain*—one of the subtlest, truest books ever written about the desert. But she could not get over her self-importance.

"Do you believe there's a metaphysics of place?" Mary Austin was asking me.

The subject frightened me. "Well, I believe we transfer the activities of the mind itself to nature—" I said.

"Oh, that old sawhorse!" said Mary Austin, snorting and blowing out like a whale. "That's Kant. You're just quoting someone."

I felt ashamed. She was very smart, this terrible fat dropsical old woman.

"No," she shouted. "I mean a *place* has a soul. Not man-made—but intrinsic, which rules the emotions of men who live there. Taos, itself—has a soul." She saw she had vanquished me and was happy.

I questioned Margaret with my eyes. Margaret was natural, unaffected, sincere. "Shall we go into the other room and watch the Indians get ready to dance?" she asked, leading me away from Mary Austin.

But there was Walter Ufer—tense, hostile.

"Light," Ufer was saying to the crowd around him. "I

deal in light. It's my life—light. When you see light it's like music. If you know light you know everything."

"Now you know you're in an art colony," said Margaret as we drifted on.

"They talk art all the time, don't they?"

"Well, not really. Romantic art. Photographic art. The outside world—nothing inner like Braque. They never heard of Cézanne."

Ralph Meyers had found us. A great big amorphic wreck of a man with a huge misshapen, divine face.

"Hello, Ralph. How are you?" asked Margaret.

Ralph Meyers admired Margaret, trusted her. "Well, I don't know, Margaret. They say I'm the worst painter in Taos." So that was what was bothering this huge, kind, homely man.

"You *may* be the best, Ralph," said Margaret.

We were both thinking of Ralph Meyers' grey-green sketches of the desert—its transientness.

Ralph inhaled deeply. "It's a dream—everything is a dream. There's nothing out there," gesturing to the universe in general. "Think of life as something intangible. Damn beautiful—but intangible. Something that hides itself from us. That's it—what escapes! But let it slip, let it slip—and then you have it. Everything in life is disintegrating, dissociating, fading—lovely, lovely." And he went on murmuring to himself.

"He's perhaps the only one here," said Margaret. "He can paint what can't be seen."

Margaret and I wandered out into the night. Couples were sitting everywhere under the portal, drinking and chattering nonsense.

178

Mabel was behind us quarreling with Spud.

"Well, let me finish my drink first, Mabel."

"But I want you to tell them to come in and dance."

"They don't want to be bothered," said Spud.

"Well, it's *my* party," said Mabel.

"It's the Indians' party," said Mary Austin. "The Indians make life wherever they go."

I drew nearer to Margaret. There was a certain peace about her intelligence. We sat alone and held hands in the dark.

"I wish Lawrence were here," I said.

"God forbid," said Margaret.

When we returned to the party inside it was a whole octave higher in excitement. The champagne glasses were clinking and the women shrilling, the artists arguing.

The Indians were dancing now, slow heavy dances, and chirping like birds. Mary Austin had joined them, her large black lace bulk awkward in their midst. More and more people got up and joined the Round Dance. Mabel, Spud, Leon Gaspard, Ufer, the Brett. The Indians wanted every one to dance.

Margaret quickly got in the circle too, her eyes gleaming. She pulled me in beside her. And I soon felt the slow even beat of the Indian drum invade me. After a while the dance broke up and Margaret and I strolled away. I felt freer— and she was glad.

Albidia, Mabel's Indian maid, was there holding a tray of sandwiches. She was beautiful. Just silence. Her black hair was banged straight across her eyes and caught behind in a special knot with a white ribbon. She wore a blue dress and floppy white deerskin boots. She was smooth, lovely.

The thing a woman is, that you want forever.

"Thank you, Albidia," said Margaret.

"You're welcome, Margaret."

We stood a while in the crowds. It was fascinating—the West! John Dunn, the stage driver was there. And Bert Phillips and Irving Couse, and Ernest Blumenschein, Buck Dunton and Joseph Sharp and Oscar Berninghaus. The first Taos artists. All dead now—and Margaret, dead.

Trinidad, Lawrence's friend—a beautiful, lithe, naked boy—was dancing, dancing, the older Indians chanting encouragingly. The Indians were the truth of life. Their joyousness was real. They sang and sang their reality.

Ai yo Ai yo.

A new Round Dance was forming, everybody was crowding in. The Indian voices rose higher and higher. The whites loved this moment, dancing shoulder to shoulder with the Indians. Yes, they loved being Indian for a short while.

The people were shouting around us now. The voices of the Indian chorus rose and fell. The soft-footed Indian girls had refilled the huge punch bowl again and again with pink champagne.

Margaret pointed out a middle-aged woman in starched white, spinsterish, wide-eyed, disdainful, at the edge of the circle. "That's Willa Cather. She's a botanist enthusiast. She's writing a novel about Santa Fe—the archbishop or something—"

Spud Johnson and Loren Mozely were showing Willa Cather a weed for classification.

"They're spiffing her," said Margaret.

Someone had plucked me by the sleeve.

Mabel.

Her eyes were bright that evening. Always the blue-ribbon, Alice-in-Wonderland hairdo—even though she was middle-aged. She was happy with being Mabel. It was an incurable self-love. "I want to show you something, Joe," and she turned her back on me and walked imperiously through the crowds.

I followed her through the living room, down the three rounded steps into the dining room and across the red-tiled floor to an old bureau in the corner. She stooped and opened the bottom drawer and got out a large bundle wrapped in a red handkerchief.

"I thought you'd like to see this, Joe."

I undid the knot. It was the handwritten manuscript of *Sons and Lovers*.

"Oh!" I cried.

My eyes went quickly to the first page: "The Early Married Life of the Morels."

The handwriting was so modest. Not small, not large, but in full possession of itself. I leafed through the blue-lined notebook in Lawrence's own writing. "There's hardly a correction," I said to Mabel.

She stood and watched my face. At that moment we were friends over Lawrence's manuscript. "I don't know what to do with it," she said.

"But it's too precious to keep out that way—someone might—" I protested.

She took the manuscript from me, tied the four corners of the kerchief again and dropped it in the bureau drawer.

"Lawrence gave it to you?" I asked.

She walked ahead of me out of the dining room and

did not answer. For a moment we were friends over Lawrence. But the moment was over. She dismissed the incident, dismissed me.

I found my way to Margaret. She looked at me inquiringly.

"*Sons and Lovers*," I said. "She has the original manuscript."

"Not really?"

"Wrapped in a red handkerchief. She hasn't the faintest idea of its value."

"Did you like seeing it?"

"It was beautiful."

We tried to find Mabel to say goodbye, but she had left the party. She was upstairs in her room reading.

Leon Gaspard was still talking. "Art—? Ha ha. Art is somesing deeper than your brains—an inewitable music that arranges *itself*. Everything your soul has known—defeat, defeat—*that* is success . . . emotional triumph. Margaret—!" he called when he saw us passing. "Did I tell you about when I was in Paris and Gabrilowitsch, Nijinsky and I—? All night, Maragret! Two o'clock in the morning—Nijinsky jumped up, yelling—"

"Leon! You old fool!" cried Evelyn, "You're drunk."

"Chust a little, Evelyn."

We went out to the corrals. Our horses whinnied as we went to them. We tightened their cinches and rode home slowly in the star-flooded night.

Margaret and I saw Lawrence once more that fall. We rode up to his ranch on horses but it was a hurried meeting. They were packing.

"We're leaving here next week," he said. "For Mexico."
Margaret and I were very sad.

Lawrence realized our concern with his going. He sat with us on the grass of the yard behind the picket fence. It was to be a short exchange between us—but he makes it warm, his being pouring out to us in the short, short moment he has to give us.

"I don't like to leave—the horses, the ranch, the life here." He looked at Margaret. He looked at me. He likes us. Margaret, he admires. He is still uncertain about me—how can he tell? But he is very sensitive, very tender to us both.

We sat on the grass. Lawrence hugged his knees.

"Yes, snow yesterday—a flurry," said Lawrence. "And look at the desert now. You'd think it was a June morning shining."

Margaret and I looked far off at the pink desert with Lawrence.

He looked at Margaret inquiringly—at her serene self-containment. At my chaotic wealth of youthful response.

"It's good to change the rhythm," he said, again referring to their leaving.

Margaret rose, I rose. We didn't want to delay his packing.

"The high thin air gets my chest," he said matter of factly. He got to his feet also now and looked at us. It was an unfinished friendship. He wasn't going to meddle in our life.

"Goodbye," said Margaret, giving him her hand. "Perhaps you'll come back next year?"

"Who knows?" he said quickly. "It was good to be alone up here." He shook our hands. But there was no intimacy

183

in his expression. It was a small intense moment between the three of us.

"*Auf Wiedersehen,* perhaps," called Frieda.

We went to our horses. Lawrence stood next to Margaret who was already mounted. The snow was dropping wet off the branches of the pine trees.

"The desert seems decomposing in the distance," he said, looking down into the valley.

"Goodbye," said Margaret.

"Goodbye," said Lawrence. He looked forlorn standing there at the white picket fence.

We rode down the steep road in the slush under the snow-dripping trees.

"Do you think he'll ever come back?" I asked.

A week later we heard they had gone.

XV

SO LAWRENCE WAS AGAIN IN MEXICO. This time with the Brett. She would be difficult. Frieda did not like her. "I detest her."

Still Lawrence needed the Brett. "She will stand between us and people and the world."

Spud Johnson and Witter Bynner could not go with them. Had Bynner had enough of Lawrence? He had contested Lawrence at every turn in Chapala—and come out second best.

Bynner's arguments were valid, admirable; the world would agree that his philosophy of life was finer than Lawrence's. Yet Lawrence's thoughts, their fervor, their originality, their far-reaching implications, immediately on being expressed in conversation, surpassed the fine old truths of civilization Bynner clung to.

Lawrence always put himself in a poor light with his pettiness. He would go into a tantrum and scream at you a sublime insight. He couldn't help it; beautiful things are born in conflict

Lawrence would accept nothing, nothing of all that had gone before him. He hated Goethe, Kant, Rousseau, Byron, Baudelaire, Wilde, Proust—all on the wrong track. Galsworthy, Ibsen, Strindberg. "I don't want to write like them. We have to hate our immediate predecessors to get free from their authority."

Dostoievski? "Thick, crude, insensitive."

Joyce? "Bores me stiff."

Old knowledge, dead knowledge, however true at its moment in history—Lawrence hated. Truth must gleam—with a fourth dimension. Bynner and Bynner's poetry did not gleam. They were tarnished by the debt they owed to the marvelous past of literature. Bynner commented on beauty. He did not undergo it, create it—as did Lawrence. Bynner did not realize that even the excellence of the past was dead, dead, dead.

Yet when Lawrence got to Mexico City he was lost without Bynner and Spud.

Lawrence believed in friendship between man and man—sworn, pledged, eternal, deep. He had never had such a friendship with a man.

He *liked* Bynner. He could hate him, be annoyed with him. But Bynner could serve as an audience. Lawrence was always cannily aware of the role his enemies played in the formulation of his philosophy. He *needed* enemies.

But Mexico again!

"My spirit always wants to go south," he wrote Catherine Carswell.

"Seltzer [Lawrence's American Publisher] still hovers on the brink of bankruptcy and keeps me on the edge of the same. But by being careful we manage to have $2000 to go to Mexico with."

To Bynner he wrote from Mexico City: "The Monte Carlo [hotel] is almost unchanged. We chose to go upstairs. Hon. Dorothy Brett in your old room, we in the one inside where the monkey, the parrot and the Chihuahua dog abode."

To Spud he wrote: "Very nice *sarapes* around: very nice: 16 pesos. Bought none yet, but have my eye on a fine white one.

"They say the next Revolution begins on Monday."

So he is in Mexico City again, he is a little slow to pick up his past eagerness for the people. He is too famous. There are luncheons, banquets, parties. The women flock around him. He holds his own with them easily—teasing, flirting lightly with them.

Miserable, in a boiled shirt, he talks before the P.E.N. Club. His speech is a failure.

He sits in Sanburn's, the famous tiled coffee house in Mexico City, with the Brett.

186

But he resents the loss of his mood—of Mexico itself—
as he stalks about the old streets of the town.

The primitiveness—had he lost it?

He walked and walked in the busy streets of the town,
where the automobiles and buses seemed to run wild. Yes,
there were the peons again in the white cotton clothes and
sandals and big hats lingering everywhere like heavy ghosts
in the street.

He didn't feel well—utterly rotten. He is quiet, tired,
low spirited. He wanted the elemental. He wanted the
savage. And here he had a cold in Montezuma's city.

Ought he to take to bed?

But the barefooted white-trousered hordes crossing the
Zocalo lured him out into the city again. He had to go out
each day and look. He had to cross the great shadeless plaza
in front of the Cathedral, where scores of little yellow tram-
cars crossed and crossed into the dark streets beyond.

He loved to linger over the things spread on the hot
pavement for sale. He would squat ten minutes looking and
looking at the little toys or poorly fired earthen bowls. He
handled each one delicately. But he was really not looking
at the things for sale—he was studying, being one with the
natives sitting the whole day over their wares. So gentle, so
quiet these people. Children.

They wore dirty white clothes, their skins were unwashed, they had lice in their glistening black hair. They
were at once fearsome, appealing. What large strong men
guarding little piles of knickknacks. There was the eternal
sun overhead—and these half-civilized, half-wild people.
He loved their untouched fierceness sitting there in the
street. What large fearsome bare feet the men had. They

were melancholy inside, they were stopped, they lived without hope.

But these people were good, honest, quiet. They were not greedy for money. They cared nothing for possessions.

The Indians are watching now as the tall sickly Englishman stoops among the pottery. Everyone along the way is curious about the stranger with the panama hat and the thick red beard.

"Cristo," mutters one of the Mexicans.

Lawrence is annoyed.

They do not know he is pondering a great book on Mexico. They do not know his urgency is for the poetic truth of the *soul* of these people—its savagery, its surging tenderness, its haughtiness, its hate.

His throat is fiercely sore now, his cold intolerable. But he pressed himself out into the city each day. He sought the very life of the nation.

He took the Brett to the Museum. "This is the great Aztec Sun Wheel," he tells her. "Look at the snakes, Brett —how they coil and coil."

An attendant is at Lawrence's elbow, insisting, "Will the señor please take off his hat?"

In a rage Lawrence snatches off his hat and walks straight out of the building.

He met Miguel Covarrubias in a café. Covarrubias was then young, glowing, smiling. He was very poor and an usher in a theater. Also he was a student of Rivera. He was eager to visit New York.

Lawrence was very gentle with Covarrubias. Covar-

rubias took Lawrence to see Rivera at work on one of his
frescoes—high up on a scaffold.

Rivera's swarthy Indians displeased Lawrence.

"They only represent the ideal from the social point of
view. Rivera is using them for his own hatred," Lawrence
commented.

Covarrubias did not understand.

"They are too ugly," said Lawrence. "They defeat their
own ends."

"But they are meant to be ugly," said Covarrubias.
"Capitalism is ugly. Mammon is ugly. The priest holding
out his hand to get money from the poor Indian is ugly.
No?"

"The poor Indian—no one ever looks at them except to
make a *casus belli* of them. Humanly they never exist for
you—!"

"But Rivera is a great painter," protested Covarrubias.

"He knows his art," admitted Lawrence. "But his impulse is the impulse of the artist's hate.

"The painting is caricature, not art. The Indians are
merely used as symbols of pathos of the victims of modern
industry and capitalism—not for the encouragement of in-
herent nobility in the opressed, never that."

"When we kill all the capitalists—!" countered Covarrubias.

So writing a book about Mexico involved controversies,
even fights about politics with modern Spaniards full of
European ideas. The moderns in Mexico had no bowels of
compassion.

He quarreled with his good friend Dr. Luis Quintanilla
in Sanborn's Coffee Shop.

Lawrence was horrified at the political situation in Mexico. It was a hypocritical disguise—this salvation for the Mexican peasants—for the *políticos'* self-aggrandizement.

They had words. Quintanilla was an aggressive Mexican —a young revolutionary. "Foreigners!" he cried. "You usually know everything about Mexico." For Quintanilla the old gods of Mexico were forgotten—dead.

But for Lawrence they were not dead. He intended to root the very life of his characters in the purity of the past. He knew the Mexican was still imbued with the past. It was not as distant, not as forgotten, as Quintanilla believed.

Lawrence had a certain heroism of thought about life on earth. His critics—even after *The Plumed Serpent* was finished—were skeptical of the power of life to mean anything beyond the literal moment. A novelist *must not* employ his prophetic insights in writing a book. His critics insisted he must *stick to the facts.*

What facts? Lawrence asked.

He was passionately attached to the beauty of life wherever he saw it. A great way of life gone astray—the Mexican—angered him. He was violent in saying this about the Mexicans' lost way of life. The thing *that was not seen* about the Mexicans—their great lost life—its poignancy, its loveliness—was his theme.

Lawrence was really sick now. His cold would not go, and his throat was raw. He was uneasy, depressed. The bottom had fallen out of his creative world. Although he seemed a god of strength—he could also catch colds and lie helpless in the little Monte Carlo Hotel bedroom.

Frieda was on the subject of the Brett again. "I detest the Brett."

Lawrence rolled his eyes heavenwards. "Very well. We'll go to Oaxaca. Probably shan't like it. We shall probably toddle back. If I'm going to waste my sweetness on the desert air, I'll damn well choose my desert." And he sneezes and spits and sneezes. How rotten he felt—his throat.

But the day before he leaves for Oaxaca he sits for Edward Weston, the photographer. It was not a success— the sitting. Neither man appraised the other man correctly.

Lawrence sat with chin up, looking down. He was rather patronizing of Weston. "You should go in for a bit more of publicity. *Vanity Fair* might like some of your less startling nudes."

As for Weston, he didn't "get" Lawrence at all. "He was in a highly neurotic state." A *creative* state would have been a better word for it.

As for *The Plumed Serpent*, when Weston read it, he said, "He makes inaccurate or misleading statements ... we were at times convulsed with laughter. Lawrence was bewildered, he was frightened, he over-dramatized his fear. The book was the emotional reaction of a sick man, one might say a dying man."

But did Edward Weston's camera interpret Mexico as deeply as did Lawrence's serene blue eyes?

And now Oaxaca! It was lovely there—eternal summer. But the revolution was all around them. The outlying villages are ruined, pock-marked with bullets. There are soldiers everywhere.

The town has been isolated for four years. The railroad from Puebla is their only road, and it is blown up constantly.

"Fancy," said Lawrence. "Being shut up here for years. How awful!"

He is disturbed, haunted with fear. He is told tales of unspeakable horrors in the mountain villages.

"Do not go out of town," they warn him. "It is not safe. You may be robbed of everything you have on—even murdered."

Is it any wonder there is a sinister vein of horror running through *The Plumed Serpent?*

"I'll have to rewrite it," he said of his novel.

So he begins in the morning to write.

He sits in the garden patio of the crumbling adobe house in Oaxaca on the Avenido Pino Suarez 43. He likes the shade of the trees, the three rocking chairs, the onyx table and the pot of carnations. He sits every morning at the onyx table with his big red Waterman fountain pen and writes in his exercise book.

He likes the cocks crowing over the wall, the Mexican women talking in the *zaguán* (entrance way). Rosalino, the sweet stupid *mozo*, his houseboy, sweeping the street, whistling, whistling. And the two green-blue parrots whistling mockingly overhead.

Mexico—?

A whole people repudiating life yet so *strong* with life. They were gay, beautiful, alive—yet melancholy inside. Yes, they lived without hope. And as he sat in the garden at the onyx table their savage mystery again came to him. The old power of the past *wasn't* lost in them.

192

Even though they themselves refused their heritage—the strange Mexican darkness that had come down and down the centuries—the past—*he* saw the utter terrible beauty of their past in them today. They needed a new faith, the old faith of the Quetzalcoatl revived. How deeply he cared and tried and tried to characterize the poetic nature of a whole nation—lost, lost in a profound reverie of the past.

Brett once more begins her slow painful typewriting.

He and the Brett get along.

Frieda does not like it. "I want the Brett to go away."

But he raved at Frieda. "You are a jealous fool."

He and the Brett have a strange mystery of friendship. He is charming and gentle with her. He takes her to see *The Thief of Bagdad* with Douglas Fairbanks in it. He is thrilled by Fairbanks' acrobatic acting.

He and the Brett stay out late one night and have several drinks in the flat of friends. He talks about the cruelty of the dark races. But suddenly he realizes it is late and he jumps up and runs home.

Frieda is in a towering rage. "I want the Brett to go away!" she insists.

He sneers at her. "You are a jealous fool."

But there is no freedom in the patio. It is almost a prison. He becomes exasperated. He wants to go out of town, but the hills are bandit-ridden.

"You will be murdered," insist his neighbors.

Is he drawn to the terror? The big-hatted, silent, dark men wrapped in their white serapes lurk everywhere. Yes, they are cruel. Dark and cruel. And they look and look at Lawrence as he passes down the street.

193

But he cannot stand the patio a moment longer. He *must* go out into the country. His blood is chilled at the idea of being murdered. Still he wants to go out and sit in the desert—and write.

"Let us try it," he says to the Brett. "Two of us must be safe. We'll take our lunch."

Frieda will not go, of course. She is cool to the Brett—to what is going on between the Brett and Lawrence.

Early the next morning Lawrence was ready with his copybook and pen. The Brett in her big cowboy hat is eager. She has her paints.

The morning is perfect; in a moment they are out of town. And there are the hills Lawrence loves so much. The whole pink-ocher valley is wild and exalted with sunshine. He loves the stiffly pleated mountains, clothed smokily with pine. And there are two white dots of a church with its twin towers. Farther still the speck of a village—so magical, alone, tilted on the fawn-pink slope. Oh, so alone, that village; it was as he wanted it, alone.

He and the Brett are happy with the great space all around them. Not a soul in sight.

"It's early still," he says.

"How brilliant the sun is," says the Brett when she understands.

Lawrence is looking at the far-off crumbling town up the slope—beautiful, isolate. "This will do," he decides.

He finds two bushes—far enough apart, but within easy calling distance. He takes off his coat and flings it over the bush and sits down in his shirt-sleeves and starts to write.

The Brett sets up her paint box and starts to paint the far mountains.

194

Two women on burros, mere specks, ride by in the distance. In the pure blue sky huge vultures are wheeling farther and farther apart.

After an hour or two Lawrence calls to the Brett, "I am finished. How have you been getting along?"

She shows him her painting proudly.

"Oh, Brett. Do look at the mountain. It has great bare toes where it joins the desert. Here, let me have a try." He sits down and gives the mountain toes. He roughens the fir trees and darkens the sky. "You are dumb, Brett, you don't look at things."

But when he gets back safely in town, unmurdered, Frieda is furious. "I want the Brett to go."

Lawrence says nothing. A great weariness is upon him—an everlasting weariness. And his throat is so sore. His bronchials. And that everlasting pain in his side.

Next morning he and the Brett start out again. He feels terrible in the radiant glory of the morning, the solitude of Mexico holding him spellbound. His heart gives a clutch at the solitude. But he loves the desert outside of town, the mesquite bushes, the occasional burro.

No bandits.

Were the bandits the mere terror of his imagination? His novel worked him up into the deeper terror of being alive. Yes, there was a terror of being alive on earth, the deep magical terror of existence alone—lost to modern man. And he, acting out Mexico's deepest meaning, was in terror too.

"Here are our bushes," he said to the Brett.

195

She sat down with her paints. And Lawrence sat down under his bush with his notebook and fountain pen.

But he could not write; the thoughts did not flow. He is moody, uneasy. Oh, his throat. Damn Frieda for giving me this cold.

The Brett has painted an endless flow of imaginary people down her empty road. Mexico—white-coated peasants moving ceaselessly down the dusty roads.

Lawrence shuts his book at last, puts his coat over his arm and looks down at Brett's painting. "Yes, yes," he says. "On the whole I think the picture is very nice—lively, amusing."

"What about tomorrow?" asks the Brett.

"I don't know. I don't think Frieda likes it."

When he arrives home Frieda is in a state. "I want the Brett to go!"

"But why!" cries Lawrence.

"She spoils all my fun—that's why!" And she runs into the garden in tears.

He goes to bed for three days. His throat, his throat. And oh, the chaotic pageantry of his mind. This book is killing him. Is it real—is it fantasy? He cannot decide. It is having its awful way with him, undoing him—brilliantly. It is awful to be sick—writing, writing of final meanings, drunk with them—*undone* by them. If only his throat didn't ache, his whole body didn't flame.

On Christmas Day he staggers to his feet. He must decorate the tree. He looks frail, transparent, collapsed. But the

196

tree—it is a sacred thing for Lawrence to deck out the tree on Christmas Day—even in warm Oaxaca.

Brett plays tennis in the morning and comes to see him in the afternoon. She gives him a lovely knife with his name on it.

"I am not such a knifey person as you, Brett, but I must give you a penny, so as not to cut our friendship." And he gives her a penny.

He is up and around again but fearful that he is ill. He fears Mexico. He fears being sick in Mexico. He is thinking again of England. "England in the Spring," he says to the Brett.

But she says nothing.

She and Lawrence are joyous together. This young woman and the sainted ghostly Lawrence—fearing his coming illness. Yet his fear inspires him. In some strange way the meaning of the book is quickened by his illness.

He and the Brett are excited, exhilarated, happy. They come into the shady patio. Frieda is sitting in a rocking chair, smoking. Her mouth tightens.

The Brett notices nothing. She is obtuse. She goes home to the Hotel Francia.

Lawrence is pale, remote, his eyes unseeing.

"I want the Brett to go away," says Frieda fiercely.

Lawrence goes immediately into the high, red-tiled barren bedroom. He felt chilly. This damnable climate. Is it hot, is it cold? The roses are blooming and it is Christmas. His throat is dry. He swallows painfully.

"I don't want Brett such a part of our life. I just don't want her," insisted Frieda.

He is hot again suddenly! What could it be?

He was writing the scene of the bandits in *The Plumed Serpent*. Men crashing in mid-air. Revolvers going off. His character Kate stabbing at bandits again and again in the throat while blood shot out like a red projectile.

Yes, the novel was running away from him. A certain creative delirium had taken over. The living Huitzilopochtli? This terrible convulsion of a nation's history—*in his mind*.

Fantasy?

No!

He felt these things—the strange blood-sodden meaning of Mexico—their cruelty.

Weren't the hills full of bandits? Wasn't the revolution *that*—the blackening blood of the past. Their dark, glittering supernatural souls shuddering to life. Kill, kill. It was elemental in the Mexican. Death.

And a vision came to him—of Mexico—because his life too was death.

His very life was death and he made of it a vision each day he woke—death. How beautifully he admitted it. And he wrote and wrote his lyric song of man's meaning— death—yet he surmounted it splendidly, with surpassing visions.

The death motif in *The Plumed Serpent* was the truth of life on earth. Death.

He thought passionately of man—how great, how admirable, was man's struggle for meaning.

"I don't want the Brett. I don't, don't want the Brett," Frieda was saying.

He was under the covers now—oh so cold, so very cold. He looked up at the black beams vermiculated with worms. The walls were done in dull Etruscan red. Red— the mourning color of the Zapotec.

His teeth were chattering.

"What's wrong, Lawrence?"

"Nothing. Is there any way to light a fire in this damnable house?"

"But it's warm, Lorenzo! It's always warm in Oaxaca."

"Nevertheless."

"I'll get a hot-water bottle." And she ran across the street to the Kulls.

When she had gone he reached out for his pen and notebook. His brain arranged and arranged itself in imagery, set itself to lovely music:

> I am the living Quetzalcoatl
> I am the Son of the Morning Star,
> And child of the deeps.
> When you turn to your wives
> As brave men turn to their women,
> The Morning Star and the Evening Star
>   shine together,
> For man is the Morning Star.
> And woman is the Star of the Evening.
> I tell you, you are not men alone.
> The star of the beyond is within you. ⚹ *christ consciousness*
> But have you seen a dead man,
> How his star has gone out of him?
> So the star will go out of you,
> Even as a woman will leave a man
> If his warmth never warms her.
> Should you say: *I have no star; I am no star,*
> So it will leave you,

And you will hang like a gourd
  on the vine of life. . . .
If you were men with the Morning Star
If the Star shone within you. . . .

"Lorenzo!" cried Frieda in the doorway. She held the red hot-water bottle. He was writing again, always writing. "You've thrown the covers off!"

"It's hot enough now," he said, putting the pen and notebook aside. You could not explain anything to a woman like Frieda.

She felt his forehead. Clammy, hot. "Do you suppose you have malaria?"

"What of it?" He got up and went into the cold damp tiled bathroom and sat down. He shivered. His stomach ached. Was his soul capable of knowing the souls of another nation?

The Brett comes later that afternoon.

Frieda is in a rage.

Lawrence has gone down the street—hurt, angry about the inconsistencies of his life—his tortured, thwarted vision, his smarting heavy chest, his women.

"You spoil all my fun!" screams Frieda at the Brett. She runs into the garden, angry, humiliated.

"Come on, Frieda," says the Brett. "Let's have a talk."

Frieda hates her. Her eyes are mistrustful of anything the Brett says. She will not answer.

Lawrence comes back—pale, sick, remote. He does not look at either. He has a strong resistance to both women now. He goes to his bed and sits down. He was chilled to the bone again. He got under the covers and quaked.

Next morning the Brett waits for him in her hotel.

He does not come.

She goes out into the famous Zocalo of Oaxaca and watches the endless streams of short white-clothed Indians crossing and recrossing the plaza. Suddenly she sees him walking under the arcades—head up. His feet move so lightly. He drifts dreamily along, seeing nothing, hearing nothing.

But he is pale, grey, shaken. His big Stetson shadowing his sunken face. There is the sickly luminosity of death to his face and a certain resurrectional life, an aura of grace, that flows from him.

Brett hurries to meet him.

"Shall we go out into the country?" he asks her.

He looks asthenic. The pale death of his face invades the very roots of his heavy dark beard.

"It's dangerous to go out of town, Lorenzo." She is afraid for him.

"I know. But we'll stick to the road. We'll walk toward Mitla."

The roads of Mexico fascinated Lawrence

From the valley villages and from the mountains the peasants and the Indians are coming in with supplies, the road is like a pilgrimage in greatest haste, dashing for town. Dark-eared asses and running men, running women, running girls, running lads, twinkling donkeys ambling on fine little feet, under twin baskets with tomatoes and gourds, twin great nets of bubble-shaped jars, twin bundles of neat-cut faggots of wood, neat as bunches of cigarettes, and twin-net sacks of charcoal. Donkeys, mules, on they come, great pannier baskets making a rhythm under the perched woman, great bundles bouncing against the sides of the slim-footed animals.

Yet the dust advances like a ghost along the road, down the valley plain. The dry turf of the valley-bed gleams like soft skin, sunlit and pinkish ocher, spreading wide between the mountains that seem to emit their own darkness, a dark-blue vapor translucent, sombering them from the humped crests downwards. The many-pleated noiseless mountains of Mexico.

It is Saturday and the white dots of men are threading down the trail over the bare humps to the plain, following the dark twinkle-movement of asses. And girls in long full, soiled cotton skirts running, trotting, ebbing along after the twinkle-movement of the ass. Down they come in families, in clusters, in solitary ones, threading with ebbing, running barefoot movement noiseless towards the town, that blows the bubbles of its church domes above the stagnant green of trees, away under the fawn-skin hills.

Now that he was in the country—what was there to be afraid of? Being murdered by bandits? Nonsense.

Yet he was afraid.

"Frieda broke out again the moment you left," he said to the Brett.

They walk down a side road, leave the constant stream of white pilgrims, and sit down in the fields.

"She made such a scene that I cannot stand it any longer. I am at the end of my tether—in despair." And he rumples his hair wildly.

"Look here, Lawrence," said the Brett. "Let us be calm and sensible. It is too much of a strain for you; it makes you ill, doesn't it?"

"Yes," he replies wearily. "It is unbearable. I shall be ill if it goes on."

"What do you want, Lorenzo?" She is delicate in her feeling for Lawrence.

He looks at her frankly.

"The only thing I can think of is to ask you not to come again to the house."

"Very well," says the Brett. "I will go back to Taos to the ranch for a while. This will relieve you of the strain."

"That will be best," he replies more hopefully. "But I don't altogether like your taking that long journey by yourself." He gives her a long strange look as he sits there in the field, leaning slightly forward.

Suddenly he leaps to his feet. "I will go and tell Frieda, and maybe things will be better."

They walk back to town among the white crowds.

But Frieda is still angry.

This thing between Lawrence and the Brett! She cannot stand it. "Why do you not make love to her?" For Frieda things must go full circle.

Lawrence avoids her anger. He feels so hot again. His book, his book! He wanted to submit to the creative wonder of his thoughts. He had a deep, deep passion for his characters. A stream of life was shaping itself deep within him—a movement *toward* something great—but ever darkly beyond. He acknowledged that wonder, the ecstasy of insight.

"Make love to her, make love to her!" cried Frieda cruelly.

Lawrence went to the sofa and lay down. His dreams were a vast choral background to Frieda's shrill voice. Could a dream be an illness?

"It is not *my* fault!" screamed Frieda.

"What is not your fault?" he said coming out of his reverie.

"That you do not make love to her."

"Did I say it was?" It was wonderful to lie weak on the bed in the hot sultry air of winter in Oaxaca!

"Only make love to her, Lawrence. And don't make a fool of yourself." She goaded him, and he lay there half dead—exalted with the meaning of Mexico.

"You are like a curate and a spinster, you two. Make love and have done with it, Lawrence."

Yes, that was another chill coming. But he must not think of his chest—it must *never* be his chest.

"Friendship, bah! Between man and woman. Why *not* make love to her?"

His fingers were thrilling now. Yes, it was malaria. He was glad. Malaria was not so bad. But the other dreadful disease—!

"Why not! I want you to make love to her. And quiet all our lives."

He turns his face to the wall and lies there shivering, his very bones are frozen. "Would you get me a tablet of quinine?"

So the Brett leaves for Mexico City—alone.

Lawrence and Frieda came down to the railroad station just in time to see her off.

204

"I wish I were coming too," he says. "But I must finish my book. Then we'll see."

He gives her a warm handclasp. "I wonder how the horses are on the ranch. You must feed them, Brett. Tell Mabel I'm all right. And Rachel—you must remember me to Rachel."

She looks at him shyly—trying to thank him for all the things he has done for her.

"I do hope you will be all right," he says, still anxious, still worried. And he shakes her hand again, warmly.

The Brett kisses Frieda. Frieda is astonished.

Brett gets into the train. They all wave and wave until the train is gone.

And suddenly Lawrence and Frieda are alone.

XVI

BUT NOW A CHANGE COMES IN THEIR lives. Lawrence becomes very ill.

His book becomes a flame in his mind. How creative a fever can be. His brain aflame, aflame with Mexico.

But there was always that undercurrent: death. He wrote and wrote—and there was the beautiful meaning of life: death. Oh, in the sky of his mind were long mare's tails aflame. Death.

And fear.

"Did Rosalino sleep in the *zaguán* last night?" he asks fearfully when dawn has come.

He is haggard after the fever, the terror of the night.

"Lawrence?" says Frieda. She is frightened. He is but a ghost of a man sitting up in bed in his soiled nightshirt.

"Where is Rosalino?"

"He is sweeping the street in front of the house."

"He did not sleep in the *zaguán* last night."

"Oh, but he did, Lorenzo."

The *zaguán* is Rosalino's home, just the passageway behind two huge wooden doors to the street. In one corner Rosalino curls up on the low wooden bench and sleeps at night wrapped in his serape, his *huaraches* on the cobblestones. To guard Lorenzo.

"Are you sure he slept in the *zaguán* last night?" asks Lawrence suspiciously.

"But yes, but yes!" insists Frieda.

Lawrence is afraid. She sees in his eyes how frightened he is. The house is like a fortress. The windows to the street are heavily barred. There is no other entrance to the house but through the *zaguán* where Rosalino sleeps.

"Call him," he demands.

The short shy boy comes and stands at Lawrence's bed. He wears a white blouse and white calico pantaloons. And his straw hat he wears in the house.

Lawrence is strange to him—someone to watch and wonder at—a sick white man dying in bed. He is flabbergasted by a man dying. Rosalino was perfectly happy—and here was a man dying. Strange.

"The señor wanted me?" He smells of the wet dust he

has been sweeping in the street. He is very strong, a dwarf in stature but perfectly made.

Lawrence looks at the silent, thoughtless Indian boy. What a dumbbell. Still he sleeps in the *zaguán* and guards Lawrence.

But did he? Could he have been out last night? Does Lawrence dare show his fear to this simple idiot?

"Have you been reading your school book?" he asks the boy.

"*Como no?*" replied Rosalino. Why not?

In fact Rosalino sits most of the afternoon in the *zaguán* learning to read and write.

"And have you written something?" asks Lawrence.

"*Como no?*" replies Rosalino. And he produces from somewhere in his white clothes a large sheet of foolscap *covered* with writing.

"Quite nice," praises Lawrence. He likes the boy. "A poem! Where did you copy it from?"

Rosalino writhed and laughed in agony. How pale the white man was. Dying, yet talking to him. Yes, the white man was dying—yet talking about Rosalino's exercise in large childlike writing.

"But you haven't any capitals—any punctuation at all," cried Lawrence, quickly seizing his pen and correcting the page. "You can't write straight ahead without verse lines!"

"*Como no?*" says Rosalino. Why not?

Lawrence hands the paper back to the proud young boy. The boy hides it away again in his billowing white blouse.

Lawrence gets up his courage at last. "Rosalino, did you sleep in the *zaguán* last night?"

207

"*Como no?*" smiles Rosalino. Why not, señor?

After he has gone to sweep the whole patio all over again, Lawrence turns his frightened eyes to Frieda.

"We must get another boy to sleep in the *zaguán* with Rosalino."

"But Lawrence—! *Two* boys to guard the house?"

"Two," insists Lawrence. And he tries to make his demand sound reasonable. But he knows Frieda knows—he is afraid, afraid.

"How much longer now on the book, Lawrence?" asks Frieda the next day.

He is very ill, tormented. Perhaps the whole thing was impossible—to invoke Mexico's past in the dark slumbering people of the present.

He would be laughed at for his great dream of beauty for Mexico. They didn't *want* their virgin selves. A great death and then a living result: a new conception of human life. He wanted something aboriginal, before the mental world came into being. Yes. Yes. Yes. Something new, something new that was old and forgotten. Fantasy—?

Yes, they would crucify him.

He spat and spat, and sometimes there was blood in his sputum. He looked at Frieda and there were tears in her eyes. He was no longer frightened now that there were two boys sleeping in the *zaguán*. But there was still a horror—his horror alone—one of insight?

"When, Lawrence?" she begged. This book was killing him, killing her. When would it be finished?

He looked up from his notebook where he had been

writing in bed. "When? If heaven is with me I shall finish this month."

Rosalino came in every morning to look at the white man dying.

Yes, it a was a certain wonder to watch a man die a little more each day. He looked and looked at Lawrence's cadaverous white face. He took his straw hat off when he stood before Lawrence's sick bed. And this sign that Rosalino knew Lawrence was dying frightened Frieda.

"Have you brought your exercise book?" asked Lawrence of the barefooted boy.

"*Como no?*" said Rosalino producing his precious paper.

But Lawrence was too ill to care. He lay in a nausea of his own fever and let days, weeks, centuries pass over him.

The door of his room stood open onto the patio where green banana trees and high flowering shrubs rose from the water-sprinkled earth towards that strange rage of blue which was the sky.

"Lawrence," said Frieda, leaning over him.

He could not, could not rouse himself. Oh, the flowers. His being, far off, was caught in a larger and larger outward motion. Everything, everything moving—his meaning, Mexico's meaning, life's meaning—moving, moving outward, slowly outward, into the nescience of space, the slow roundward motion like hawks going away, away against the will of the world.

"Lawrence," said Frieda again.

The little Mexican maid came in now, barefoot, with a

cup of tea, her flounced cotton skirt swinging, her long black hair down her back.

And Rosalino, hatless, his jaw dropped, came in too. No, the Gringo hadn't died yet. Rosalino came into the room a dozen times a day on the slightest pretext. He didn't want to be away when the white man died.

"Lorenzo," said Frieda. "Do you want the tea?"

A century passed before he could bring himself to answer. In the flush of fever he saw England. His head was humming like a mosquito, his legs were paralyzed and his soul was as good as dead.

Yes, he was ill, frightfully ill. Frieda was there. Rosalino was there—the little barefoot maid with the birdlike voice —and the Greater Day of Mexico—men of a dying race to whom the busy common day is nothing, nothing.

The Greater Day. He was of it now—the Greater Day.

He wanted to go home. England!

But he was too ill—dying? Rosalino was there constantly with his hat in his hands—as though in church. And Frieda crying, crying—his death?

Dark-blue shadows moved from the side of the patio, disappeared, then appeared on the other side. Evening had come, and the barefoot natives in white calico flitted with silent rapidity across, and across, forever going, yet mysteriously going nowhere, threading the timelessness with their transit, like swallows of darkness.

The window of the room opened on to the tropical parched street. It was a big window, came nearly to the floor, and was heavily barred. Past the window went the natives, with the soft light rustle of their sandals. Big straw hats balanced, dark cheeks, calico shoulders brushed with the silent swiftness of the Indian past the barred window-space. Sometimes children clutched the bars and gazed in, with great shining eyes and straight blue-black hair, to see the foreigner lying in the majesty of a white bed.

"Lorenzo," pleaded Frieda.

He was too ill to open his eyes.

One morning Frieda saw the room sway sideways.

A picture fell to the floor. Then the room moved the other way. The door swung open of its own accord. And there was a roar outside, a colossal roar. Frieda was frightened.

Rosalino, who was in the room, crossed himself.

The floor trembled and trembled.

"What is it?" asked Frieda, terrified.

"*Es un terremoto, señora.*"

"An earthquake—!" She looked quickly at Lawrence on the bed. He slept peacefully—a death sleep.

She saw the beams of the ceiling move slowly and the roar was deafening. "Rosalino, what shall we do!"

"Nothing, señora. You die or you don't die. But don't go out into the street." He crossed himself again and waited.

Night came. All the dogs and the horses and the asses howled in the night. A wind came and sucked the air out of the room. Frieda gasped and gasped for breath.

To her horror she saw the black beams move again in the roof.

"Will the roof fall, Rosalino?"

"Sometimes," he admitted.

All that night the house was jolted by the shocks. Suddenly the bed jumped off the floor.

Lawrence slept on quietly.

The next morning was bright and the earth was solid again.

"Has it gone?" asked Frieda.

"For a while," said Rosalino.

"Will you dare go down town for me?"

"As you like, señora."

"Will you go down to the Plaza and ask the doctor to come?"

"*Porque no?*" And why not? Putting on his big hat and taking a last look at Lawrence.

An hour later Rosalino was back.

"Will not come, señora."

Lawrence was awake now.

"Lorenzo," said Frieda, "the doctor will not come."

"He's afraid," said Lawrence.

"Afraid?"

"Afraid to have an Englishman die on his hands."

"He says—if you will come to the Plaza, to the hotel down town—"

"No," said Lawrence. Ever no, to his illness.

This moment in his life—illness, death—was like the little day of the rest of mankind. But outside whispers the Greater Day. And the time will come when the walls of the little day shall fall . . . and men shall find themselves outdoors in the Greater Day.

And little men will shudder and die out like clouds of

grasshoppers dying into the sea. Then tall men will remain alone in the land, moving deeper in the Greater Day, and moving deeper.

"We must get him down to the hotel, Rosalino," said Frieda.

"He is dead?" asked Rosalino, preparing to enjoy the event.

"No. No. But we must get him down town."

"*Como no, señora*," said Rosalino, always happy to please.

Lawrence was awake now.

He listened to their dialogue. The white ones passed and passed his window in the dark. Life was a void suddenly. He had lost all the world in his sultry illness. "There is no help, O man. Fear gives thee wings like a bird, death comes after thee open-mouthed, and thou soarest on the wind like a fly. But thy flight is not far, and thy flying is not long. Thou art a fish of the timeless Ocean, and must needs fall back.

"Cease then the struggle of thy flight, and fall back into the deep element where death is and is not, and life is not a fleeing away. It is a beauteous thing to live and be alive. Live then in the Greater Day, and let the waters carry thee, and the flood carry thee along, and live, only live, no more of this hurrying away "

"No more of this hurrying away!" he said suddenly.

"What, Lawrence?" said Frieda.

He looked so frightened—so in need. And death was in his eyes. Yes, he knew now he was going to die.

"You'll bury me in this cemetery here," he said grimly.

"No. No." she forced her laugh, "it's such an ugly cemetery, don't you think of it."

One more, one more thing he struggled to say to Frieda. "If I die, nothing has mattered but you, nothing at all." And he lay there helpless unable to turn over. All during the earthquake he lay silently, waiting until the tremors ceased.

The earthquake was at last over and they carried him to the Hotel Francia downtown where he lay exhausted, frightened.

The doctor came, an educated Indian. He too was frightened. The man was dying, and his death would be on his head. But the powers in Mexico City had telegraphed him: "This is a famous man—do everything. You are not to let him die!"

What could he do with a man in a torpor—dying? He had malaria, typhoid, and that other dread disease.

The doctor was frightened—but the powers in Mexico City had said, "Do everything! But you are not to let him die."

What could he do? Inject quinine in his wasted leg. Give him doses of calomel for the searing pain of his intestines. For the other dread disease—there was nothing to prescribe.

One morning the dying man came alive and looked at the frightened doctor, pumping and pumping his leg with quinine until it was paralyzed.

"England," said Lawrence.

"What's that?" said the Indian doctor.

"I think we shall stay in Devonshire a while," quite awake now.

The doctor withdrew the needle and looked at the sick man.

214

"I break my heart over England when I'm away from her," said Lawrence.

Strange a dying man could talk so naturally.

Do everything, they had wired him from Mexico City. *This is a famous man. You are not to let him die.* But how could a mere telegram from the government three hundred miles away save a man already in the third stage of consumption?

Lawrence was murmuring now: "Beautiful it is to be dead and quite departed."

The doctor looked at him in silence, and understood. *Beautiful it is to be dead.* It was the refrain which hums at the very center of every Indian heart, where the Greater Day is hemmed in by the lesser day.

"We shall go to Mexico City and see about a ship," decided Lawrence. But he was asleep again.

The last sleep? The doctor didn't know. He was afraid, afraid this famous man would die on his hands.

"So perhaps we shall be in England by March," said Lawrence, coming back from the dead once more.

The doctor left the room. What, what can you do with a dying man—enjoying voyages of death?

After days Lawrence crawled out into the Plaza of Oaxaca in the pale sunshine. The arched arcades, the low yellow baroque Spanish buildings stood back with a heavy sick look as though they too felt the endless malaria in their bowels. The yellow cathedral leaned its squat, earthquake-shaken towers, the bells sounded hollow.

Lawrence sat on one of the broken stone benches, while

tropical birds flew and twittered in the great trees and natives twittered and flitted in silence.

His body was sick with the poison that lurks in all tropical air. He wanted to get out, get out of this ghastly tropical void into which he had fallen.

"We'll go. We'll go straight to Vera Cruz," he said to Frieda. "With luck we should sail on March 10th—land in England March 25th or thereabouts."

The doctor said nothing.

"My wife hates Mexico and I no longer like it."

The doctor said nothing.

"I shall take the MS of Quetzalcoatl with me and get it typed. It is finished. It will probably make them open their eyes—or close them: but I like it very much indeed."

The doctor felt sorry for this dying man.

"Do you think I can leave, Doctor?"

"Well—?" said the doctor. "A little revolution has broken out again. They've destroyed a little wooden bridge. And so there is no railroad out of here, señor, for the time being."

Ah, that little thread of railway—a single narrow little track. It was so easy to break the thread with one plant of dynamite. And to the north was three hundred miles of wilderness.

"I want to get to England," said Lawrence.

At last the train came again—two coaches with white-clothed natives—and on the roof sat Orozco-fierce soldiers with cartridge belts and rifles.

216

Lawrence crawled into his seat. Frieda was terrified. She was crying. She cried all the way as the little black train ran through the savage loneliness of the Mexican landscape.

He had only a frail, thin thread of life as he sat there on the seat beside her. He was mysterious with death—yet lyrically alive to the beauty of life still.

"We shall go direct to Vera Cruz," said Lawrence.

Frieda did not answer. She cried and cried. She sat with a dead man. His time was over. His life all gone now. He was doomed. The strain was too much for her. She cried and cried.

"N', lass, give over. We'll soon be in England and all will be well."

When they got to Mexico City, Lawrence lay exhausted in his little hotel room.

"Phone the Hamburg-Amerika line," he demanded of Frieda.

"But Lawrence—! Let us wait a little while until you're rested."

"Nay—" dropping into the old dialect. "Phone about a boat from Vera Cruz."

Again she was crying.

"What's amiss?" he said softly.

She sat down on his bed. The terror of his coming death affected her.

"Phone, lass. We'll go to England."

At last she had the courage to telephone the Hamburg-Amerika line about a boat.

"There's one!" she said "From Vera Cruz on the 17th —the *Rio Bravo*."

"Where do we land?" asked Lawrence.

217

"In Plymouth—about April 3rd."

"Ah," said Lawrence thoughtfully. "Very well, secure two passages for us."

He walks the streets of Mexico City again while they wait for the *Rio Bravo* to sail.

He looks very ill, a pale green. People stare at him as he goes in and out of the alleyways crowded with people. What a sick man to go crawling up and down. But he cannot resist the mystery of Mexico.

Frieda has a doctor come and see him, Dr. Uhlfelder.

The doctor is a very truthful man. He examines Lawrence's chest again and again.

"We've passage on the *Rio Bravo* sailing from Vera Cruz on the 17th," Lawrence tells the doctor.

Again the doctor listens to Lawrence's chest, listens to his heart.

"My wife wants to go to Germany to see her mother," he further explained.

The doctor stood up and looked at Frieda.

"Mr. Lawrence has tuberculosis."

Lawrence quickly looked at her with unforgettable eyes.

"Take him to your ranch, it is his only chance. He has tuberculosis in the third degree. A year or two at the most."

She looked back at the doctor cheerfully. "Now we know, we can tackle it. That's nothing. Lots of people have that."

So there would be no England for Lawrence as he

wished. He looked down quickly at his hands. "Really there is a doom on all of us in Mexico."

The trip north to El Paso was a crucifixion for Frieda.

Lawrence was so weak and ill. She too was broken. "He is ill. He is doomed. All my love, all my strength will never make him whole again."

At the border they were stopped by the immigration officials. They did not want Lawrence to enter the United States. They were very insulting. A doctor examined him. Frieda fought for two days to get him across the border. Lawrence was an emigrant. He was sick with tuberculosis. He could not enter.

The doctor examined him again. It nearly killed him— he was so weak, so utterly gone. No, they wouldn't let him enter.

At last Frieda prevailed.

The American Embassy in Mexico City helped her. They wired the officials at the border. Yes, he was an important person. Let him pass.

And the Lawrences crossed into the United States March 29, 1925.

They arrived on the Del Monte Ranch April 1.

The mountains were snowy, the wind wild and cold, but the sun bright.

"I'm not altogether here yet," he wrote his friend, Mrs. George R. G. Conway, in Mexico City, "bit of me still on the way, like luggage following."

It was to be the last happy year he would spend on his ranch. He was very ill.

219

Lawrence did not believe in his illness. It was an inconvenience, a bother. In a sense it never existed for him. His chest was half gone. He could barely drag himself through doors and down strange streets. And stand up shakily and be examined by hostile doctors. He was exhausted. Yet it was nothing—this illness. Still he had to live with it.

He also had to live with his greatness. Greatness is purgatory—a harassment of the soul. Visions flourish and die—and leave one irritable, exasperated, petty. Especially so in Lawrence.

Lawrence believed in his own greatness.

"I shall change the world for the next 1000 years."

Still he was a very lonely man, almost friendless, living far up a mountain alone with two women who were constantly quarreling over him.

Lawrence's greatness is his Creativity.

Not the creativeness of man. Not the creativeness of a Picasso nor of a Shakespeare.

But the Creativity of the Universe. The Incomprehensible.

Lawrence's genius is his final mergence with the great Creative Cause of the Universe itself. All Lawrence's life was a groping toward a oneness with the Creative strength of the Universe—the vast spiritual flames that brought life into being. Man's tragedy was his contrariety, his hostility, his resistance to the Creative power of the Universe.

The Universe itself is Creative, he decided.

"All existence is surging toward a consummation into being.

"Man, as yet, is less than half grown.

"There is only one law of the Universe: Spontaneous Mutation.

220

"There is no cause and effect sequence in the unfolding of the Universe. The universe flows in infinite wild streams.

"Only man tries not to flow, repeats himself over and over in mechanical monotony of conceit."

This is Lawrence's great discovery: The Universe itself is Creative. It is an even greater discovery than Einstein's. Einstein saw only the physical manifestations of the Creativity of the Universe. Lawrence saw the great dark depths of the Universe itself surging into being.

XVII

THAT SPRING IT SNOWED AND SNOWED. I remember the mood of our life rather than the order of events.

We were still isolated in the grandeur of the valley. There was nothing to our life but our love—and the fact that Lawrence was coming back. Just the mention of him lightened our hearts, his name alone—Lawrence—had a power to quicken the meaning of life in one.

What did Lawrence really mean to us that cold spring long ago when we awaited his return?

I suppose first he could bring into words the unbelievable secret of life. We were sensitive to this secret—but could not word it. Life was quiet, beautiful, but impossible to express.

Lawrence expressed it.

He saw the dark lost things and brought their meaning back into life again. He made things live poignantly: a cypress tree, a rose unfolding, the long, long ago of any country.

Winter was intoxicating when Lawrence wrote of it. He could reveal the invisible. Life was pure, exquisite, every time we read him. Everything was fine about him, deeply understood, free. He was free, unwavering, confessing his hates so valiantly. Everlastingly wondering, poetically. Asserting what he believed so violently, yet pulsing with uncertainty, with life itself.

Perhaps we over-experienced him. No, I do not think it is possible to exhaust Lawrence's meanings—they are so vast, so unbelievably beautiful, so infallible—one slips into his horizonless world so easily.

I have some memory now of Margaret and I going to see Lawrence and Frieda the first week they got back from Mexico. It was April—and cold.

They were in Tony's house. Mabel had not come back from New York. She was not even to see him that year. In this life Lawrence and Mabel were never to meet again.

Lawrence was in the little adobe house in his big ten-gallon hat. Frieda was there too. They seemed lost without a welcome from Mabel.

We stood, it seems to me now, before a bureau with a mirror above it. I do not remember what we said. Lawrence was thinking of repainting the bureau. He loved to paint things.

Frieda stood by with frightened eyes. Lawrence was quiet. He did not seem ill. Preoccupied. The everlasting thoughtful eyes—thinking, thinking.

I did not know that he had almost died in Oaxaca a month ago. His illnesses were always kept a secret, but I do remember that Frieda was anxious as we stood talking, Lawrence and I, in the dark spring room of Tony's house.

They seemed ill at ease. Mabel was not there and they were uncertain of their right to be in Tony's house.

I remember Lawrence's saying that after Mexico, Taos was rather chilly.

He looked at me inquiringly. He always looked at me inquiringly, begging me, challenging me to come to life.

I thought of him as English that day—all reticences. And Frieda was anxious. There was something different in his face. A faraway contemplation. How could I possibly know that he had almost died? Even though he was deathly sick, he disguised it—was polite and gentle with Margaret and me.

We understood this was not the moment to call—yet they were so nice to both of us.

"Have you been here all winter?" asked Frieda.

"It was lovely," said Margaret.

Lawrence looked at her admiringly.

Yes, he was thinking of painting the bureau. We turned to go.

"We're going up to the ranch next week," he said. "You must come up when it gets warm."

"We'd love to," said Margaret.

We went out into the snow-flying spring. Across the way pigeons were circling and lighting on their pagoda-like roosts before Mabel's big house.

Lawrence looked very drawn, but I thought nothing of it. They speak in all the books of his pallor. I never really noticed it when I was talking to him.

"Goodbye," said Frieda, relieved that we were going.

"Goodbye," we said.

"Come in, Lawrence," said Frieda. "Do not stand out in the cold."

We went to our horses.

"I'm glad they're back," said Margaret.

I said nothing. I could not understand the meeting. Now I do, almost fifty years later. He had been given a short reprieve from death. He was aware of it, and was profoundly moved by his illness in Mexico. He was chastened by death.

He had so little time left—and so much still to say. His two greatest books were still to come: *Lady Chatterly's Lover* and *The Man Who Died*.

The Brett was now compelled to live at the Hawk Ranch, two miles away, because she got on Frieda's nerves.

Lawrence wrote her, "It's no good our trying to get together—it won't happen. . . . The halfness of your friendship I also hate, and between me and you there is no sensual correspondence."

But of course, the Brett came up every day on her horse.

He was quietly active now on the ranch. He milked his black cow Susan at six in the morning and after tea in the evening. He irrigated when the water from the Gallina was running. He saw to a rather small garden and he chopped wood. He writes endless poems about birds, beasts and flowers and countless letters to people all over the world. He begins a play to be called *David*, a very beautiful play.

Yet only six weeks before he had been dying in Oaxaca.

But he isn't quite well yet. He lies in the sun a great deal. The wind is ice cold. Then suddenly it is mild and warm and very beautiful. Spring. He watches the first crocus come through the red earth under the pines.

So he was better. The ranch was good for him. He was himself again.

The desert swept its great fawn-colored circle below like a beach, with a long mountainside of pure blue shadow closing in the near corner, and strange bluish hummocks of mountains rising like wet rock from a vast strand, away in the middle distance, and beyond, in the farthest distance, pale blue crests of mountains looking over the horizon, from the west, as if peering in from another world altogether.

Margaret and I saw a great deal of Lawrence that summer.

Lawrence loved simple joyous relations. He liked to *do* things around the ranch. He was always trying to get me to do things with him. Milk the cow, and go to the spring for water, or extract honey from a beehive in a tree trunk.

"You think too much, my lad."

Sometimes he talked about literature—Melville, Whitman, Joyce, E. M. Forster, Proust, Henry James—as we sat in our heavy boots on his wooden porch. He explained the great meaning of literature to me, and so seriously. Perhaps he knew my secret. I wanted to write. As he talked he took me on spiritual voyages I had never known before.

Lawrence tried to discover why men die—why whole cultures die. He came to the conclusion it was because they denied life deep within them and so they died. Or rather they went on living—but were dead.

The living secret of life was sex. Sex was not sensuality.

225

Sex had a Promethean quality. Sex quickened our spirit. It vivified the deepest life within us. Neither nations nor men ever attained life's true meaning without being imbued with sex. Sex was not a simple function of the body. It was a spiritual catalysis—*the secret*—which created our imaginative depths.

Modern man was disembodied mind. He was in anguish. He was spiritually dismembered—his hopes, his passions spreading like wild fire—nowhere.

Life was a deep reunion within us—an instinctive meeting of our living fires. And what inspirited us, awakened meaning in us, was sex.

And so the world, because it cared more for non-life— money, war, politics—chose to stigmatize Lawrence's great discovery as merely something dirty.

Lawrence's whole life was the need to avoid the disastrous, crippling effects upon his spirit of world-wide condemnation of his works.

Much of his irritation, his pettiness, was despair.

In the meantime there was the play *David*.

He lay outside his little room on the porch in the sun every morning and began writing his play *David*.

How easily, how sensitively he translated himself back to biblical times. Saul and David and Jonathan.

Ida Rauh moved him to do *David*.

The whole play is a *Song of Solomon*. There is an archaic joyousness to the whole drama.

He gives an excitement to the Bible. It is charmingly heretical. It identifies itself powerfully with the ancient

Jewish conflict: man's joy versus God's commandments.

This is Lawrence's secret heresy: to make God's chosen people pure with love of life—yet stricken with their fate—to be tyrannized over by their life-jealous Jehovah.

David is really a lost book of the Bible. Its approximation of the mood, the somberness, the *exact* religious meaning of a peasant people 4000 years ago is a modern miracle. Lawrence is again a prophet, a voice out of the past. *David* has all the Jehovah-wrath of the Jews, their laments, their delight in sacrifice. Their eternal concern with bread and God and iniquity and idolatry. The everlasting urge of the Jews to *disobey* God—the everlasting urge to *worship* Him.

A terrible God the Jews wanted—one who promised them only death and the rending of the kingdom of Israel. One who would not relent.

David has the greatness of the *Song of Solomon*. There is a delicious anguish running through Saul's speeches. It is Lawrence's lyric greatness, apologizing, justifying the Jews' paganism.

The conflict is not between sin and God. But between the beauty of life's urge and God's jealousy. Lawrence's theme—to the end.

He had almost died in Oaxaca—and he was turning to the Bible for meaning. Almost death—and he suddenly sought the Holy Ghost The Word. The Father. The whole play becomes pure prophesy.

It is his final testament.

Life on the ranch went on as usual. Susan, the damned cow, is off again, always vanishing in the trees. Lawrence shouts at her; cursing her violently, threatening to kill the bloody thing. Susan simply stands and looks at him.

The Brett takes up their mail every day.

Frieda is white with fury, almost unrecognizable. She strides up to the Brett and says in a choking voice, "I don't want you up here every day. I won't have you on the place. You are a mischief-maker. I hate you, hate you!"

Brett stares at her amazed. "Oh, go to hell!" says the Brett, daughter of Lord Esher. "I won't be bossed by you!"

Frieda turns and goes indoors and bangs the screen door in Brett's face.

The play is going wonderfully.

The Brett is typing furiously. She still spells badly.

"Look here, Brett. Sometimes you spell it *Johnathan*, sometime *Jonathane*. Have you never heard of *Jonathan*? It's the bunk the way you spell—with my copy right in front of you."

"I know, it's terrible," she says sadly.

"Cheer up, Brett. I do like the way you explore a word's spelling with the typewriter."

Ida Rauh has come for a week. She stays with the Brett at the Hawks. She is very exhausted by the altitude, almost 9000 feet. Ida has a very biblical, Old Testament head, black touseled hair. She could have been any of the heroines of olden times: Medea, Salome, Helen of Troy. Ida Rauh was the inspiration for *David*. She is to be Michal—wife of David.

But *David* is finished.

He wants to read it to Ida and the Brett.

They ride up to the ranch on horses.

They go into the sitting room. Lawrence is waiting for

228

them with the Brett's badly typed manuscript in his large hands. Frieda is lying on the bed smoking.

Lawrence begins to read in the slightly shy, bashful way he has. He has invented little songs for the play. He sings them in a soft voice.

He lives every part. In some subtle way he changes his voice as the characters alter from Saul to David to Samuel and then to Michal. He makes a woman's voice sound lovely.

He reads and reads. His voice is becoming hoarse. It's evening now. They have tea, but he reads on about Michal and David.

He sings again the lovely songs he has written for his play.

Ida is very moved by the beauty of the play Lawrence has written for her.

When Lawrence is finished, Ida is silent.

Lawrence looks at her inquiringly.

"Lawrence," she says softly. "I am too old to play the part of Michal—so young, so radiant a creature!"

Lawrence is appalled. He has written the play for Ida. Yet she cannot see herself in the part of Michal.

"The songs!" says the Brett. "You must write out the music for the songs."

Lawrence gets a piece of paper and rules it with lines. He begins to hum and tap out the tunes, jotting down the notes with a pencil. He hums softly, tapping the rhythm lightly on the table.

Suddenly Frieda says roughly to Lawrence, "Oh, you get on my nerves! Get out—go away— I don't want to hear you!"

Lawrence replies in a quiet, deadly voice, "You are impudent. Don't be so impertinent."

Ida gets up, throwing an indignant look at Frieda. She goes into the kitchen and sits on the kitchen table. The Brett follows. They listen intently to Lawrence, still humming in the other room.

David reached the peak of biblical tragedy. It is far beyond anything achieved by the Elizabethans. One must go to Aeschylus for its equal. Its prophetic wonder is unsurpassed. It is charged with poetic insights:

"Kings come and pass away, but the flame is the flame forever. . . .

"For that which is without name is lovelier than anything named. . . .

"And Saul hath seen a tall and rushing flame and hath gone mad for the flame rushed over him. . . . Saul yearneth for the flame; thou for tomorrow's glory."

XVIII

FRIEDA ASKED AFTER SWINBURNE every time she saw us. He appealed to her. He was handsome, blond and daring. What a hero he would make in a Wagner opera.

It was his daring that fascinated her most, and his charming sarcasms. He was a *man* in the ordinary sense. Powerful in a weak way. Self-possessed. He was tall, devilish—understandable. Lawrence was so intangible. What she had with Lawrence was just a reflection of his greatness—and his greatness was never wholly graspable. She lived with his pettiness not his greatness. "Just try it sometime—living with a genius!"

Swinburne Hale wasn't forever surging with visions like Lawrence. There was a kindness, an ordinariness about Swinburne that soothed her tired soul. Swinburne *might* have been her man. His roguish gestures, his presentability his irresistible handsomeness. They could have had a life together with his gallantries, his sympathy for her lot—his love making. His insatiableness matched hers.

Frieda saw only Swinburne's handsomeness, his devilish smile. Lawrence, of course, saw the unspeakable inner chaos of Swinburne. What conversations, what quarrels he and Frieda had about Swinburne I do not know, but years later when we told Frieda that Swinburne had died she was taken aback. Her eyes started at something in *her* life that had been touched. "He was a splendid man—but with a bad destiny," she said.

There was no peace in the desert for Swinburne.

He became over-aware of everything—the mountains, the sage, the dawn—but in a hateful chaotic way. What a contempt he had for life, the beauty around him. He would stand in the doorway of his cabin and mock the full moon forging slowly up over the first ridge.

He hated the haze-less orange sunsets and the desert night with its countless stars drifting westward.

He stood in the door of his cabin and looked at the vast sage wilderness. The end of the known world. He sneered

231

at the night wind. The emptiness of beauty around him. Was it hate, was it love—?

No, it was shame. Shame, shame that he was going mad. He could no longer make words on paper—only curse the beauty of the darkness. A certain poetry of insanity was now realizing itself within him. The stars halted in the sky and waited for his song.

He took to shooting at flocks of grackles in the sky, cursing as they swerved over him. Once he shot a crow and made a thick, bitter stew. He annotated the Bible, started a dozen poems—but his imagination always failed him. They were blank moods—arabesques of nonsense. He felt the purity, the fragility of the lovely undulating sea-bottom world about him. But he could not word it.

He was ashamed now that he had no words—no words for the beauty of—?

What do you do with things beyond you?

The proper thing was to go mad. Escape. Fail. Repudiate God, Mamá, Papá. Harvard! Ought I to shoot my horses?

One morning he came across the field and sat in the sun against the ruined wall and talked to Margaret and me. "I'm going back East."

He looked at Margaret to counsel him. "Yes, Bob."

"I—?" he gestured to the beauty of the desert all around us. He was tired, worn with his disease. "You are free," he said to Margaret. "Free! You always were free."

He was having trouble now—and we were concerned.

"Don't know why I'm not free. Mamá, Papá, New England. Why in hell did they call me Swinburne? Mamá, Papá. Oh, God!" putting his big face in his hands.

"Don't you think you've discharged your debt to Mamá and Papá and their idea of life by now?"

Swinburne tilted his chair down to the ground, got up wearily. He stood a moment facing us in his big Stetson and high-laced boots. His face was heavy, ugly—a bad man from Owen Wister's *The Virginian*.

"Don't tell Margaret—ever," he said to Margaret. "I am going to New York to meet Shakespeare. There's a certain word he'll tell me." And he turned and walked slowly across the field to his log cabin.

A month later Margaret's father wrote her that Swinburne had been committed to an asylum in Connecticut where he sat in his room and talked brilliant nonsense for twenty-four hours a day. He had been overtaken at last by his destiny—the dark. He was at last released. And happier than he had ever been in life.

I had a letter from Lawrence: "Do come and see us. Next week perhaps.... Could you bring us some meat from Cummings?"

We were happy to have the short note in his careful handwriting.

"Shall we ride?" I asked.

"No, we'll ask Ruth Swaine to take us."

Ruth was in awe of Lawrence. She was quiet around him. She came for us in her big open Buick early in the morning. It was a nice day in May or June.

We stopped in Taos at Mr. Cummings', the butcher, and got an eight-pound roast.

We drove north across the desert a little way from the mountains. It was very dry. The sage was tarnished. All the arroyos we passed through were waterless, silent. There were bleached bones of horses that had died in the winter, and skulls of rams with enormous spiral horns.

"I hope we'll make it," said Margaret. It was always a question of whether we'd make it to the Lawrences.

When we arrived at the bottom of the deep Hondo Gorge we heard the water echoing loudly. Overhead the sky was a dark blue. We forded the steep current by the old distillery and started up the crooked wagon track among the pines. Almost immediately the car lost power. It went slower and slower.

I could not think of the car. It was so beautiful under the trees. The pines rose higher and higher, and the desert dropped below us—luminous—a whole sea of beauty, a pink immensity.

"I think we ought to get out," said Margaret.

We walked beside the slow-moving car.

I could see the far ranges on the horizon. One by one they revealed themselves and the distance of the blazing sea of desert enlarged and enlarged, and floated away as I looked back.

And the light—!

Hundreds of miles of pure unsubstanced light. Living light that found further and further snowy summer ranges. How splendid was light. In the Beginning there was Light.

The car was hardly moving. Margaret was pushing it on the other side. I put my shoulder to it. But it was no use, it was going to stop. I pushed again and the car started.

"We'll get there," said Margaret.

The car had gone round a bend and left us behind. The light was beautiful below us. The First Light of the world. The living light of the desert.

234

We ran in the woods. We caught up with the car and jumped on the running board. But the car immediately stopped and we had to get off and push.

"Ruth," called Margaret. "We'll walk behind. It's only a mile or so."

The car picked up speed and Margaret and I were left farther and farther behind.

"One could live here—and look down on life," I said. We stopped again in the stillness of the pines.

"Yes, isn't daylight wonderful. It's the *soul* of life," said Margaret.

"And night—? I don't like the night."

"Why not, dear?"

"Because it's too full of meaning. Impossible meanings. Things surging in me."

She thought a while of what I was saying there in the woods. "One's spirit must always remain inflected. It is the only reality," she said at last.

We walked hand in hand up the narrow-rutted road between the pines.

Lawrence was waiting for us behind the white picket fence. He was all dressed up for us in a white shirt and blue velvet pantaloons.

"Gave you up," he said.

"The road is very steep," said Margaret. The car was boiling.

"It *is* steep," he agreed.

We were near him now—under his spell. And there was the stillness, the truth of the man, the truth of *us* in consequence.

"It's lovely here," said Margaret looking around in the clearing.

235

We could see Frieda in her tight bodice and full skirts come out on the porch and throw away the dishwater—and the chickens scramble toward it.

"The mornings are cold and delicate," said Lawrence. He looked at Margaret intently. "There's no real season here—snow blowing in summer. And hot sun in winter. After England—" he trailed off and looked at Ruth Swaine.

"This is Ruth Swaine," said Margaret, introducing her again. "She had a car and—"

"It's no joke driving is it?" he said to Ruth by way of acknowledging her. "Heartbreaking it's so uneven."

Ruth could not answer and he understood.

"We brought you some meat," said Margaret.

"Ah?" Had he forgotten he had asked us to bring him meat in his letter?

I got the meat in the brown butcher paper and gave it to him.

"Shall we put it in the larder on the tree?" looking at me.

Lawrence and I walked slowly up the hill to the pine tree.

Margaret and Ruth went to the house to see Frieda.

He gave me the meat to hold while he got a little ladder. He stood under the huge pine tree on the very top rung and opened the screen door of the little larder. "Mabel is still in New York," he said looking down at me. Was it a question?

I handed up the meat. He reached for it, took off the brown paper, and carefully hung the meat on the hook. He was quite pleased.

"We bought a buggy and Trinidad will drive us," he said closing the screen door. "He's really like a girl, you know, with his two braids." He got down from the ladder, folded it, and laid it on the pinecone-strewn ground.

His eyes wandered here and there about the woods. He seemed to be monitoring every tender moment of nature around him: the many birds coming and going under the trees, the huge shadows straying up the wild high mountains, and the light of the desert below us.

His talk was casual, polite—but his thoughts, his ungrasp able self was deep in another world. It swept through him forever this momentous drama of life. His blue eyes told you that.

"We still have three horses. But they are down at the Hawks. The grass must grow a bit," gesturing to the alfalfa field. "Shall we look at the cabins?"

We went across the clearing to a large double cabin.

"This was the Danes," he said opening the door to the empty cabin. "They were very fine. We thought of buying a boat and sailing the ocean—the Danes and I."

A memory was upon him now. I did not know what to say of the half-empty house. There was only a bed, a bureau, a washstand, a blackened fireplace.

"Perhaps you and Margaret will come sometime and stay overnight."

We went out into the clearing again. We were to look at the houses then. That was what he wanted to do today. Look at his little domain of white-chinked log cabins under the huge pines.

He pointed to a small log cabin. "That was the Brett's. She's down at the Hawks this year. She wanted to come up here, but Frieda said, 'No.' We go painting, however, all of us," he confided. "Do you paint—?"

237

"No, we just live down there," I said rather lamely.

"It's best," he agreed. "Say your say anyway you want it. Live your own life."

We walked toward another cabin, Lawrence's own cabin. The door was open, and in the tiny room I saw a cot with a red Mexican blanket and a small table. A little window opened on the green woods. There was a long rather crude painting on the floor—the ranch houses and the far pink distance through the pines.

"The Brett's," said Lawrence, realizing I was looking at it. "But I did the cow—rather wild, isn't she? But you should have seen the Brett's."

We laughed at that picture long ago.

"Oh, you write with a pen?" I said.

"It's not working very well," he said picking up the large red Waterman and showing me. "The nib is worn."

There was something fleeting in his eyes—a poetry of thought he could not put from him. Something was ending in him—and there was a new beginning too.

His conversation was so ordinary, his relation with you so natural—yet there were momentous goings on behind his blue eyes. He was being swept on into his surging destiny—into the momentousness of life. How calm his eyes, how quick his soul, realizing every significance of man. He was so near, so near life's meaning. He was far off in the final sweep of things. Yet he was there with you in an ordinary way. It was beautiful to see, to be near the fluency, the serenity of his being.

"I was so ill down in Mexico," he confided.

I looked concerned. Yet he was Lawrence to me everlastingly. One never thought of Lawrence in terms of

238

health. Just what he said. He had wondrous visions, hoping, hoping to draw you into their splendor—the shimmering perfection of the universe. But one could not respond.

"The doctor was very frightened. Thought I'd die," he said, looking at me directly now.

But he had gone on. There was the radiance of life—inwardly. He did not care for anything but the glory of the moment; how it changed and changed; it was rare, new —beautiful. If he had died—? That too would have been a poetic experience, a flickering last moment of insight. Perhaps death was only another beautiful mutation.

"Malaria—I was a month in bed. Could hardly crawl."

What could I say? I was thinking only of all the wonderful thoughts in his eyes.

"Shall we go down and have tea?" he asked me.

We went across the clearing where Frieda and Margaret sat at the table under the pines.

XIX

I HAD ANOTHER NOTE FROM LAWRENCE: "Do come up sometime. I've been in bed again with a chill. Nothing much. . . . Bring some books. Whatever you have. Gibbon. The Decline and Fall. I feel like reading something heavy."

It rained and rained that summer. Terrible cloudbursts

in the mountains. The arroyos all ran down the sage slopes with thick wide flows of muddy water. Two bridges were washed out on the highway between Ranchos and Taos.

It was a very muddy valley. Our dirt roofs all leaked. We spent the night putting tin cans where they would catch the water. Our bed was soaked.

"Will it ever stop!" I cried.

"This is just the rainy season," said Margaret. "We need the water for the alfalfa field."

"The Lawrences expect us," I said.

"Well, we can't go now. There's no road."

"I wonder why they live up there?"

"Oh, after Europe—it's so high and pure an experience—and unrelated."

"I don't like being unrelated," I said.

"If you were a European and crowded in by millions of other people, you would long to be unrelated for a while."

"I suppose he'll go back to Europe," I said.

She did not answer. Neither of us wanted him to go.

We did not get up to the Lawrences for three weeks. I do not remember in whose car we went, but the road had been washed away in several places. It was a harrowing experience.

I collected a carton of books for him. Poems. History. A book on psychoanalysis by Tridon. A novel by Swinnerton. A novel by E. M. Forster. It is so long ago, but I remember the books were tumbled into a Pet Milk carton.

He was waiting for us again—in his white shirt and blue pantaloons. He liked to dress up in that quaint, individual way he had. His color was better—not tanned.

"I've been lying in the sun," he said.

240

He looked at Margaret quite anxiously. "A bit rough the road."

"Very rough," said Margaret.

He laughed. "No one's been up. I hear Mabel is back?"

"It rained so," said Margaret. "We haven't been anywhere."

"Hello. Hello. Hello!" said Frieda coming down the steps. Had she been crying? No, her eyes were always sad. There was a laughter-sadness in Frieda's blue eyes. "We knew if anyone could come up that road it would be you, Margaret."

The four of us walked toward the sunny porch. The mountain light was filtering through the trees. There was a smell of wet pine still from the rains. And that silence of the trees Lawrence always seemed a part of.

"We saw the most beautiful star fall last night," cried Frieda. She confided her childlike wonder of life to everyone.

"Very softly," said Lawrence.

"And the dark—?" questioned Frieda. "Is the darkness beautiful where you are too?"

"Yes," said Margaret.

I carried the box of books toward the house.

"I didn't have a copy of Gibbon," I said.

"Ah, well," said Lawrence.

On the porch he poked through the box of books. He found a copy of Thomas Mann and curled his nose. "Still learning his medium. Loves his sickness—not life. Awfully banal. Even the murders in *Macbeth* are alive. But not Mann."

"But Thomas Mann is a great author, Lawrence," protests Frieda, the German in her roused. "You are not God."

"Don't be a fool, Frieda. He's stale. He's full of disgusts and loathing of himself."

"You know so much!" said Frieda, and she went into the house and slammed the screen door.

Margaret went into the kitchen after her.

Lawrence and I sat down on the steps of the porch.

Everything in the woods was so motionless around us. The balsam trees were so still. The mountains higher and higher above us.

Lawrence was silent. He was thinking about Frieda's attack.

We both sat with our heads in the sun. We both wore heavy boots and tucked-in trousers.

"Do you like American writers?" I asked.

"Well, your Whitman—he's so near the quick of the universe."

"But in your *Studies of Classical American Literature* you didn't like him."

He laughed but would not defend his contradictions. "And Melville—?"

Brett, in her big cowboy hat and orange blouse, was tying her horse to the white picket fence. She came up and showed him the long picture of the woods and the cabins I had seen on the floor of his room the time before.

His face looked tired, but only for a moment, then he said in his high, preacher's voice, "Quite nice, Brett. But it needs more color."

"The mesa—?" She looked to him for everything in life.

"A lot more, Brett. I'll see what I can do."

"Shall I leave it then?"

242

"Yes, in my cabin."

They were working together on this awkward little painting of the ranch.

"Where is Frieda?" asked the Brett.

Lawrence rolled his eyes heavenwards. "In her lair."

The Brett acknowledged me now with a guarded smile and went into the kitchen.

"Melville—?" said Lawrence, picking up the conversation the Brett had interrupted. "The fight with the whale is too wonderful. It's the strangest, most wonderful book in the world," he said. He could only be talking about *Moby Dick*—the battle for life, the doom of the white civilization. The white race dooming itself—hunting down and killing Moby Dick—*life*.

"It's a great book," he said, looking at me sincerely. "Tiresome style. But when he forgets he is writing—! He gives us sheer comprehension of the world. Then he is wonderful, he commands a stillness in the soul. That book awed me."

He picked up the cat and held it prisoner between his knees. His talk was a sort of reverie that afternoon.

I wanted to ask him about so many writers.

We talked about E. M. Forster.

"A bit like you," he said. "His beard."

Then we got on Joyce.

"They say we are alike," he laughed. "But I don't see us as the same."

"What about *Ulysses*?" I dared ask.

"Read the last chapter," he jeered. "That's all."

We came to Poe.

"Poor Poe! He was a little out of his wits. Pushed it to

243

the verge—his soul. Too heightened, too frenzied this seeking of his—wanted the extreme in everything. No limits. Especially to love and ecstasy. Really Poe was unappeasable. More. More. A too heightened experience of life is just death."

"You seem to prefer the older American writers?"

"You've done nothing since," he said quickly.

"Perhaps not."

"But at least you're free of us. And you've gone down very very deep—in the last century. Down to the quick—not quite understanding it."

"Well, it was easier the last century. They were closer to—?" I couldn't quite say what.

Yet he understood.

"Yes, to the frontier. The crisis in your history. Everyone was *real* then. But they were all a little cowardly, you know, in their way. Poe and Hawthorne. When they got to the center of the matter—when they got to the quick—they didn't know what to do about it. A little afraid of the truth. Went moral before the throne of God—the old boys. They got to the quick—and then missed."

"But you do like Whitman?"

"But oh, that Allness. You can't become the whole world."

I saw he was getting irritated now. His own ideas irritated him.

"But he was a very great poet. We haven't anything like him in England. Nor in France. Little, little poets. Innovators. But Whitman—he meant so much to me because he *struck out* across the wilderness. There was nothing beyond him and he tried to find a way. A new, unopened way. He was great," he said again. "Probably your greatest.

244

He broke through. *The Open Road*. His soul took the open road. No goal. He left the soul free."

A sort of rhythmic enthusiasm seized him—his phrases were created and shaped so brilliantly in his complaining voice.

"What do you think of Henry James?" I asked.

"A wet-leg."

I looked surprised.

"He never got to the Edge," sneered Lawrence.

I couldn't always understand Lawrence. His fierceness? Now I know it was for any one who had not gone to the very bottom of life.

"Do you like any of the moderns?" I dared ask.

"Well, there's so much false frenzy today in literature. Ego. Self-consciousness. Mr. Proust, tearing and tearing himself to pieces—his smallest emotions shreds. The great ones of the past had tremendously powerful *permanent* emotions. Not wholly graspable in words.

"But you Americans: Your consciousness is pot-bound—safe. European consciousness still has roots of memory grasping down to the heart of the world. But in America —life is good! You're all having a good time. You don't go very deep. You're concerned with yourselves—childishly. Not with underlying impulses. *New* underlying impulses. You've got to break through."

The cat escaped him now and ran into the weeds. Lawrence looked at me and smiled his grave inquiring smile.

The Brett came out of the kitchen.

"BRETT!" he shouts. He frightens her. "Come to tea tomorrow."

"It's not the day. Is it wise?"

She listens intently in her ear trumpet for his answer.

"Oh, yes."

She looks relieved. She's only to come three times a week. Frieda won't have it any other way.

"I'm going fishing in the Hondo—early," she said. "They're biting like mad."

"We'll cook them—if you catch any," he patronizes.

"I'll whistle first," says the Brett.

She went to the picket fence and mounted her horse clumsily and rode off into the trees.

Lawrence looked at me. I realized he would not continue talking. He was tired and white. He was waiting for us to go.

Margaret came out from the kitchen and Frieda stood behind her in the doorway.

"You must come again," said Frieda.

Lawrence went to the picket fence with us. He stood there in his white shirt and velvet blue trousers. The French trousers Brett has loaned him: the ones she bought in Paris in 1915.

"It's best by Arroyo Hondo—if you want to save time. There's a bad bridge, however. Do watch the road. I must hunt Susan. Goodbye. Come again."

He waved and turned toward the ranch house.

We crept down the badly rutted road.

The next evening the Brett arrives in the dark and blows her whistle.

Lawrence comes out of the house.

"Look!" she cries, opening her bag. Twenty-five fish.

246

"Really, Brett, you are a wonder. Come in and we'll cook them."

"It's not the day I should be here, Lawrence. Frieda won't have it."

"I'll see," and Lawrence goes up to the house.

The Brett remains by the barn.

Presently Lawrence returns. "Frieda is hopeless," he says with a laugh.

The Brett finally understands and lowers her horn and laughs too. She's not permitted to come in today. How silly it all is. She gets on her horse again and rides down to the Hawks.

But life on the ranch even in the midst of so much beauty becomes a strange desuetude. Lawrence is restless and unhappy. His throat is sore again. His bronchials. He never uttered the word *tuberculosis* in his life. It was always his bronchials. "I want to get out of America," he decides. "America sends everybody a bit loco."

This restlessness is his very life. England! "I have a bit *Heimweh* for Europe. The Mediterranean for the winter ... the Adriatic might be nice: real peasants still."

In the meantime he lay in the sun—and read *Adventure* magazine, "very exciting and really good." He built a shed for Susan. He exhausts himself carrying a log.

"I feel as if I have hurt something inside me."

Frieda comes out, with her cigarette hanging from her lip. "I will help," and she stoops and picks up the log easily with one hand and walks off.

247

They all paint a great deal. The Brett is painting last year's Indian camp below the trees.

"What a muff you are, Brett," he says cheerfully. "Let me try."

They exchange canvases. The Brett paints in a long mesa of pine trees.

"BRETT!" he shouts. "Look at my Indians. Aren't they much better than yours?"

"I don't know," replies the Brett. "Mine are good too."

"Not so good as mine. There is something vital you leave out. Some spark. Don't you think so?"

"Yes," replies the Brett meekly.

But he is restless, sad, depressed.

Frieda lies on the bed smoking. The Brett and Lawrence are sitting at the table having tea.

Suddenly it is all too much for him. He hates Frieda. "My life is intolerable with this incessant hostility. It's like being caged up with a tiger," he cries.

"You are bad-tempered," storms Frieda.

"I wish I could go straight to Italy." He takes a sip of tea and pushes the cup away irritably. "Oh, how I want to get away!"

The next day all goes well. Lawrence milks the cow. A certain peace possesses him. A warm affectionate loving mood. At supper he sits in the lamplight and eats thoughtfully. Afterwards he sings songs to Frieda and the Brett.

But the next day he cannot bear anything. He hurries off into the woods. He comes out carrying Smoky, the hen, headless, with wings still flapping. "I chopped off her head," he says, "to relieve my feelings."

Frieda flies into a temper and rants at him. "You want

248

to make a god of yourself! You are no more important than I am. I am just as important as you are!" She makes a low curtsy and puts her tongue out at him. "If only you were a gentleman; if only you were well-bred, like me—an aristocrat instead of a lower-class man! Bah! You are not a gentleman!"

He is finishing *The Plumed Serpent*—sending it off to Seltzer. "I still say this is the most important of all of my novels."

He felt shaky still. He had to lie down most of the time, but he *thought* he was getting better. It was lovely weather. He loved the flowers, the scarlet cactus, and he liked to ride up Raspberry Canyon behind the ranch. And he liked to go along the ditch with a shovel. He liked the big pine in front of the house. *His* tree.

He felt miserable and ill at times and couldn't do a thing. Europe would be better—the sea.

Frieda is painting now too. She sits—big, warm, bounding creature—in her tightly laced peasant bodice and red skirt and carefully sketches a pot of flowers.

Lawrence comes in from the woods, snatches the painting out of her hands, throws it on the ground and stamps on it.

"Why! Why!" screams Frieda.

He does not know himself, he is so tired with his illness going on and on each day.

"Because you've got your perspective all wrong. You don't know how to paint!"

"I am just as important as you are!" shouts Frieda.

Lawrence laughs his bitter laugh when she says that.

Frieda begins to cry.

Lawrence and the Brett go out on the porch and read most of the afternoon. He reads very slowly, intently.

The Brett gets her horse, and rides home.

Lawrence goes into the kitchen and then the bedroom.

Frieda is lying on the bed smoking her cigarette.

Lawrence lies down beside her. He puts his hand tenderly on her cheek.

"Lawrence," she says softly.

X X

ONE OF THE LAST TRIPS we made to the Lawrence Ranch was with Sara Higgins.

Lawrence had perhaps really cared for Sara in his shy way. Two years before they had taken rides together in the sage, and whatever was between them was very lovely —but the secret of history.

Sara came back from New York that fall of 1925 for a few days. She had a divorce from Victor and was happy. She was staying at Mabel's. Sara and Mabel had a great friendship. They had secrets together. Sara was Mabel's closest friend.

Sara was still very lovely, but she had changed. She had been very successful in New York—famous, in fact, in photography. She had found herself, but it was a dangerous self she had found, a commercial self.

She had had fine insights into a pure world of art when she was a young girl in Santa Fe. She was a miracle of innocence. And men like Lawrence and Maurice Sterne and George Bellows and Marsden Hartley and Leon Gaspard had seen this instinct to life in her and were happy knowing her. But suddenly she had discovered she had a facility in photography. She was successful. She was making $20,000 a year.

"How could she!" I asked Margaret.

"Well, New York is hard to resist. Especially if you have talent."

"Yes, I know, but she had something else. She had the real thing. How could she sell out?"

"The easiest way of life today is commercialism."

"But what will Lawrence say?"

I remember that ride Margaret, Sara and I took to the Lawrence Ranch in the fall of 1925. It was about twenty miles as the crow flies. All the way across the valley we could see the ragged green patch—Lawrence's Ranch—high in the dark forested mountains.

It was a beautiful autumn day. There was a splendor about the earth. A splendor in being alive. There was a golden silence everywhere. We were silent too. the universe was silent.

How empty, how marvelous was the earth.

We loved the great lava plains to the west—vast out-pourings, vast deluges of lava still flowing from long rents radiating from San Antonio Peak, the Mother Vesuvius of it all.

I liked to trace the purple surges across the horizon,

251

piling up here and there in low rhythmic peaks, then on again in wide black glaciers, until it had all spilled into the roaring Rio Grande 20,000 years ago. There was a magic about riding horseback straight across the desert. Things came to you. The big things came to you.

Northward, above the Lawrence Ranch a group of barren mountains uplifted themselves—heights dominating heights—a great mural, a multitude of peaks and spires in wonderful profile against the white northern sky.

We had lunch and rested under some cottonwoods. We were all very happy together.

"I'm so tired, so tired," said Sara.

"It's only about fifteen miles now," said Margaret. "We'll make it by sundown."

We mounted and let our horses gallop across the golden afternoon desert!—a horizontal solitude. The stillness threw us all into a state of wonder.

We walked our horses in the pungent sage. Each moment enlarged itself into a lifetime. The Lawrence Ranch was still there before us—still high in the afternoon mountains. We were drugged with fatigue. The horses stumbled and stumbled in the sage. I lost myself in the interminable nothingness of thought.

We had risen. There was a splendor to the setting sun.

Below us the golden evening plain was strewn with tiny clumps of sage lengthening their ragged shadows toward eternity. The sage was gold, the cottonwoods streaming from the dark canyons were gold, the far-off lonely windmill was made of gold. Dust from a flock of sheep was a golden geyser in the still evening, and the undulating lava ranges on the horizon were golden too.

252

Taos was far below us—a golden scattering of houses on the plain twenty miles away, its many golden windows blinding me.

There is no distance in the West. Just isolated phenomenon, huddled mud towns or single shacks in the sage, or lonely riders—no distance between any of them—just the immensity of wonder.

You rode all day toward a village and never got there. Yet you were there all the time. You and the village and your loneliness in the sage were one. You and the village and the mountains were one. You were everlastingly moving nowhere—just galloping, galloping, in the golden eternity of the sage.

The mountains before us were distilling magenta shadows in their ravines, slashing themselves deeply with purple-blacks. But the plain remained forever golden, and Taos was still far behind us, burning to the ground in golden ashes.

The world was low and lonely, an endless horizontal experience, on and on in the calm alluvial flow of gold—of sunset. Only the isolated buttes here and there seeking to rise above the horizontal solitude that went on and on in the Golden mind of God.

We rode on now in the bright unity of creation. The blazing town far below us, the golden mountains, the lowering red universe on the horizon—rose and rose in the everlasting silence of our thoughts. Three riders in the golden tide of sage draining from the darkening mountains before us.

We had come to the foot of the mountains and were going up, up through the tall pines. Oh, the heavy sharp aroma of that lane of pines. It is Lawrence to me. A fifty-year-old memory. The sharp smell of the pines on the lonely mountain road to the Lawrence clearing.

There was a gate. "I'll open it," said Margaret. She got down quickly and pressed her shoulder against the aspen pole and took off the wire and let Sara and me pass.

We waited dumbly while Margaret did up the gate again.

"There!" she said. She mounted heavily and we were walking slowly in the twilight of the pines.

The sun was very low now—setting a whole world of golden minutiae adrift on the plain below us.

"I hope he'll remember me," said Sara.

"Oh, he'll remember you," said Margaret.

The sun as they spoke burned its way deeply into the sea's horizon—crests beyond crests of stone. The mountains stood out strangely—black riddles, black masterpieces eternalizing the last conflict of lights glancing from the golden ruins of the world. The sky sprang out violet. Night fell instantly making the pale moon, Margaret, and I one.

"I can't ride much more," said Sara.

"There's the alfalfa field." A white horse was grazing in the moonlight.

We skirted the field slowly. There were thick stands of firs up all the silent gorges behind the ranch.

"It used to be an old goat ranch in the '80s before Mabel bought it and gave it to Lawrence," said Margaret in her clear low voice. "There's the fence."

We saw the low cabins now, their roofs shining dully in the moonlight. And the trees crowding in everywhere.

254

"Are they there?" asked Sara.

"I don't think so," said Margaret.

There was no light in any of the cabins. I heard the night wind soughing through the pines.

"I'm so tired," said Sara.

We rode to the white picket fence and dismounted. We loosened our horses' cinches and let them graze on the grass, trailing their reins after them. We sat on the steps of one of the cabins and waited.

Sara was exhausted. "Where could they be?" she fretted.

Margaret and I were overcome by the stillness. It was a living stillness, a vast meditation, if you like, of the night. A magnificent surge, this silence, of the earth's last meaning. Wave on wave of beauty—choiring.

We heard a sound up the mountain. Voices.

"Let us gallop a bit!" Lawrence's shrill voice from a distance.

"All right." The Brett.

"Lawrence!" It is Frieda cautioning.

"Spud!" cried Lawrence. "Are you coming?"

"They're quite high up still," said Margaret.

We sat and waited in the moon shadow of the cabin.

"I wonder if he'll remember me?" worried Sara.

We listened to them coming down and down the mountains. We heard them laugh and call to each other, their British voices sharp and clear. Suddenly they are in the clearing—four riders strung out. Lawrence is first, of course, then Brett and Spud, and Frieda last. They are very happy, they laugh and laugh. What lovely gaiety as they trot toward us. They are all carrying branches of yellow aspens.

255

"Hello," said Margaret. "We heard you up the slope."

"Yes! We've been up to the peaks!" shouted Frieda, and she waved her large branch of aspens in the moonlight.

"Have you waited long?" asked Lawrence, concerned.

"No. No," said Margaret. "We were listening to the wind in your trees."

"Ah," said Lawrence. "We quite forgot you were coming. It was nice up the mountain."

"Hello, Sara. Hello!" cried Frieda, flopping off her horse. "How nice of you to come." Even in the dark Frieda was radiant.

"Hello," said Sara, not daring to go to Lawrence first, instead to Frieda. "You live so *high*."

"Yes, yes. The ranch is 8500 feet. But we were at 10,000 today."

"Ten thousand five hundred," corrected Lawrence irritably.

"And this is the Brett!" said Frieda.

The Brett held out her horn to Sara.

"How do you do?" said Sara.

When the Brett understood she replied, "How do you do?"

Spud shrank back and would not join the circle.

I looked at Lawrence and saw how tired he was. His face was very white. He seemed to crouch over as though in pain.

We stood an embarrassed moment waiting for Lawrence. "You must be tired," he said. "Come in the house and we'll make a fire. But first let us turn the horses loose in the pasture."

"Joe could do that," said Margaret.

256

"Oh, no," said Lawrence. "We'll all do it. Come along, Brett."

I gathered up the reins of our three horses. The Brett and Lawrence took the reins of their four horses.

We went to the picket fence.

"We'll unsaddle them here—and just turn them loose." I saw he was very, very tired. Yet he was the host that chill autumn night and he could not let himself be tired. I undid the cinches and pulled off the saddles from our horses.

"Can you manage?" he asks.

"Oh, yes, yes."

I took off the sweat-smelling blankets and then the bridles. The horses—seven of them—scampered in the moonlit alfalfa field. And then suddenly as one pack of wild horses they dash down the steep slope into the pine forest.

"We'll find them tomorrow," said Lawrence. He looked a moment across the clearing through the crowd of pines and then down, far down, to the motionless desert in the moonlight.

We turned and went back. He was utterly exhausted.

There was a light in the kitchen. And a duller light in the living room of the larger cabin.

"Frieda will have lighted a fire."

He stopped before another cabin. He went up the steps and opened the door. This was to be our cabin for the night. "Will you be comfortable here?"

"Oh yes!"

"I'll fetch you a lamp. You'll need some things."

We went to the house. All the women were talking

excitedly. Frieda's voice rang and rang, but I saw her give Lawrence a quick look of concern as he came into the kitchen. He avoided her.

"We're having dumplings!" shouted Frieda. She stood over the stove, strong and healthy.

Lawrence went up to Sara, who was quite sensitive to her meeting with him again in this high, high place. "How have you been?" he asked. He let his eyes flicker over her young face, her young body.

"All right. I live in New York now."

"It's a house of cards—isn't it? It doesn't materialize. And the people—quenched."

But I saw he was too tired to be anything but pleasant.

"Frieda, have we a lamp?"

"In the pantry—and they'll need a washbasin and water. I'm so glad you came," she shouted to Margaret and Sara. "It does Lawrence good to have people come. We're alone up here, you know, and Lawrence gets irritable."

I waited while Lawrence got the things from the pantry. I stepped to the doorway of the living room. A fire was burning. Spud was sitting far back on the bed reading. He looked at me, and I looked at him. But we said nothing.

I went back into the warm kitchen where the women were talking—Frieda, Margaret and Sara. The Brett was silent as she listened with her ear trumpet.

Margaret was saying something now, and Frieda was saying, "Ja. Ja."

Lawrence brought the lamp and the washbasin.

"Will you take a pitcher of water?" he said to me.

I dipped some water from a pail into the large enamel pitcher he gave me.

258

We went outside and crossed the patch of moonlight to the other cabin. He stopped a moment. Then in his strange shrill voice he said, "I haven't milked Susan."

"Isn't it too late?" I said.

"Yes," he hissed. His life revolved around that cow. His love of her, his hate of her and the exasperating way she always ran into the woods when it was time to milk her.

We went into the cabin and put the washbasin and the pitcher on the table. I heard him panting.

"It's chilly. Shall I light a fire?" he asked.

"Oh, no. We're used to it. It's fall."

"After supper then, I'll light the fire for you."

I didn't want to say *I* could light it as well as he. I didn't want to diminish by one iota his own strength. He was so tired, so utterly tired, and yet he wanted to be, *must* be a good host.

"Are you sure you'll be all right—here for the night—you and Margaret?"

"Oh yes, yes."

"Sara can have the other room," nodding. "Mabel used to sleep here. But she doesn't come now. See here, she's left her moccasins."

They were very wide white moccasins Mabel had left hanging by their white laces from a nail in the wall.

We went back to the kitchen.

"Lawrence, we're going to eat now," shouted Frieda. Perhaps she always shouted because of the Brett. "Spud! Spud! Come and eat."

Spud appeared languidly in the doorway of the living room.

"Spoodle," said Lawrence affectionately.

We all sat down around the farmer's table in the log cabin high in the mountains fifty years ago.

The light from the kerosene lamp was very dim.

I remember Lawrence's tired white face and Frieda's rosy health. She carried the burden of the conversation. Spud and the Brett were silent. Sara sat next to Lawrence. Margaret and I opposite them.

It was Lawrence who served us from the stove. Frieda sat, a queen—and radiated queenliness.

"And Lawrence made the bread," shouted Frieda. She passed us a little wooden paddle with white slices of bread. It was very good.

"Are you cold?" said Lawrence to me, suddenly jumping up.

"Oh, no, no," I protested.

"Would you like to sit here? There's a draft where you are."

"Yes, the house is cold at night," agreed Frieda. "The wind comes through the cracks."

"Here," said Lawrence. "Shall we change places so you won't be in the draft?"

I got up and took his place. He wanted it so.

"Lawrence!" shouted Frieda. "Aren't you going to give them some of your whiskey?"

Lawrence jumped up again. "Would you like some?" he said to me. "It's bootleg."

"It is very raw—awful," said Frieda.

"Will you have a bit?" pleaded Lawrence.

"Yes," I said. I didn't know what I was in for.

Lawrence went out into the chill night in his little checkered coat.

"He keeps it in the vegetable cellar," said Frieda.

Lawrence came back with a huge sticky bottle of what appeared to be varnish. He got a tumbler and started to pour.

"Oh, that's enough!" I cried.

He handed me a half-glass of bootleg whiskey. He looked at me curiously as I drank it. It was truly awful. It burned my mouth and throat.

"Brett!" he cried. "Will you have some?"

Brett listened and listened, then replied, "Mercy, no!"

Everyone laughed at the Brett.

Lawrence poured himself a good half-glass and drank it down. "It's good," he said. "It's rotten—but it's good." He was in brighter spirits now, not as tired. He was quite gay with our being there. He cared so much for the conviviality of life and friends.

"Shall we go in the other room?" shouted Frieda. "It's so nice by the fire. And Lawrence will tell us stories. Ja!"

We all got up and went into the other room, a pioneer log cabin room with an adobe fireplace and a mantle with bric-a-brac on it. Frieda's sentimental things.

It seems to me we all sat far back on the bed against the wall. Lawrence in front of us on a chair, as would a teacher before a class.

"Lawrence, tell them about the people on the boat," cried Frieda.

Lawrence sucks in his cheeks and rolls his eyes heavenwards—then makes fastidious gestures with his hands. He gets up and shrinks away—then suddenly relents and allows himself to be overcome.

"That was Beverly ———." Frieda named a famous

movie actress of the twenties. "She was very beautiful."

Lawrence mimicked a very beautiful woman with his white sunken cheeks. How fascinating he was as a beautiful woman.

Sara howled with delight.

"We picked up a whole cinema company in Tahiti," he explained, sitting down in the rocking chair again. "And they were all drunk—the whole trip."

"The women were all naked and always going into the men's cabins," shouted Frieda.

"They had little handkerchiefs for nightgowns," said Lawrence, his heavy hands showing us the size.

Sara could not contain herself and she screamed with laughter.

"And now, Lawrence, tell them about San Francisco."

Lawrence got up shakily and walked, oh so carefully, across the room. But suddenly he almost lost his balance and he put his arms out to save himself. He looked frightened. He turned around carefully, almost fell, got to the wall at last, and slowly felt his way back to his rocking chair.

"We were twenty-five days at sea—and we were still land-sick. The floor would go up and down."

His act over, Lawrence sat there in his rocking chair serenely, as though posing for his portrait, a mockery in his lovely eyes.

"And now New Orleans, Lawrence," said Frieda.

Lawrence became the guide on top of a bus as he took us through a famous cemetery in New Orleans under water.

Sara could bear it no longer and she got up and pulled

Spud to his feet. "Come on, let's go and wash the dishes, Spud."

Frieda got up too and they all went into the kitchen leaving Lawrence rocking silently in the chair and Margaret and I facing him on the bed.

He seemed in another mood now that his charades were over.

I knew he was thinking of Margaret and me. In spite of all that play acting—he really only wanted to give us advice. Lawrence yearned to give everyone he met advice.

"Will you go to England?" asked Margaret.

"It would seem best," he said. "Perhaps I made a mistake forsaking England and moving out here into the periphery of life."

He was talking about England but thinking of us. He kept his large hands folded in his lap and rocked back and forth.

"Joe and I—" began Margaret.

But he interrupted. "What you have to do is to stick to the good part of yourselves. Face the facts of your lives and live *beyond* other people. You can't help being more or less damaged by other people. After all you will have your life together," looking at me. "Not what vulgar people *call* life—but you and Margaret—what you have together. Live it *intensely*. And it is so lovely here where you live. But the greatest virtue in life is real courage—and that you have," looking at Margaret with finality.

Yes, Margaret had the courage. He was giving her the advice—not me. My fate was really in Margaret's hands. He knew that.

"Lawrence!" said Frieda in the doorway. "Spud and Sara

have washed the dishes." She sang her sentences—inflected them in her guttural English.

She smiled—and it was a signal the evening was over.

"Very well," Lawrence said, rising. "I'll take them to the cabin."

He rose, still another self. He could change and change before your very eyes. Always this moody far-offness. All the while he was smiling at you so sensitively.

We went out on the little porch Lawrence had made. The moonlight filtered whitely through the huge pines.

"Good-night. Good-night. Good-night," shouted Frieda.

Lawrence went ahead of us. Margaret, Sara and I followed. He always hurried. He was in the cabin lighting the wick of the little lamp, before we arrived.

"There's but one lamp," he apologized.

"Oh, there's moonlight," said Margaret. "Sara can have the lamp."

He held the dim old-fashioned lamp in his gnarled hand a moment to see that the wick was properly turned up. Then he handed it to Sara.

She took it carefully and looked at him. "Shall I ever see you again?" She asked.

He gave a slight whinny. He liked Sara. He liked her premonitions. He went to the door and turned and with an odd smile said to all of us, "Good-night."

"Good-night," we said.

Sara sat down on the bed and cried.

"Isn't he wonderful! Every word he says suggests so much. He is so infinite in his understanding of you. I always feel so magnificent when I'm with him. He sort of creates a longing in the sweetest part of my heart. A tenderness, a fear for *him*. But also the impossible greatness of life."

"Yes," agreed Margaret.

It was very beautiful the next morning when we awoke. The sun shone strongly on the pines. There was a circus of bird life among the trees.

"Jays," said Margaret. She had been brought up in the Maine woods.

We listened to the charivari of birds in the pines outside. Our love was so perfect that morning long ago. We did not want to get up and break the spell.

I was a burden to her with my intensity, my indirections. I must have been very difficult for someone so gentle, so serene as Margaret. But I loved her. Some blind fierceness in me loved her everlastingly.

"I'm going to walk around," I said getting up.

What a simple whitewashed bedroom it was in the bright daylight, a stark room in which to be born or die. A kind of room that was Lawrence—the plank floor, the small barn-sash windows, the quaint crooked bed.

"You won't bother him, will you?" said Margaret. "You know he writes in the morning."

"No. No. I just want to be outside." I put on my shirt and stuffed my trousers in the tops of my boots.

I opened the door and there was the magnificence of the morning Lawrence loved. And the silence. You came alive in the morning—in the utter stillness of the forest. The desert was far, far below. How absolute the morning desert is, sweeping up to the ponderous black mountains.

265

There was smoke coming from the kitchen in the larger cabin but I did not go near it. I went through the white picket gate. The horses were grazing calmly near the house.

Coming along the edge of the field was the Brett riding her horse awkwardly. She stood in the stirrups and leaned a little forward, her orange blouse ballooning behind her. In her hand, of course, was her brass ear trumpet.

I went into the forest under the dark pines. The early sun shot down from the peaks and made a golden twilight under the shaggy branches. I found the spring and drank. I seemed alone in the world, a lost feeling possessed me. I could not bear it—this utter nothingness of the spirit.

There were no jays now, no squirrels chattering, just the loneliness, the early morning sunlight, the silence—and Lawrence—sitting under a huge pine writing, his eyes on the far splendor below of the morning-pink desert.

How easily, how quickly he wrote on a pad on his knees. But with a strange intensity too. He needed the outdoors, the distance to inspire him.

I backed away and left him sitting there under the huge pine.

When I got back to the clearing Frieda came out on the porch and threw some water to the chickens.

"Isn't it wonderful in the morning?" she asked.

"Yes," I agreed.

"You see there's the moon still," she pointed to the faded moon in the morning sky. "I would like to have a telescope and look at the moon and the stars."

"I—I came across Lawrence," I said. "I'm sorry."

"Under the tree? Yes, he likes to write under a tree. Don't worry. He's never bothered. Even with people around him, he writes. And do you think Sara is happy not being married to Victor?"

"I don't know," I said. "She has so much ahead of her in life."

She thought of that a moment. Then said boldly, "Ja. Ja. You're right, Joe. But we all have. You and Margaret most. You will break through, Joe, I know."

I was embarrassed. But I realized Frieda's and Lawrence's insights were merely different phases of the same genius. "I think I'll see if Margaret is up," I said.

"Ja. Ja. And come to the kitchen when you wish. The Brett is here. We'll all go riding."

I went to the cabin. Margaret was up and dressed in her riding breeches and black boots. Her large silver concha belt glittered wherever she went about the room.

"Was it nice?" she asked looking at me calmly. She was beautiful that morning, strong and refreshed.

"It's so strange up here. Beautiful but awing. Frieda says I'll break through." I wanted Margaret's assurance.

She smiled and kissed me.

Sara was in the doorway. She looked tired, forlorn. She had city-puffy eyes and her hands were nervous. "I couldn't sleep," she said, throwing herself in Margaret's arms.

She experienced life intensely. But even Lawrence couldn't save Sara from her destiny—commercialism.

She looked at me. "Do you have a cigarette?" Sara couldn't do without a cigarette a moment longer.

"I didn't bring any." In those days I did or didn't smoke as the mood suited me.

"Do you think that Lawrence would have a cigarette?"

"No, he doesn't smoke," said Margaret. "I'll have coffee in a moment. That will help."

We ate happily. Lawrence's bread was wonderful toasted.

"Frieda made the jam," said Margaret. "It's choke-cherry."

"I *hate* that kind of jam," said Sara. She had barely nibbled her toast. She looked at me defiantly because she knew I thought her childish. "I'm so lame. Do you suppose there's any way down the mountain without riding a horse?" she pleaded. "Perhaps Mabel would come for me?"

"Mabel doesn't come and see them any more," said Margaret. "I'm afraid you'll have to ride back."

After breakfast we went across the clearing to the kitchen.

Frieda and Spud were finishing the dishes. Spud was thin and withdrawn, a monk who did not like to talk.

"And did you sleep?" asked Frieda of Sara.

"Wonderfully," lied Sara. For the Lawrences she was keeping up the bluff of still being real.

"And have you seen Mabel?" asked Frieda, rather fearfully.

"I'm staying with her."

"She doesn't come and see us. She sulks. It's just as well."

Frieda was efficient about the stove, pushing kettles here and there. It was a compulsion to mention Mabel, her enemy.

"I think Mabel was really my mother," said Sara. "She taught me so much. All the things about people I could never have known. She has such a restless curiosity about life."

"But she is *bored*, Sara!" said Frieda, "Everything dies in her."

"I have found her a fascination," said Sara. She was really Mabel's staunchest friend. "It's an excitement to be with her. She wants life—"

"But only for herself." It was Lawrence's sarcastic voice hissing behind us.

I looked at him. There was an indifference, a spent thing about his body. He had been writing.

"Don't you like her?" asked Sara. She wanted the truth.

"She has no center," he said with finality. He sat down on the chair and mopped his pale white forehead. Yes, he was tired from the concentration of writing. He looked at Frieda as if he didn't want anything but to be with her in the little kitchen, to fight with her, love with her.

"Well, I like her." Sara would not drop the subject.

"She's an egoist. She can't forget herself."

"But you admired her at first," insisted Sara. She dared challenge Lawrence.

"Her dauntlessness, yes. But that empty vortex of her ego—!" He rolled his eyes upwards, showing only the whites. "She burns without any center."

Neither Margaret nor I could stand the quarrel. We did not know what Lawrence would say next if pushed too far.

Frieda stood waiting at the stove. Her eyes were nervous, darting here and there. Her smile never left her face.

Sara didn't care. She wanted to defend Mabel. To disagree with Lawrence was to inspire him.

Suddenly Frieda could stand it no longer. She discharged all her venom at Lawrence, "You lovely phoenix! You are the bird and the ashes and the flame all by yourself.... I don't exist."

"Yes, possibly," said Lawrence dryly.

269

They were each reciting their parts fiercely, and Margaret and I were distressed.

The Brett was in the doorway of the kitchen. She wore her huge cowboy hat.

"Brett!" screamed Frieda. "I won't have you here every day."

"I have caught the horses," said the Brett calmly to Lawrence.

"Our lives are so easy if nobody makes any mischief!" Frieda shouted at the Brett.

"And were they far?" asked Lawrence, looking at the Brett civilly.

"Just behind the clearing in the woods, standing rump to tail, swishing the flies from each other's faces," she described lovingly.

Lawrence got up rather shakily, I thought. "Shall we ride down to the Hawk Ranch? We're painting down there you know. The plain below the big house." He looked at Frieda defiantly. He and the Brett were painting together, and he liked the anger it caused Frieda.

Frieda bit her lower lip and said nothing. She could not cope with the situation today.

"It's a short ride," said Lawrence. "Then you and Margaret can go on from there." He did not mention Sara. He was angry with Sara—a sure sign that he had a special feeling for her.

"What about the cow?" I asked.

"Oh, I've milked the cow—quite early. She was bursting."

"Ja," said Frieda. "Three quarts! They had a regular battle in the woods—she and Lawrence—before she would come in and be milked." She was smiling again. The storm had passed.

Lawrence took his big hat from a peg on the wall and put on his little checkered-black-and-white coat. It was too small, and his large white wrists stuck out from the sleeves.

"Well, then," said Lawrence.

We all went out on the porch relieved.

"Goodbye, Sara. Goodbye, Margaret," said Frieda, her eyes, her soul, bright again.

"Goodbye, Frieda," said Margaret.

Sara hugged her, for she knew she would never see Frieda or Lawrence again.

I saw it was not convenient to shake Frieda's hand. I went down the steps.

"And Joe!" she called. "You are the real thing. Just get out of life what *you* want not what *they* want. You will be a success in your own living way."

Lawrence whinnied at Frieda, taking it upon herself to give others advice.

Lawrence and the Brett's horses, Prince and Aaron, were saddled. Brett had also bridled our horses and tied them to the picket fence.

"Oh, thank you," said Margaret.

The Brett offered her horn inquiringly.

"Thank you for getting our horses," repeated Margaret.

"It's quite easy unless they run away. When they run it takes the morning!"

Lawrence was coming from his little house now in his big hat. Under his arm he carried an enormous canvas. He gave the painting to the Brett and mounted his grey gelding.

271

She handed him back the huge canvas and went to her horse.

"We're painting on the same picture," he explained. He waited patiently while Margaret and I saddled our horses. "Are you stiff?" he asked Sara by way of making up with her.

"Terribly." She laughed.

We were all mounted now and outside the fence and we headed through the woods—down, down, down—Lawrence ahead of us—hunched over, his short coattails flying—like the headless horseman.

He always rode ahead of us, very fast, down the sharp-smelling lane of pines.

We came to the big lonely house of the Hawks that forever faced the valley like some lost Pharaoh's tomb in Egypt.

"Oh, the view!" cried Margaret.

"Yes," said Lawrence. "Perhaps the most beautiful in the world."

We all looked with Lawrence at the vast sweep of earth.

Finally he turned to us. "The Brett and I are going on a bit to do our painting." It was his way of saying goodbye.

I saw he was anxious that we separate. He was eager to go over the hillside and paint the vast scene below with the Brett. "Painting is more fun than writing," he explained. "Much more of a game and costs the soul far less."

The Brett wheeled her horse around and Lawrence's horse followed.

"Goodbye," said Margaret.

He smiled his wistful smile over his shoulder at all of us. "Come again. Do come up again. In a week or so. We're going soon you know."

We watched them go over the hill into the pines to a higher vantage point where the Brett and he could paint a while.

Margaret and Sara and I turned our horses toward the desert below for the long ride home.

X X I

LAWRENCE BECAME MORE RESTLESS NOW. He is strangely sad and depressed.

"The Mediterranean is glittering blue today."

Frieda said nothing.

Every morning he rounds up Susan and milks. Every morning from eight to ten he sits under the huge pine tree and writes.

"Venice is lovely in autumn if it's not too crowded."

Frieda purses her lips grimly.

After tea he has another battle with Susan. But he finally wins and she lets herself be milked placidly.

"September would be lovely in Bavaria," he says as he hands Frieda the milk pail.

Frieda lays the things for supper. They are quite alone on the ranch now; there was really nothing to be done. Susan's cow shed is finished. He is very proud of it. And there is no alfalfa this year—the weeds took over.

"And Scotland," he says at supper, "the heather is out on the moors. The days last until 9 o'clock. And the silent lochs—the sea running in for miles and miles. Like the twilight morning of the world. Scotland is very beautiful."

"It rains and rains, Lawrence," said Frieda, passing him the potatoes.

"There is no fish as good as in Italy," he counters. And he gets up and goes out to lock the chicken house so the skunk won't get his hens.

Next morning Susan is waiting for him at the new cow shed. How boring. No fight today. He milks her matter-of-factly, bunting his head into her belly.

"I think Italy agrees with me better than America does."

He takes his irrigating shovel and goes up the ditch to bring down water. He loves to irrigate—and feel the water running softly over his black rubber boots.

The Brett has not been up for several days, so he has not been painting. There's really not much to do. Milk Susan. Write two hours every day—short things. See after the rather small garden. Frieda will not even quarrel.

"I don't feel myself very American; no, I am still European," he ruminates.

Frieda is doing the washing again. She washes the sheets very white as he has taught her.

"I'd be quite glad to be out of America for a time. It's tough and wearing," he insists. And he goes to the woodpile and chops a bit of wood for Frieda.

He brings a little armful of kindling into the kitchen and dumps it in the woodbox. "I have a sort of feeling I should like to go to Russia." He stands there, panting, at Frieda's brightly polished stove.

"You are a fool!" shouts Frieda. And she goes into her room, lies down on her bed and starts to read a book.

274

The Brett comes and they all three go riding.

He gallops gaily through the woods on Aaron, snatching off his little tweed hat and stuffing it in his pocket.

"How he does love it!" Frieda says to the Brett.

But at supper he is very depressed. "My life is intolerable. People come, and they suck the life out of me, to bring life into themselves. I am tired, sick to death of people and everything. I don't want to go to England. I wish to go straight to Italy."

He is very white. After all he has had a terrible hemorrhage in Oaxaca only a few months before.

"Look here, Brett. You have plenty of money. It is much better for you to travel a bit than to stay here for the winter alone. Have you ever been to Italy?"

"No," says the Brett.

"Everyone who can ought to see Italy. I may be there this winter. Why don't you go to Capri?"

"So that's it!" cries Frieda, getting up in a rage and going to her room and slamming the door.

Lawrence's eyes twinkle.

The terrible fights with Frieda go on and on. They vilify each other. Lawrence is really vicious. And she takes advantage of his weakness as a man whenever she can.

Frieda grows quite wild with the ordeal of Lawrence's rages. They fight and fight.

In utter desperation she turns to the Brett for sympathy. "I am not used to playing second fiddle. I am just as important as Lawrence, don't you think?"

"We all are," replies the Brett. "In one way—but not perhaps in another. He is a great creative artist and that makes a difference."

Frieda thinks a while. "He always wants to be boss," and she is disgusted.

But Lawrence *is* boss. They are going back to Europe.

They start tidying up the ranch, cleaning the barn and making arrangements for the horses and the cow. They are both very depressed. They are in a state over leaving. But they must go.

Mabel has not seen them the entire year. She holds her grudge against Lawrence. He has not bowed to her. But to whom has Lawrence ever bowed? Certainly not to Mabel.

Their relationship was ended. "You can't do anything for people—ever," he decides.

Perhaps Mabel felt the same about Lawrence. She too felt she had a destiny. She believed she had a power. She could have helped Lawrence. Lawrence just didn't realize what she was offering. So she dropped him.

They were never to meet again.

"I think I will go straight to Italy. I would rather. What's the use of England?"

So the die was cast. They will leave the ranch—forever. But he does not realize this.

"Come up tomorrow, Brett, and help us tidy up for packing!" he calls after her as she rides away into the dark.

The last time Margaret and I saw Lawrence was less than a week before they left. We rode up on horses and stayed the night.

276

It was still very beautiful. Their life went on as usual but there was a sadness everywhere because he was going.

"Ja. We are going," said Frieda. "Lawrence cannot really stand America any longer. He wants Europe."

I remember every moment of that last meeting.

Lawrence and I sat again on the worn boards of the porch.

He talked to me of literature that day. "The novel," he said, guessing that I wanted to write, "is a great discovery; far greater than Galileo's telescope. The novel is the highest form of human expression so far attained.

"Great novels, to my mind, Genesis, Exodus, Kings, by authors whose purpose was . . . big.

"In every great novel who is the hero all the time? Not any of the characters, but some unnamed and nameless flame behind them all. Just as God is the pivotal interest in the books in the Old Testament.

"Character is the flame of man.

"It is the flame of a man which burns brighter or dimmer, bluer or yellower or redder, rising or sinking or flaring according to the drafts of circumstances, changing continually, yet remaining one single separate flame, flickering in a strange world.

"In the great novel the felt but unknown flame stands behind all the characters. If you are too personal, too human, the flame fades out.

"The novel is too serious today. The people in serious novels are so absorbedly concerned with *themselves*. Those wearisome sickening little personal novels! Proust: a four-teen-volume death agony in *what I am*. 'Did I feel a twinge in my little toe?' asks every character. Adolescent.

"The great relationship, for humanity, will always be the relationship between man and woman. And the relationship between man and woman will change forever.

"The novel is a perfect medium for revealing to us the changing rainbow of our living relationships.

"The novel is the one bright book of life.

"To be alive, to be man alive, to be whole man alive: that is the point. And at its best, the novel, and the novel supremely, can help you. Only in the novel are all things given full play."

He looked at me that last afternoon and told me these things so seriously.

"I liked your *Sea and Sardinia*," I dared say.

"Oh, I think I have a copy. I'll give it to you." He got up and went into the house in his lithe natural way. A moment later he was back. "It has disappeared. They take them and take them. I can't keep a copy of anything. I even don't have an English copy of the First Edition of *The Rainbow*. Shall we milk Susan?"

Susan stood off from us in the woods. She was wild. *Two* men to milk her? She would not come near. She stood there snorting and snorting. No, she wasn't going to be friends with any stranger.

"It's my trousers," said Lawrence. He was all dressed up again in his blue pantaloons and white shirt for our coming. "She doesn't like these trousers. Doesn't recognize me unless I'm in the corduroys. Come now—" he said to the black cow.

But Susan turned wildly and fled.

278

"I'll have to change," said Lawrence. "Will you come to the cabin?"

We walked across the clearing to his little cabin.

"It's very tiresome. She knows it's me. But she'll not have these blue trousers while I milk her."

I waited outside while he sat down on his cot and took off his boots and changed his trousers.

A moment later he came out into the evening sunshine smiling—in his worn white corduroys. He was pale, sensitive and life-giving, his eyes always on you, asking you to understand—yourself.

We went down to the pasture. Susan was very docile now that he had on his corduroy trousers.

"There, you see," taking her by the halter. He brought her to the cow shed, then took a galvanized pail and turned it over to sit on and started to milk Susan. But oh, what a miserable cow was Susan—however famous. She gave scarce three quarts. But Lawrence was very happy milking her. He smiled when he got up and showed me the frothy milk.

Next morning we had breakfast with Frieda and Lawrence in the little farm kitchen.

Lawrence and Frieda were very still. They were in secret communication—a fight? But they were very polite to us.

I remember the red jam, the burnt toast, the ranch coffee —for us—but tea for Lawrence and Frieda.

Again there was Lawrence's concern that we be comfortable. "Shall I heat the coffee? We don't know how to make coffee—we English."

"Oh, it's very nice," lied Margaret.

He was always the perfect host. Even though he was white and tired and had quarreled violently with Frieda (had she been crying?), he was a perfect host.

"It's quite chilly at night," said Frieda, looking at Lawrence defiantly. She dared him to take exception to that.

"You are so high," said Margaret.

Lawrence still said nothing. He was not going to make up with Frieda this morning.

"And the cottonwoods," said Frieda. "They are *golden* now. And the aspens—!" She wanted to be happy—but Lawrence did not want her to be happy.

We sat there in the little kitchen that last day—the autumn, golden in the hills above us. The huge pines and firs nearly black all around us. The sun was bright on the breakfast table. Yes, it was chilly. Fall had come early.

"A lovely moment, a beautiful moment," described Frieda.

"But it will not last," said Lawrence.

Brett was in the door—quite frightened.

"The horses!" she said.

"What, Brett?" asked Lawrence.

"They've run away overnight," said the Brett. She was out of breath.

"The scoundrels!" said Lawrence rising.

"Why don't you let Joe head them back?" said Margaret.

"Yes, Lawrence," said Frieda. "You go and write and we'll catch the horses."

Again they were man and wife. He trusted her judgment. The quarrels, the fights—they were just dramatics. Whatever she really wanted he always wanted too.

"Very well," he agreed. "But watch out for Azul. He's

foxy. You catch him, Joe," he said to me. "And we'll all ride down with you and Margaret to Valdez."

"Ja," said Frieda.

Lawrence smiled and went out on the porch and to his cabin to get his red fountain pen. He must write every day of his life.

The Brett and I went to the white picket fence. My black Indian pony, Ak, still stood under the pine trees waiting for me.

I went up to him and bridled and saddled him.

The Brett looked on fascinated.

"Ours are quite unmanageable when they run away."

The Brett and I mounted and started into the woods—hunting for Lawrence's horses. We rode side by side under the big boughs of the pines. The Brett was very alert and looked intently neither to right or left but only in the distance.

"How many were there?" I asked.

Although we were riding knee to knee she did not answer. I liked her that day—she *must* find those horses for Lawrence.

After we had ridden fifteen minutes straight down the mountains through the pines, she turned her frightened eyes to me. Lawrence's horses were lost and she could not bear the thought.

"Perhaps they're back near the ranch house," I said.

She kept on riding straight down the mountain. She had not heard me.

"It's to be their last ride, you know. With you and Margaret. They leave on Thursday. But I shall wait a while. Go later—to Capri. Lawrence says I ought to see Italy."

She rode swiftly down the hill.

281

We came to a fence. The far end of the Lawrence Ranch.

"Oh, dear," she said, looking at me helplessly.

"They're back at the ranch," I said again. "They'd stay near your haystack."

She listened intently now, her eyes widening. "Of course!"

We galloped back up the mountainside. The Brett was very young, very happy that day as she stood in her stirrups and rode back to the ranch—to Lawrence.

The horses were standing under the pines by the white picket fence whisking their tails—waiting for us.

We saddled them.

I went into the kitchen.

Margaret and Frieda were talking.

"They were right here all the time near the haystack," I explained.

"Of course," said Frieda. "The Brett gets hysterical—too much Lawrence is all."

Margaret and I laughed.

Lawrence came into the room. He looked very calm. He handed Frieda what he had written that morning—several pages torn from a notebook. Frieda took the sheets and put them on the shelf. She would read them later.

"We'll go, Lawrence," she said. "I have the lunch and Joe has got the horses."

"Very well," said Lawrence. He was in a far-away mood. Things didn't really exist for him. He had been writing and nothing mattered. Writing had this lost effect upon him.

Margaret and I went outside to the horses.

Very soon Lawrence and Frieda came out of the house. He walked meekly behind her, carrying the lunch things in paper bags.

"We'll have lunch by the river in the Hondo," Frieda said smiling.

Lawrence said nothing. He tied the various little paper packages on the back of his saddle, then he stood by Frieda's horse and held the bridle. She mounted heavily, but not to Lawrence's liking, for he gave her a contemptuous look. She looked down defiantly.

Yet he was very meek that day—until he got in the saddle, then he was a very daredevil. He rode poorly but recklessly off into the woods.

"There you have him!" shouted Frieda. "At his worst— at his best."

But Lawrence, his checkered coattails flying, had already disappeared in the trees.

We rode very hard to catch up with him. The sun was hot under the heavy pine-smelling trees.

It was a very lonely road—the road to Valdez. Straight through the woods. You can still take it today—fifty years later. It was very narrow and went up and down the hot gullies.

We strung out single file.

Lawrence, Frieda and the Brett were silent. This was to be their last ride.

The horses plodded in the hot hillside-woods. Even Lawrence could not get Aaron to go. He looked back occasionally to see that we were following properly. But he said nothing. His face was very white. He loved New Mexico; riding in its great mountains was life to him.

We came to a crest among the trees.

"There it is!" cried Frieda.

We looked down at the Hondo River far below in the gorge. We all cried out and dashed down the zigzag trail to the water's edge. The Lawrences were happy at that moment. It was as though they had discovered the Pacific.

"Shall we cross?" said Lawrence. He dashed right into the snow-foamy water and was waiting for us on the other side. He jumped down and started undoing the thongs on the back of the saddle and taking off the paper packages of the lunch things.

Frieda dismounted heavily and looked around. "How nice. How wonderful." Her whole being expanded with the simple beauty of the scene. It was very wild. Just the piñon-dotted mountains coming down to the stream.

It was the last lovely spot on earth and it was here we were to say goodbye to Lawrence.

The Brett had gathered the reins of Frieda's and Lawrence's horses and was bending over him.

"Shall I let them graze?"

"Yes, do, Brett. There's grass." He was kneeling in the sand, opening the lunch things. He always was the one who took charge of occasions.

I tied our horses to a tree in the riverbed, a dry island. I didn't want to take any chances of their running away.

None of us carried a watch in those days. But it was noon.

Lawrence soon had the camp set up. The bread, the jam, the cold meat neatly laid out. He jumped up and quickly gathered driftwood for a fire. Yes, he was going to do it all. We didn't dare help him. He crouched again and got the

284

fire blazing between three stones. Then he ran to the river with the coffeepot.

"How wonderful! How wonderful that we are here," cried Frieda again. "Here you get the special feel of New Mexico. It is a revelation this place, to be here by this river, coming out of the mountains. Almost too fierce, but real and beautiful." She merely stood there and took joyful possession of the water-rushing canyon.

"Shall I cut the meat?" said the Brett to Lawrence.

He gave her a knife and she was soon cutting slices of cold mutton. But he watched that she did it correctly.

He looked up at Margaret. "I feel a little relief that we're going." He let his eyes linger on hers waiting for her understanding.

"We are very sorry that you are going," Margaret managed to say.

But he could not, could not, make a personal response to her. His eyes drifted away across the stream to the higher and higher piñon-dotted mountains. "It's always great and splendid here."

We all sat down or rather knelt among the lunch things. I seem to remember white-enamel plates and Lawrence handing them to us.

"We'll put the shutters up tomorrow," said Lawrence. And he looked at the Brett.

"Oh, then you're going quite soon?" Margaret dared ask.

"Ja," said Frieda. And there was a wistfulness in her eyes. She must go where he went—on these torturous odysseys about the world.

"Rachel and William will take good care of our things. William will come in a wagon for the better things. The

285

silverware, the rugs, the beds—the pictures." He laughed at the idea of the pictures.

"And the mattresses," said Frieda.

Lawrence rolled his eyes heavenwards.

"Yes, the pack rats will eat them to pieces otherwise."

"And what will you do with your animals?" asked Margaret.

I could hardly eat. It was so distressing—the details of their going.

"Oh, the horses can stay in the alfalfa field until December—until the big snow comes. Then William will take them to his ranch and feed them till spring when we will come back again."

When we will come back again.

Margaret finished eating her sandwich. She got up. "We ought to go. You know it's a long ride back to Ranchos. And it's late."

Lawrence jumped up too.

We stood a moment awkwardly. Then a warm expression came over Lawrence's pale face. He extended his thin hand to each of us.

"Till we see you," he said.

We went to our horses tied to the trees.

Lawrence stood there a moment and watched us mount from a distance, then went back to Frieda and the Brett.

Margaret and I took the steep trail up the side of the canyon, looking down upon the three of them still sitting by the river eating—Lawrence, Frieda, the Brett. When we got to the very top of the canyon we waved to the three small figures below us.

But they did not wave back.

286

EPILOGUE

LAWRENCE NEVER CAME BACK TO AMERICA.
I had had a picture postcard from him from London, Ludgate Hill, dated October 26, 1925.

Mr Joe Foster
Ranchos de Taos New Mexico U.S.A.
How are you all! It pours with rain here, so we are fleeing South. Send a line sometime—c/o Curtis Brown 6 Henrietta St. London. W.C. 1.
                    D. H. Lawrence

He died four years later in Vence on March 2, 1930.
Frieda wrote of his death:
"Since Doctor Max Mohr had gone, we had no doctor, only Mme. Martens the cook. She was very good at all kinds of tisanes and inhalations and mustard plasters, and she was a very good cook.

"My only grief was that we had no open fireplaces, only central heating and, thank goodness the sun all day.

"Lawrence made such wonderful efforts of will to go for walks and the strain of it made him irritable. If I went with him it was pure agony walking to the corner of the little road by the sea, only a few yards!

"How gallantly he tried to get better and live! ... And

I wanted him to live at any cost. I had to see him day by day getting nearer and nearer the end, his spirit so alive and powerful that the end and death seemed unthinkable and always will be, for me.

"And then Gertler sent a doctor friend to us, and when he saw Lawrence he said the only salvation was a sanitorium higher up. . . .

"Lawrence had always thought with horror of a sanitorium, we both thought with loathing of it. Freedom that he cherished so much! He never felt like an invalid, I saw to that! Never should he feel a poor sick thing as long as I was there and his spirit! Now we had to give in . . . we were beaten.

"With a set face Lawrence made me bring all his papers on to his bed and he tore most of them up and made everything tidy and neat and helped to pack his own trunks, and I never cried. . . . His self-discipline kept me up, and my admiration for his unfailing courage.

"And the day came that the motor stood at our little house, Beau-Soleil. Achsah Brewster came before we started with armsful of almond blossoms, and Earl Brewster travelled with us. . . .

"And patiently, with a deep silence, Lawrence set out on his last journey.

"At Toulon station he had to walk down and up stairs, wasting strength he could ill afford to waste, and the shaking train, and then the long drive from Antibes to the 'Ad Astra,' at Vence.

"And again he had to climb stairs. There he lay in a blue room with yellow curtains and great open windows and a balcony looking over the sea.

288

"When the doctor examined him and asked him questions about himself he told them, 'I have had bronchitis since I was a fortnight old.'

"In spite of his thinness and his illness he never lost his dignity, he fought on and he never lost hope. Friends brought him flowers, pink and red cyclamen and hyacinths and fruit . . . but he suffered much and when I bade him goodnight he said, 'Now I shall have to fight several battles of Waterloo before morning.' I dared not understand to the full the meaning of his words.

"One day he said to my daughter, 'Your mother does not care for me anymore, the death in me is repellent to her.'

"But it was the sadness of his suffering . . . and he would not eat and he had much pain . . . and we tried so hard to think of different foods for him. His friends tried to help him. The Di Chiaras and the Brewsters and Aldous and Maria Huxley and Ida Rauh.

"H. G. Wells came to see him, and the Aga Khan with his charming wife. Jo Davidson did a bust of him.

"One night I saw how he did not want me to go away, so I came after dinner and said: 'I'll sleep in your room tonight.' His eyes were so grateful and bright, but he turned to my daughter and said, 'It isn't often I want your mother, but I do want her tonight to stay.'

"I slept on the long chair in his room, and I looked out at the dark night and I wanted one single star to shine and comfort me, but there wasn't one; it was a dark big sky, and no moon and no stars.

"I knew how Lawrence suffered yet I could not help him. So the days went by in agony and the nights too;

289

my legs would hardly carry me, I could not stay away from him, and always the dread, 'How shall I find him?'

"I slept on his cane chair several nights. I heard coughing from many rooms, old coughing and young coughing. Next to his room was a young girl with her mother, and I heard her call out: 'Mama, Mama, je souffre tant!' I was glad Lawrence was a little deaf and could not hear it all.

"After one night when he had suffered so much I told myself: 'It is enough, it is enough; nobody should have to stand this.'

"He was very irritable and said: 'Your sleeping here does me no good.' I ran away and wept. When I came back he said so tenderly: 'Don't mind, you know I want nothing but you, but sometimes something is stronger in me.'

"We prepared to take him out of the nursing home and rented a villa where we took him. . . . It was the only time he allowed me to put on his shoes, everything else he always did for himself. He went in the shaking taxi and he was taken into the house and lay on the bed on which he was to die, exhausted. I slept on the couch where he could see me. He still ate.

"The next day was Sunday. 'Don't leave me,' he said, 'don't go away.' So I sat by his bed and read. He was reading the life of Columbus.

"After lunch he began to suffer very much and about tea-time he said: 'I must have a temperature. I am delirious. Give me the thermometer.' This is the only time, seeing his tortured face, that I cried, and he said: 'Don't cry,' in a quick compelling voice. So I ceased to cry anymore. He called Aldous and Maria Huxley who were there, and for the first time he cried out to them in his agony. 'I ought to have some morphine now,' he told me and my daughter, so Aldous went off to find a doctor to give him some. . . . Then he said: 'Hold me, hold me, I don't know where I am, I don't know where my hands are. . . . Where am I?'

"Then the doctor came and gave him a morphine injection. After a little while he said: 'I am better now, if I only could sweat I would be better . . .' and then again 'I am better now.' The minutes went by, Maria Huxley was in the room with me. I held his left ankle from time to time, it felt so full of life, all my days I shall hold his ankle in my hand.

"He was breathing more peacefully now, and then suddenly there were gaps in the breathing. The moment came when the thread of life tore in his heaving chest, his face changed, his cheeks and jaw sank, and death had taken hold of him. . . . Death was there, Lawrence was dead. So simple, so small a change, yet so final, so staggering, Death!

"I walked up and down beside his room, by the balcony, and everything looked different, there was a new thing, death, where there had been life, such intense life.

"The olive trees outside looked so black and close, and the sky so near; I looked into the room, there were his slippers with the shape of his feet standing neatly under the bed and under the sheet he lay, cold and remote, he whose ankle I had held alive only an hour or so ago. . . . I looked at his face. So proud, manly and splendid he looked, a new face there was. All suffering had been wiped from it, it was as if I had never seen him or known him in all the completeness of his being. I wanted to touch him but dared not, he was no longer in life with me. There had been the change, he belonged somewhere else now, to all the elements; he was the earth and sky, but no longer a living man. Lawrence, my Lorenzo, who had loved me and I him . . . he was dead. . . .

"Then we buried him, very simply, like a bird we put him away, a few of us who loved him. We put flowers into his grave and all I said was: 'Goodbye, Lorenzo' as his friends and I put lots and lots of mimosa on his coffin. Then he was covered over with earth while the sun came out on his small grave in the little cemetery of Vence which looks over the Mediterranean that he cared for so much."

NOTES AND SOURCES

page 3

l. 5 Luhan, *Lorenzo in Taos*, p. 18. "I had sent him some powerful letters and I had used a lot of willing on him."

l. 12 Frieda Lawrence, p. 91. "Very few people wanted to be friendly to us in those days. I was a Hun and Lawrence was not wanted."

l. 19 D.H.L. to Catherine Carswell from St. Ives, Cornwall, 7 November 1916. *Letters*, p. 379. "Because there, I know, the *skies* are not so old, the air is newer, the earth is not tired."

page 4

l. 4 D.H.L. to Mabel from Taormina, Sicily, 5 November 1921. Luhan, *Lorenzo in Taos*, pp. 5–6.

l. 12 Lawrence, "New Mexico," *Phoenix*, p. 142.

l. 16 Helen Green Blumenschein, anthropologist, writes: "The periods of Indian occupation in Taos Valley were from 900 A.D. to 1300 A.D. After 1300 A.D. the entire valley was abandoned by the Pueblo Indians, except perhaps for the Taos Pueblo." However, recent excavations in the summer of 1970 by Dr. Florence Ellis demonstrated that the Tewa Pueblo at Tsama was still occupied when the colonization of New Mexico (1598) began. The bones of sheep and cattle of European origin and an early Bible hinge found in the Tsama ruins indicate early Spanish contact. Tony Luhan once said or rather gestured in the author's presence to indicate that the Taos Indians originally came from across the river near Ojo Caliente, N.M.

l. 24 Lawrence said of the Pueblo in "Taos," *Phoenix*, p. 100: "Taos Pueblo affects me rather like one of the old monasteries. When you get there you feel something final."

page 5

l. 16 D.H.L. to Mabel from Taormina, 28 December 1921. Luhan, *Lorenzo in Taos*, p. 13.

l. 20 D.H.L. to Mabel from Thirroul, N.S.W., 9 June 1922. Luhan, *Lorenzo in Taos*, p. 24.

l. 29 Aldington, p. 122. "Whatever else may be denied Lawrence there can be no doubt he had a great attraction for many women." In his youth there was Jessie Chambers, Helen Corke, Louie Burrows, Agnes Holt, a Mrs. Davidson, Mrs. Alice Dax, and Jane. "I met Jane and kissed her good-bye—my heart was awfully heavy." Who was Jane? There was also an unknown married woman who initiated Lawrence into sex.

Moore, *The Intelligent Heart*, p. 93. Another married woman who told Mrs. Hopkin over the phone, "Sally, I gave Bert sex. I had to. He was over at our house, struggling with a poem he couldn't finish, so I took him upstairs and gave him sex. He came downstairs and finished the poem." Later in his mature years there was Ottoline Morrell, Mabel Luhan, and Dorothy Brett.

Aldington, Richard (1892–1962). English poet, novelist. A leading Imagist poet. Husband of "H. D.," Hilda Doolittle, (1886–1961). Hilda Doolittle gave Lawrence a room in her flat in London after he and Frieda had been put out of Cornwall. Aldington wrote many books including a biography of Lawrence, *D.H.L. Portrait*.

page 6

l. 4 D.H.L. to Austin Harrison from Kandy, Ceylon, 11 April 1922. *Letters*, p. 549.

l. 8 D.H.L. to Mrs. A. L. Jenkins from Kandy, Ceylon, 28 March 1922. *Letters*, p. 547.

l. 10 D.H.L. to Robert Pratt Barlow from Kandy, Ceylon, 30 March 1922. *Letters*, pp. 548–49.

l. 14 D.H.L. to J. M. Murry from Los Angeles, 24 September 1923. *Letters*, p. 585.

ll. 17–20 D.H.L. to Martin Secker from Taos, N.M., 19 September 1922. *Letters*, pp. 556–57.

l. 23 D.H.L. to Mabel from Sydney, N.S.W., 3 June 1922. Luhan, *Lorenzo in Taos*, p. 23

l. 30 D.H.L. to Mabel from Thirroul, N.S.W., 20 June 1922. Luhan, *Lorenzo in Taos*, p. 25.

l. 32 Frieda Lawrence to Mabel from Thirroul, N.S.W. Luhan, *Lorenzo in Taos*, p. 25. "We don't know a soul here, rather fun. Nobody has 'discovered' Lawrence."

page 7

l. 6 Hapgood, Hutchins. Author, journalist. A radical-conservative devoted to Mabel Luhan. "I believe," he said *in 1912*, "that the prevailing standards in art, politics, industry, literature and morality are uninteresting and unvital and they stand in the way of true progress and of intenser and fuller life for all of us."

l. 9 Luhan, *Lorenzo in Taos*, p. 297.

l. 15 Luhan, *Movers and Shakers*, pp. 80–81. "If you had lived in Greece long ago, you would have been called a hetaira. Now why don't you see what you can do with this gift of yours?"

page 8

l. 3 D.H.L. to Mabel from London, 22 January 1924. Luhan, *Lorenzo in Taos*, p. 136. "I'm not going to think of you as a writer. I'm not going to think of you even as a knower . . . the essential you, for me, doesn't know and could never write."

l. 9 O'Neill, Eugene (1888–1953). American playwright. Wrote *Anna Christie, Desire Under the Elms, Mourning*

Becomes Electra, and other plays. Awarded 1936 Nobel Prize in literature. Mabel Luhan wrote of O'Neill: "[he] loved the sea, and for whom it seemed, really, to have been designed. . . . Gene was often drunk. . . . Gene's unhappy young face had desperate dark eyes staring out of it and drink must have eased him." *Movers and Shakers*, p. 484.

l. 10 Hartley, Marsden (1877–1943). American landscape painter. One of the first Americans to practice expressionism. Mabel Luhan said of Hartley: "—that gnarled New England spinster-man who came to New York with his tragic paintings of New Hampshire and Maine landscape where the trees were fateful, and Hartley told me how Stieglitz kept him from starving." *Movers and Shakers*, p. 72.

Duncan, Isadora (1878–1927). American dancer. A daring, dynamic innovator who danced almost naked before huge audiences all over the world. She greatly influenced the modern dance. Isadora and Elizabeth Duncan were friends of Mabel Luhan. She said of Isadora Duncan: "Isadora always dressed like an antique statue.

"I went to see her dance with her young girls from Russia. It seemed to me I recognized what she did in the dance. Power rose in her from her Center and flowed vividly along her limbs before our eyes in living beauty and delight. . . .

"She seemed to be hungry for children—many children—since her own two had drowned in the Seine. . . . The glamorous way Isadora herself saw life was immediately apparent all about her." *Movers and Shakers*, pp. 319–20.

l. 12 Brisbane, Arthur (1864–1936). American journalist, editorialist. Friend of Mabel Luhan. Encouraged her to write articles for Hearst papers.

l. 14 Reed, John (1887–1920). American journalist adventurer. In love with Mabel Luhan. Sympathizer with Russian Revolution. Buried within wall of Kremlin. Wrote *Ten*

Days that Shook the World, an eyewitness account of the Russian Revolution.

l. 18 Eastman, Max (1883–1969). American author. Edited the magazine the *Masses* until it was suppressed during World War I. Husband of Ida Rauh.

l. 19 Robinson, Edward Arlington, "E. A." (1869–1935). American poet. Mabel Luhan said of Robinson: "I have never seen anyone else, except Duse, with quite the depth of imprisoned heat in the eyes that this man had. He turned these infinitely dark eyes upon me, black burning deeps. No ocean has ever seemed so deep, no night so unendingly deep as those eyes. Was he conscious of the fire within? Did he know the singular discomfort he caused by the black flare of his glance?" *Movers and Shakers*, p. 126.

l. 22 Stokowski, Leopold (1882–   ). U.S. orchestra leader. Friend of Mabel Luhan and Dorothy Brett.

Duse, Eleonora (1859–1924). Italian actress. Her acting combined simplicity with emotional power. Romantic attachment with Italian poet D'Annunzio. Mabel Luhan knew her in Italy.

l. 23 Lewis, Sinclair (1885–1951). American novelist. Wrote *Main Street* and other books. Awarded 1930 Nobel Prize for literature. Friend of Mabel Luhan.

Galsworthy, John (1867–1933). English novelist and dramatist. Wrote the Forsyte novels. Awarded 1932 Nobel Prize for literature.

Gish, Lillian (1896–   ). Renowned film actress. *The Birth of a Nation*. Friend of Mabel Luhan.

l. 24 Wilder, Thornton (1897–   ). American novelist. Wrote *The Bridge of San Luis Rey, Our Town*, and other works. Friend of Mabel Luhan.

l. 26 Craig, Gordon (1872–1966). English scene designer and play producer. Son of Ellen Terry. His poetic abstract scene designs and productions of Ibsen's plays and Shakespeare's *Hamlet* (Moscow Art Theatre, 1912) greatly contributed to modern selective realism in scene design. Friend of Mabel Luhan in Florence, Italy.

l. 27 Bergson, Henri (1859–1941). French philosopher. Man knows matter through intellect, but more important through the *élan vital*. Time is duration in terms of life experience. Bergson came to Mabel Luhan's salon on Fifth Avenue. But "—he never came back."

Davidson, Jo (1883–1952). American sculptor, best known for busts of famous contemporaries. Frieda wrote that just before Lawrence died "Wells [H.G.] came to see him and the Aga Khan with his charming wife. Jo Davidson did a bust of him [Lawrence]." Frieda Lawrence, p. 295.

l. 28 Goldman, Emma (1869–1940). American anarchist, deported to Russia in 1917. Mabel Luhan says of her: "I knew she stood for killing people if necessary . . . but Emma herself . . . a homely motherly sort of person. She didn't look frightening . . . rather like a severe warm-hearted school teacher. . . . What will power! Sheer strength in that jaw and no sensitiveness. . . . Berkman (Emma Goldman's lover) tried to kiss me in a taxi once and this scared me more than murder would have done." *Movers and Shakers*, pp. 57–58.

Lippmann, Walter (1889–   ). American writer, syndicated columnist. Confidant of Mabel Luhan. She said of Walter Lippmann: "He was so strong and young and opinionated and rational. . . . He might lose his glow, but he will never lose an eye," as her friend Big Bill Haywood had lost an eye in a fight. *Movers and Shakers*, p. 119.

l. 29 Sanger, Margaret (1883–1966). American leader in Birth Control Movement. Organized first International Birth Control Conference, 1925. Friend of Mabel Luhan. Mabel says of her, "Margaret Sanger was an advocate of the flesh. It was her belief that the attitude toward sex in the past of the race was infantile, archaic and ignorant." *Movers and Shakers*, p. 70.

298

l. 30 Robinson, Boardman (1876–1952). American painter, cartoonist. Murals in Rockefeller Center, New York. Made prisoner with Jack Reed by the Russians in Kholm, Galicia. Later Robinson became an enemy of Mabel Luhan because her affection for Jack Reed had lapsed while Reed was in prison.

page 9

l. 5 Wolfe, Thomas (1900–1938). American novelist. Wrote *Of Time and the River* and other books. Visited Mabel Luhan in Taos.

page 10

l. 21 Hearst, William Randolph (1863–1951). Journalist. Founded a news empire which numbered eighteen newspapers at his death. Opposed internationalism.

page 17

l. 21 Brett, p. 53, writing of Tony: "A strange magnificence clothes him."

page 18

l. 5 *Naestsan Biyin* (Happiness of All Things), Curtis, p. 417. This may not have been the song Tony sang that day. But Tony was always singing Indian songs to Mabel wherever they were.

l. 24 A Washoe-Paiute song in Austin, p. 107.
Now I know why when we met
It slipped
So easily into loving.

page 20

l. 15 Luhan, *Lorenzo in Taos*, p. 4.
l. 22 Ibid., p. 3.

page 25

Beach, Sylvia. An American living in Paris made literary history when in 1922 she published James Joyce's *Ulysses* then banned in every English-speaking country in the world. Her bookshop Shakespeare and Company on the Left Bank was the literary center for such writers as Ernest Hemingway, Ezra Pound, George Antheil, Gertrude Stein, Sherwood Anderson, Scott Fitzgerald, Paul Valéry, André Gide, Jules Romains. The author knew Miss Beach very well and used her remarkable library while he lived in Paris in the early '30s. Miss Beach was decorated with the Legion of Honor in 1936 for her services to literature. Beach, pp. 92–93. "The next book I was obliged to turn down was *Lady Chatterly's Lover*. I didn't admire this book . . . D. H. Lawrence was a man of great personal charm. It was always a matter of wonder to me why a writer so greatly gifted never seemed to have the power to produce what his readers were expecting of him. As a man he was very interesting—fascinating. I could understand the devotion of Lawrence's friends and why women pursued him across countries and over seas.

"It was sad refusing Lawrence's *Lady*, particularly because he was so ill the last time I saw him that he got out of bed to come to the book shop and had a flushed, feverish look. It was distressing trying to explain my reasons for not undertaking other publications than *Ulysses*. . . . It was difficult to tell him I didn't want to get a name as a publisher of erotica, and impossible to say that I wanted to be a one-book publisher—what could anybody offer after *Ulysses?*"

l. 26 Lawrence's friends had included some of the most brilliant men of his time:

Moore, *The Intelligent Heart*, p. 94. Enid Hilton writes: "Every Sunday evening was open house [at the Hopkin's home in Eastwood] when my mother served wonderful 'snacks' and we made music, talk, readings, or just plain fun. Philip Snowden, Ramsay MacDonald [eventually to become Prime Minister of England], Beatrice and Sydney Webb and others of the then 'forward' group visited us frequently, and these Lawrence met. He was a silent or an almost violent leader of the conversation. . . ."

Hilton, Mrs. Enid, née Hopkin. Childhood friend of Lawrence. Helped distribute *Lady Chatterly's Lover* in England. Mrs. Hilton has perhaps the most realistic feeling for Lawrence of any of us who knew him.

Lawrence also met Lord and Lady Asquith (son of the Prime Minister) at Lady Ottoline Morrell's estate at Garsington Manor.

Asquith, Lady Cynthia (1887–1959). The daughter of Lord and Lady Elcho. Married to the Hon. Herbert Asquith, son of the Prime Minister. The Asquiths met Lawrence in 1913 and remained his friends throughout life. Lady Asquith has said of Lawrence in *Remember and be Glad*, p. 133: "Some electric elemental quality gave him a flickering radiance . . . one could see at once he was preternaturally alive."

Asquith, The Hon. Herbert (1881–1947). Son of Herbert Henry Asquith, Prime Minister of England (1908–16). Met Lawrence in 1913. Asquith wrote of Lawrence, ". . . it is impossible to be with him five minutes without being struck by the passionate vividness of his perceptions and by the power of expression which seemed to well out of him as though it were coming fresh from a spring." Asquith, p. 182.

Morrell, Lady Ottoline (1873–1938). Patroness of intellectual circle, at Garsington Manor, which included Lawrence, Bertrand Russell, J. Ramsay MacDonald. Lawrence did a cruel picture of Lady Ottoline as Hermione in *Women in Love*. For a time the friendship was broken off. She writes of him, "He was so natural . . . his mind so vivid and flame-like, his whole being so active and alive." *The Nation and Athenaeum*, XLVI (No. 25, March 22, 1930), 859.

Lady Ottoline also introduced Lawrence to Bertrand Russell who took him to Cambridge where he met the giants of the English intellectual world. Lawrence reacted with rage.

They were "dead, dead, dead." He quarreled bitterly with all of them, notably with Russell.

At first Russell and Lawrence were friends. "I felt him to be a man of certain imaginative genius," said Russell. "I thought that perhaps his insight into human nature was deeper than mine. He says 'facts' are quite unimportant, only 'truths' matter. I do not think that in retrospect [his ideas] had any merit whatever." Russell, pp. 14–15.

Russell described Lawrence's "blood-consciousness" as "rubbish." Lawrence, in turn characterized Russell in *Women in Love:* "His mental fiber was so tough as to be insentient." Although these seemed to be bitter personal quarrels with "superior people," Lawrence was really taking the measure of England itself, its society, its politics, its academic world, in fact the achievement of civilization itself. He turned away to a more profound concept of mankind. *The Rainbow* was suppressed not because it was obscene but because Lawrence was against the war.

page 26

l. 1 D.H.L. to Mabel from Palace Hotel, San Francisco, Monday. No date. Luhan, *Lorenzo in Taos*, p. 28.

l. 8 Luhan, *Lorenzo in Taos*, p. 36. "The Lawrences seemed to be intensely conscious of Tony, and somehow embarrassed by him. I made out, in the twinkling of an eye, that Frieda immediately saw Tony and me sexually, visualizing our relationship."

l. 25 Ibid., p. 37. "The meal was an agony—a halt—an unresolved chord, for me at least, and for Lawrence. Frieda continued her noisy running ejaculations and breathless bursts of emotional laughter. Lawrence hid behind her big body. I scarcely saw him, but we all knew he was there, all right."

page 27

l. 5 Ibid., p. 38.

l. 19 Frieda to Mabel Luhan from Vence, France. No date.

Tedlock, p. 234. "But he is very thin, only weighs 44½ kilo."

l. 23 D.H.L. to Catherine Carswell from Taos, N.M., 29 September 1922. *Letters*, p. 560.

page 28

l. 18 This description of Mabel is taken from the original manuscript of the novel Lawrence and Mabel commenced and never finished. See note on p. 40, l. 24 regarding Dr. Keith Sagar. See also Frieda Lawrence, p. 158, for Lawrence's description of Mabel to his mother-in-law. ". . . American, rich, only child, from Buffalo on Lake Erie, bankers, forty-two years old, has had three husbands. . . . Now has an Indian, Tony, stout chap. She has lived much in Europe—Paris, Nice, Florence—is a little famous in New York and little loved, very intelligent as a woman, another 'culture-carrier,' likes to play the patroness, hates the white world and loves the Indian out of hate, is very 'generous,' wants to be 'good' and is very wicked. . . . Terrible will to power."

page 29

l. 9 Frieda Lawrence, p. 136.

l. 10 The manuscript deposited was another book on Lawrence written by Mabel Luhan.

l. 15 Luhan, *Lorenzo in Taos*, p. 58.

l. 17 Ibid., p. 59.

l. 27 Ibid.

page 30

l. 3 Ibid., p. 61.

l. 13 Frieda Lawrence, p. 136.

l. 19 Luhan, *Lorenzo in Taos*, p. 62.

l. 21 Ibid., p. 64.

page 31

l. 1 Ibid., p. 64.

l. 4 Ibid. Frieda Lawrence, p. 136.

l. 24 D.H.L. to Mabel from Kandy, Ceylon, 10 April 1922. Luhan, *Lorenzo in Taos*, p. 19. "I still of course mistrust Taos very much, chiefly on account of the artists. I feel I never want to see an artist again while I live."
Frieda to Mabel from Thirroul, N.S.W. No date. Luhan, *Lorenzo in Taos*, p. 25.

page 33

l. 4 Lawrence, "New Mexico," *Phoenix*, p. 146. "Never shall I forget the Indian races, when the young men, even the boys run naked, smeared with white earth and stuck with bits of eagle fluff for the swiftness of the heavens, and the old men brush them with eagle feathers, to give them power. . . . It is a vast old religion, greater than anything we know: more starkly and nakedly religious. There is no god. No conceptions of a god. All is god."

page 34

l. 25 Nin, p. 71. "I proceed by intuition." See also Brett, p. 247. "I never know when I sit down what I am going to write. I make no plan; it just comes, and I don't know where it comes from."

page 36

l. 1 Frieda Lawrence, p. 137. "It's your business to see that other women don't come too close to me."

l. 3 Luhan, *Lorenzo in Taos*, p. 61.

l. 14 Ibid., p. 66.

l. 16 Ibid. "I remember trying to write things out for him in my bedroom at Santa Fe, but it was an agony for me. I was not a *writer*."

l. 28 D.H.L. to Mabel from Villa Mirenda, Florence, Italy, 21 May 1926. Luhan, *Lorenzo in Taos*, p. 303.

page 37

l. 1 Luhan, *Lorenzo in Taos*, p. 65. "You've got to remember also things you don't want to remember."

l. 7 Ibid., pp. 69–70.

l. 22 D.H.L. to J. M. Murry from Del Monte Ranch, 2 February 1923. *Letters*, p. 568. "I got your note just now, via Kot, about Katherine. Yes, it is something gone out of our lives. . . . What is going to happen to us all? Perhaps it is good for Katherine not to have to see the next phase. We will unite up again when I come to England. It has been a savage enough pilgrimage these last four years."

l. 24 D.H.L. to Catherine Carswell from Del Monte Ranch, 17 December 1922. *Letters*, p. 566. "Why do they read me? But anyhow, they *do* read me—which is more than England does."

page 38

l. 11 Luhan, *Lorenzo in Taos*, p. 72.

l. 18 Ibid.

page 39

l. 15 Ibid., p. 73. "You don't *know* your floor until you have scrubbed it on your hands and knees!" he announced.

l. 18 Ibid. "Frieda appeared to enjoy the row. She had on a full, striped, cotton skirt, with a peasant bodice lacing up her plentiful bosom."

l. 27 Ibid., p. 75. "He was generally kind when he had one at a disadvantage."

page 40

l. 5 Ibid. p. 76. " 'I'm not laughing,' replied Tony, his shoulders still shaking. 'It's very nice.' He meant he was not being mean—he was just feeling happy."

l. 17 Ibid., p. 79.

l. 20 Dr. Keith Sagar of the University of Manchester has since discovered this manuscript in the University of California at Berkeley and has given the author a copy. The "novel" Lawrence wrote in collaboration with Mabel Luhan is only six pages long.

l. 24 Luhan, *Lorenzo in Taos,* p. 87.

page 41

l. 5 Ibid., p. 89.

l. 10 Ibid., p. 90.

l. 23 Ibid.

l. 26 Ibid.

page 42

l. 3 Mabel Luhan's ranch originally belonged to William L. McClure in the '80s. It was an old sheep ranch.

l. 16 Merrild, p. 51.

l. 18 Merrild, p. 51.

l. 22 Luhan, *Lorenzo in Taos,* pp. 91, 101. "I went away, down to Santa Fe, the day before they were to leave, to show them I didn't care—but in reality because I couldn't bear to see them go."

page 43

l. 8 Merrild, p. 54. "Lawrence, like a good sport, wanted to do his turn, but we never let him. It was too dangerous, the crank would kick back."

page 44

l. 3 Merrild, p. 56.

l. 7 Merrild, p. 58. " 'Are you afraid?' Lawrence asked. 'No,' I answered, 'not for myself, but there are four of us, and we are all human, and I have seen how you get irritated and annoyed with people and how rapidly you grew tired of the art colony. Even Mabel hardly lasted a month. . . .' "

l. 16 Merrild, p. 59. " 'I know we will get along,' said Lawrence.

" 'Win him over, Götzsche,' shouted Mrs. Lawrence as we started off."

Merrild, pp. 60–61. Merrild ended up by saying, "But Lawrence is so vastly complex that one never knows what will happen next."

l. 23 Merrild, p. 62.

l. 25 Merrild, p. 57.

l. 27 Merrild, p. 57.

l. 30 Merrild, pp. 62–63. " 'Just call us Lorenzo and Frieda,' said Frieda."

page 45

l. 6 D.H.L. to Catherine Carswell from Del Monte Ranch, Questa, N.M., 17 December 1922. *Letters*, p. 566. Catherine seems to have been his most trusted friend at this time.

l. 18 D.H.L. to Mabel from Del Monte Ranch, Sunday. No date. Luhan, *Lorenzo in Taos*, p. 108.

page 46

l. 2 Luhan, *Lorenzo in Taos*, p. 109.

l. 5 Ibid., p. 112.

l. 7 Ibid.

l. 12 Ibid., pp. 112, 113. "Walter Lippmann replied, 'It's your own fault. Don't you know that you can't make a pet out of a snake.' "

l. 15 Frieda Lawrence, p. 136. Luhan, *Lorenzo in Taos*, p. 113. "He [John] had felt Lawrence's antagonism to him —and he had hated my concentration on him."

page 47

l. 5 Luhan, *Lorenzo in Taos*, p. 113.

l. 9 Ibid.

page 48

l. 11 Walter Ufer to the Danes from Chicago, February 16, 1923. Merrild, p. 160. "Tell Lawrence I understand him better and better each day."

l. 14 Luhan, *Lorenzo in Taos*, p. 85. "Lawrence said of Walter Ufer to Mabel Luhan, 'That canaille—that *canaille!*' "

l. 1 Frieda Lawrence, p. 137. Taos Valley becomes extremely cold in winter. On January 5, 1971 the temperature stood at —40° F. in Questa, N.M. where fifty years earlier Lawrence got his mail.

l. 6 Lawrence, "Compari," *The Complete Poems*, p. 499.

l. 18 Merrild, p. 99. "We reminded him that we were not just out for a walk but were trying to reach Lobo peak [alt. 12,106 ft.], and had to keep going in order to get there and back before sundown. . . . I remember we thought it was fine for him to get some real exercise. 'That will build him up, it will only do him good.' "

l. 22 Lawrence, "Mountain Lion," *The Complete Poems*, p. 402.

l. 30 Merrild, p. 111. "I feel I should die if I had to live here. . . . The whole country, the mountains, the air, it is so hopelessly empty. Even the birds don't sing, it is all dead! It needs to be lived in. . . . There is too much menace in the landscape."

page 50

l. 11 Merrild, p. 100. "He had done his best to follow us, even to the point of exhaustion. He was very brave."

l. 13 Merrild, p. 101. "Frieda was angry at this incident in the snow. 'You two should see to it that he doesn't get so tired when you are out together. He can't stand it, I tell you. I know best.' "

l. 31 Merrild, p. 132.

page 51

l. 23 D.H.L. to Catherine Carswell from Del Monte Ranch, Questa, N.M., 17 December 1922. *Letters*, p. 566.

l. 26 D.H.L. to J. M. Murry from Del Monte Ranch, Questa, N.M., 30 December 1922. *Letters*, p. 567.

page 52

l. 24 Merrild, p. 152. "The deep psychic disease of modern

man and woman is the diseased, atrophied condition of the intuitive faculties. . . . Sex is the road of which intuition is the foliage and beauty the flower." This is the gist of Lawrence's entire philosophy.

l. 26 Merrild, p. 153.

l. 31 Merrild, p. 86.

page 53

l. 31 Merrild, p. 232.

page 54

l. 4 Merrild, p. 232.

l. 6 Merrild, pp. 224–25.

l. 23 Merrild, p. 235.

page 55

l. 5 Merrild, p. 235.

l. 18 Merrild, p. 236.

l. 24 D.H.L. to J. M. Murry from Del Monte Ranch, Questa, N.M., 25 February 1923. *Letters*, p. 570.

l. 28 Merrild, p. 252. "Among them was a large 8x10 of Mabel, the one she had sent overseas to Lawrence. On the back it says: 'Mabel Dodge 5 years ago just come to Taos.' "

page 56

l. 10 Lawrence, "New Mexico," *Phoenix*, p. 142.

l. 16 During this winter of 1922–23 at the ranch the Meta Lehmann incident occurred. Miss Lehmann was a little "gone" on the Indians, in fact had an Indian lover. She also studied the occult and Eastern religions. She spoke Indian and the Indians liked her. She was a lost soul, but attractive to men. The Danes were her protégés. When she turned up at the Del Monte Ranch to see the Danes, Lawrence became violently puritanical. See Merrild, pp. 148–50. " 'This Lehmann woman,' he said. 'She can't stay with you. Why, it's absurd. I won't have her. You must get your Lizzie right away and take her down to Taos.' However, the Ford would not work and Miss Lehmann had to walk the entire eighteen miles back to Taos in the snow." The author and his wife knew Meta Lehmann very well.

page 61
l. 11 Hale, p. 12.

page 63
l. 16 D.H.L. to J. M. Murry from Hotel Monte Carlo, Mexico City, 27 April (1923). *Letters*, p. 572.

l. 17 D.H.L. to Catherine Carswell from Hotel Monte Carlo, Mexico City, 11 April 1923. *Letters*, p. 571.

page 66
l. 22 Lawrence, *The Plumed Serpent*, p. 93.

l. 28 This was the real reason Lawrence did not write about the United States. It lacked the elemental reality so necessary to inspire his genius. "Life in America is empty and stupid." D.H.L. to Frieda's mother from Del Monte Ranch, Questa, N.M., 28 June 1924. Frieda Lawrence, p. 168.

page 67
l. 9 The Zocalo is the large central plaza of present-day Mexico City. The Cathedral of Mexico City stands near the ruins of the great Aztec temple of Huitzilopochtli.

See Bynner, p. 20. "He liked to lean against a low railing over a street corner deeply excavated and see ancient shadows below him on Aztec pavements and stairways which the digging had exposed."

page 69
l. 24 D.H.L. to J. M. Murry from Oaxaca (Mexico), 15 November 1924. *Letters*, p. 631.

l. 29 Lawrence, *The Plumed Serpent*, p. 71.

page 70
l. 11 Ibid., p. 61. "Only they get an excitement out of wom-

en, as they do out of chili. . . . But after the moment they don't care. They don't care a bit."

page 71
l. 10 Ibid., p. 72.

page 72
l. 7 Bynner, p. 235.
l. 10 Bynner letter to Eunice Tietjens. Bynner, p. 165. "I usually care very little for his writings; but when he begins on any animal or bird, I am spellbound."

page 73
l. 5 Bynner, pp. 51, 54. "His [Lawrence's] nerves exploded. Fortunately people were too intent on the ring to notice him, and only a few of them heard a red-bearded Englishman, risen from his seat, excoriating cowards and madmen . . . he sickened suddenly, plunged away from us, treading toes, and lurched down the row toward the exit."
l. 21 Bynner, p. 72.

page 74
l. 28 Bynner, p. 77. " 'And can you tell me what happened?' asked Frieda. 'Did you ring a bell?'
" 'All of them,' said Bynner."

page 75
l. 10 Bynner, pp. 37–38. " 'Lorenzo, I am going to see the town,' said Bynner. 'There is no reason why I should give in to your whims. You're not going to boss me.' "

page 76
l. 19 Frieda to Edward Gilbert. No date. Tedlock, p. 344. "You are wrong saying L. is disregarded. He is there in the human consciousness all right. . . . He was great enough to know life goes on and there is no ultimate word."

page 78
l. 19 Bynner, p. 219. "From the begining Lawrence thought

of himself as Jesus; and at the begining his thought was
humble. . . . When, as a dying man in France, he was
reviewing his life and wondering what he had made of it
and writing *The Man Who Died*, his story of Christ, he
found himself a ghost not of himself but of Jesus.

"There was in Lawrence [said Norman Douglas] . . . a
strain of Christ, prophet and sufferer . . . although in Jesus
we find less hysteria than in Lawrence, whose Messianic
utterances are delivered in shrill tones."

page 79

l. 5 Bynner, pp. 160–62 passim. "When Isabel brought the
eggs, Lawrence asked her if there was not danger when
men scaled walls and broke panes in doors. '*Mucho*,' said
Isabel."

Bynner asked Frieda later, "But didn't he see there was no
broken glass on the floor?"

"*Ach!*" replied Frieda indulgently, "It was more exciting to
see a knife in the moonlight."

l. 25 Kate in *The Plumed Serpent*, p. 103. "In this country
she was afraid. But it was her soul more than her body that
knew fear."

Skrebensky in *The Rainbow*, "I am not afraid of the darkness in England. . . . But in Africa it seems massive and
fluid with terror . . . the blacks know it. They really worship, really the darkness. . . . "

l. 27 Bynner, p. 151.

page 80

l. 17 Aldington, p. 128. "But anyone who thinks those two
weren't in love with each other is crazy. How else could
they have endured one another? Frieda the survivor, writes
in her large generosity that Lawrence gave her 'a new
world.' Of course he did, but it was through her that he
had a world to give. . . . He could only live and work
with a woman to back him. After he met Frieda no other

312

woman was possible. Indeed he came to depend upon her far more than she upon him; and her influence may be seen in almost all his writing after 1912."
Bynner, p. 142.

l. 25 D.H.L. to Bynner from Chapala, Mexico, 2 May 1923 (afternoon). *Letters*, p. 572.

l. 28 D.H.L. to J. Middleton Murry from Chapala, Mexico, 26 May 1923. *Letters*, p. 574.

page 81

l. 3 Bynner to Edward Nehls (25 May 1956) thirty-three years later. "The 'beach where [Lawrence] used to sit' is now a severe boulevard which gives me a pang while I remember the simple village we lived in. The tree under which he sat and wrote is gone long since and the beach close to it where fishermen cast nets and women washed clothes has receded a quarter of a mile. But the mountains still surround what is left of the lake and, as a village somewhat inland, Chapala would still have charmed us had we come upon it in its present state." Nehls, vol. II, p. 499 (note 118).

l. 8 Lawrence, *The Plumed Serpent*, p. 69.

l. 26 Ibid., p. 93.

page 82

l. 9 Ibid., pp. 229–30.

page 84

l. 5 Idella Purnell Stone to Bynner. Bynner, p. 84.

l. 7 Bynner, p. 62.

l. 11 Bynner, p. 165.

ll. 16–17 Bynner, p. 145.

l. 18 D.H.L. to Bynner from Monte Carlo Hotel, Mexico City, 29 October 1924. Bynner, p. 252. "Disagreeable, with no fun left in him [W. Somerset Maugham]."

Maugham, Somerset (1874–1965). English novelist, play-wright. His most famous novel is *Of Human Bondage*. Met, quarreled with the Lawrences in Mexico City.

page 85

l. 10 Bynner, pp. 31, 61.

l. 14 Bynner, p. 62.

l. 16 Bynner, p. 62.

l. 24 D.H.L. to Knud Merrild from Chapala, Mexico, 27 June 1923. *Letters*, p. 576.

l. 29 Idella Purnell's words, quoted in Bynner, p. 179.

page 86

l. 9 D.H.L. to Bynner, care Seltzer, 5 West 50th St., New York, 14 August 1923. *Letters*, p. 581.

l. 14 D.H.L. to Merrild, care Seltzer, 5 West 50th St., New York, 7 August 1923. *Letters*, p. 579.

l. 19 Merrild, pp. 312, 313. "Lawrence was not the same as he had been at Del Monte. Obviously he was not in his right environment. Who is, living in a hotel room?"

page 87

l. 5 Merrild, p. 314.

l. 17 Merrild, p. 319.

l. 20 Merrild, p. 319. "It might have been possible for us, indi-vidually, to get on ships, but three dilettantes on one ship was too much to expect."

l. 27 Merrild, pp. 323–27 passim. "There is no paradise. Fight, fight. That is life."

page 89

l. 5 Merrild, p. 314.

l. 18 Merrild, p. 320. " 'You see,' we said, 'the girls are pining to dance with the mysterious man in the red beard.' "

page 90

l. 3 Merrild, pp. 327–29.

l. 10 Merrild, p. 327.

l. 14 D.H.L. to J. M. Murry from Los Angeles, 24 September 1923. *Letters*, p. 585. "California is a queer place—in a way it has turned its back on the world and looks into the void of the Pacific. It is absolutely selfish, very empty, but not false."

l. 20 D.H.L. to Bynner from Navajoa, Mexico, 5 October 1923. *Letters*, p. 587.

page 91

l. 7 Kai Götzsche to Knud Merrild from Guadalajara, Mexico, 22 October 1923. Merrild, p. 341.

l. 11 D.H.L. to Knud Merrild from Navajoa, Mexico, 5 October 1923. Merrild, pp. 333–34. "In Minas Neuvas we did nothing but drink beer and whisky cocktails."

l. 17 Kai Götzsche to Knud Merrild from Guadalajara, Mexico, 10 November 1923. Merrild, p. 348.

l. 20 Kai Götzsche to Knud Merrild from Guadalajara, Mexico, 10 November 1923. Merrild, p. 348.

l. 25 Kai Götzsche to Knud Merrild from Guadalajara, Mexico, 15 October 1923. Merrild, p. 338.

page 92

l. 7 Merrild, p. 343.

l. 12 Merrild, p. 314.

l. 20 Merrild, p. 315.

l. 26 Kai Götzsche to Knud Merrild from Guadalajara, Mexico, 22 October 1923. Merrild, p. 340. "Somehow it becomes unreal to me now. I don't know why. The life has changed somehow, has gone dead, you know I shan't live my life here."

page 93

l. 3 Kai Götzsche to Knud Merrild from Guadalajara, Mexico, 25 October 1923. Merrild, p. 343.

l. 12 Merrild, p. 350.

l. 19 Kai Götzsche to Knud Merrild from Mexico City, 18 November 1923. Merrild, p. 350. "It is biting cold here in Mexico City; we are using our overcoats."

page 94

l. 3 Koteliansky, Samuel Solomnovich ("Kot") (1882–1955). Student radical in Russia under the Czar. Came to England on scholarship from University of Kiev to do research in economics. Lawrence helped Koteliansky translate Ivan Bunin's *The Gentleman from San Francisco* from the Russian. Later Koteliansky was afraid of being implicated in the publicity surrounding the Lawrence paintings. (D.H. L. to G. Orioli, his Italian publisher from Kesselmatte, Gsteig b. Gstaad [?13 September 1928] *Collected Letters,* Moore, p. 1090.) Frieda said of Koteliansky: "He did not like me but he loved Lawrence and he used to cheer Lawrence by roaring Russian songs at him." Bynner, p. 201.

l. 6 Gertler, Mark (1892–1939). English painter, educated at Slade. Friend of Lawrence, Dorothy Brett, the Gilbert Cannans. It is thought he was the sculptor Loerke in *Women in Love.* Gertler committed suicide in 1939.

l. 9 Carswell, Catherine (1879–1946). Scottish writer. Devoted friend and biographer of Lawrence. Wrote *The Savage Pilgrimage: A Narrative of D. H. Lawrence.*

l. 11 Cannan, Gilbert (1884–1955). English novelist and playwright. Friend of Lawrence. With John Drinkwater founded the Manchester Repertory Theatre.

page 95

ll. 6–13 Brett, p. 21.

l. 27 Moore, *The Intelligent Heart,* p. 323.

l. 30 Ibid., p. 323.

l. 32 Ibid., p. 324. There are three firsthand accounts of this famous supper in the Cafe Royal: Brett, p. 21; Catherine Carswell, p. 205; and Murry in Nehls, p. 302. Mabel Luhan's account is secondhand.

l. 7 Moore, *The Intelligent Heart*, p. 323.

l. 14 Brett, p. 22. "For several days you are sick in bed. I [Brett] come to see you. You are sitting up in bed in a red knitted shawl, looking very pale and ill and hurt. . . ."

l. 3 Brett, p. 23. "Later . . . your anger that the painters of today never faced life itself."

l. 14 D.H.L. to Bynner from 110 Heath St., Hampstead (England), 7 December 1923. *Letters*, p. 597.

l. 26 Brett, p. 27.

l. 14 Brett, pp. 31–32. "Later, Frieda, on her hands and knees sweeps up the broken china with a dustpan and a brush.

" 'Strange, isn't it,' I [Brett] say to Murry, 'to hear Lawrence use the 'thee' and 'tha' of the Yorkshire dialect?' "

l. 21 Brett, p. 33.

l. 22 D.H.L. to J.M. Murry from Baden Baden, Germany, 7 February 1924. *Letters*, p. 602.

l. 8 D.H.L. to J. M. Murry from the *Cunard, R.M.S. Aquitania*, Monday, 10 March. *Letters*, p. 605. "Landed at last. . . . The passport officials looked askance at Brett travelling alone—called her 'this girl.' I got so *mad*."

l. 10 Brett, p. 34.

l. 1 Curtis, p. 63. The Ghost Dance was an anguished spiritual rebellion against the extermination of the Indian. It was a religious movement. The Ghost Dance promised the return of the buffalo and the disappearance of the white man. It was crushed by the U.S. army in 1890 by the murder of Sitting Bull and the massacre of a band of Sioux at Wounded Knee, S.D.

page 108

l. 26 Ufer, however, greatly admired Lawrence. Merrild, p. 160. "Tell dear old Lawrence, really he is a man, that I wish him so much happiness."

Lawrence underestimated Ufer's accomplishments. Merrild, p. 331. "In November I must again go to New York to serve on the National Academy Jury."

That year, 1923, Ufer was also asked to exhibit at the Rome International. Merrild, p. 339.

A friend of the author Ufer was vital, urgent and excitable—an extremely kind man.

page 114

l. 23 Eddington or Whitehead, probably. I had been studying them in philosophy in the University of Wisconsin.

page 121

l. 20 Douglas' estimate of D.H.L. in Nehls, vol. II, p. 11. "Lawrence never learned to be succinct . . . diffuseness is a fault of much of his work . . . pages and pages of drivel. Those endless pointless conversations! That dreary waste of words."

page 128

l. 4 Hale, p. 50.

page 139

l. 30 Brett, p. 243.

page 146

l. 1 The importance of Swinburne Hale to Frieda Lawrence is mentioned in a letter she wrote to Mabel from London, on August 8, 1926, almost two years later. Luhan, *Lorenzo in Taos*, p. 308. "Arabella [Mrs. Richard Aldington] loved my Indian rings . . . the one Swinburne Hale gave me. I feel superstitious about them, thinking they bring me luck and always wear them."

l. 12 After Lawrence's death Frieda received many letters

misinterpreting Lawrence's message. She could be brilliant and cutting in defending him.

Frieda Lawrence to Edward Gilbert from Taos, N.M., 25 November 1951. Tedlock, p. 338. "Lawrence 'was a way of life,' his living and thinking were one and the same activity. There were no 'thought processes.' What he wrote came out of his living and thinking like daisies out of the soil. . . .

"You see Lawrence as a great man and yet in the same breath you affirm he did not find what he wanted, he could not think, he could not formulate his ideas; so what the hell *do* you see in Lawrence?"

Frieda Lawrence to Edward Gilbert from Los Angeles. No date. Tedlock, p. 342. "When I think of him, there was a splendor, a magnificence about him that I cannot possibly connect with failure. It is just absurb to call L. a sexual weakling, anything but: with his intensity . . . you don't know how a man like he was, could give himself, body and soul. I experienced this miracle. . . ."

Frieda Lawrence to Edward Gilbert. No date. Probably Hollywood, January 1952. Tedlock, p. 343. "You haven't understood, being an intellectual, that Lawrence wrote like a tree puts out leaves and grows tall and spreads. It was not a cerebral conscious activity. That was his genius. . . . You are wrong in saying L. was disregarded. He is there in the human consciousness all right. . . ."

page 148
l. 1 Frieda Lawrence to her mother from Del Monte Ranch, 26 October 1923. Frieda Lawrence, p. 171.

l. 11 Frieda Lawrence, pp. 48, 51.

page 149
l. 8 D.H.L. to Willard Johnson from 110 Heath St., Hampstead (England), 9 January 1924. *Letters*, p. 599.

l. 19 Bynner, p. 95.

Brett, pp. 138–39. "How thin he [Spud] is! . . . His face is as thin as his body: the delicate beaked little nose; the sharply cut, full lips. . . . He might be a Chinese ascetic from some old, old Mandarin family: . . . he is Chinese to me: he has also something of their reserve; he keeps his inner life hidden away, carefully guarded."

page 150
l. 24 Ted and Bobby Gillett. Bobby was the sister of Betty and Bill Hawk.

page 151
l. 9 Brett, p. 122; Bynner, p. 150.

page 155
l. 21 D.H.L. to Mabel Luhan from London, 22 January 1924. Moore, *Collected Letters*, p. 773.

page 157
l. 9 Luhan, *Lorenzo in Taos*, p. 189. " 'Something like a Holy Russian idiot?' I asked. 'Perhaps,' he answered."
l. 21 Brett, p. 52.

page 158
l. 8 D.H.L. to Mabel Luhan from Lobo (ranch). No date. Moore, *Collected Letters*, p. 788.

l. 10 Brett, p. 95.

l. 23 Aldington, p. 263. "No doubt he could write as easily in a ship's cabin or a hotel bedroom as in his own cottage, while he gave no time to elaborate 'plotting' and 'construction.' With him a story or a novel blossomed as spontaneously as a poem. In his case inspiration was a fact, and the moment it failed he stopped writing, as we have seen he did at some point with most of his novels. Then he would continue or finish off in a white heat of creative energy. The method obviously had its defects as well as advantages, losing in balance, finish, solidity what it gained in spontaneity, energy, and zest."

l. 25 Brett, p. 137.

page 159
l. 3 Brett, p. 138.
l. 9 Brett, pp. 99–100.
l. 23 Brett, p. 103.
l. 27 Brett, p. 76.

page 160
l. 11 Alice Sprague, a friend of Mabel's from her early days in Buffalo. Luhan, *Lorenzo in Taos*, p. 211. "She [Mrs. Sprague] continued to smile and smile and to consider Lorenzo an avatar, and Clarence [Thompson] a potential genius."
l. 16 Luhan, *Lorenzo in Taos*, p. 200.

page 161
l. 8 Mabel on Jaime. Luhan, *Lorenzo in Taos*, p. 183. "Quite suddenly Jaime arrived in Taos. He strode in one day on his rope-soled sandals, his small Spanish feet, . . . wide Mexican trousers, his blue beret far back on a head of long, crinkly hair. . . . Jaime was prepared to worship Lawrence as a hero, and he was determined to impress him. . . . Lawrence couldn't endure [it]. After a few days Lawrence was scolding and snubbing him."
l. 13 Luhan, *Lorenzo in Taos*, p. 184.
l. 18 Brett, p. 127; Luhan, *Lorenzo in Taos*, p. 172.
l. 26 Brett, p. 127.

page 162
l. 8 Brett, p. 127; Luhan, *Lorenzo in Taos*, pp. 172–73.
l. 23 Brett, p. 116.

page 163
l. 23 Brett, p. 139.

page 167
l. 9 Brett, p. 141.

page 168

l. 14 Brett, p. 143.

page 169

l. 1 One wonders if this observation on Mabel's part is cogent. Luhan, *Lorenzo in Taos*, p. 253.

l. 12 D.H.L. to Mabel, from Ranch. No date. Luhan, *Lorenzo in Taos*, p. 255.

l. 26 Luhan, *Lorenzo in Taos*, p. 257.

page 171

l. 10 D.H.L. to Willard Johnson—*Just back from the Snake Dance*. No date. *Letters*, pp. 615–18. "The pueblos of little grey houses are largely in ruin, dry raggy bits of disheartening ruin. One wonders what dire necessity . . . drove the Hopis to these dismal grey heights and extremities. . . . As for the hopping Indian and his queer muttering gibberish and his dangling snake—why, he sure is cute! He says he is dancing to make his corn grow. What price irrigation, Jimmy?" This cynical attitude of Lawrence toward the Indians is what angered Mabel.

page 172

l. 1 Luhan, *Lorenzo in Taos*, p. 267. "He had written a dreary terre à terre account . . . of the dance, a mere realistic recital that might have been done by a tired, disgruntled businessman. It had no vision, no insight, no appreciation of any kind." Later Lawrence said to Mabel, "I know you didn't like that article of mine. I'll try and do another one."

l. 24 Luhan, *Movers and Shakers*, p. 511. "Anything 'religious' was anathema to him [Brill]. He consistently tried to remove every vestige of my belief in an inner power. "He had not much use for my radical friends and he considered that their beliefs were generally only rationalized prejudices . . . and that when they got together they only bolstered up each other's complexes."

322

l. 25 Luhan, *Lorenzo in Taos,* p. 271.

l. 27 D.H.L. to Mabel from Kiowa, Friday evening. No date. Moore, *Collected Letters,* p. 809.

To which Mabel replied, "Do you mean I should serve the concrete? Such as get up deliberately in the morning and begin deliberately to *make* myself *do* things? Such as housework?" Mabel to D.H.L. from Taos, N.M., September 1924. Luhan, *Lorenzo in Taos,* p. 274.

page 173

l. 7 Luhan, *Lorenzo in Taos,* p. 270.

l. 15 Ibid., p. 279. Lawrence answered on a post card: ". . . If you want to write your apologia pro vita sua, do it as honestly as you can. . . . You haven't enough restraint in you for creative writing, but you can make a document. Only don't go at it too slap-dash—makes it unreal."

l. 19 Ibid., p. 272.

page 175

l. 29 Mabel alternately insulted and appealed to me.

page 180

l. 8 Other Taos and Santa Fe artists often seen at Mabel Luhan's parties were Kenneth M. Adams, Paul Burlin, Natalie Curtis, Burt Harwood, Ralph M. Pearson (etcher), John Young-Hunter, Gustave Baumann, Robert Henri, Sheldon Parsons, Julius Rolshoven, John Sloan, Ward Lockwood, Howard N. Cook, Catherine Critcher—first and only woman member of Taos Society of Artists, Joseph A. Fleck, E. Martin Hennings, Joseph A. Imhoff, Emil Bisttram, Thomas Benrimo, Cady Wells, Louis Ribak, Barbara Latham, Gisella Loeffler, Rebecca Salsbury James, Ila MacAfee, Gene Kloss, and Beatrice Mandelman.

page 181

l. 15 Luhan, *Lorenzo in Taos,* p. 192. "I never cared for that manuscript, once I had it. . . . I cared so little for that great bundle of finely written pages . . . that two years later I gave it to Brill in payment for helping a friend of mine. I suppose he still has it." Brill's son sold it to the library of the University of California at Berkeley. Its value now is in the tens of thousands of dollars.

page 183

l. 8 Brett, p. 155.

l. 14 D.H.L. to J. M. Murry from Del Monte Ranch, Questa, N.M., 3 October 1924. *Letters*, p. 623.

l. 21 Brett, p. 155.

l. 25 D.H.L. to J. M. Murry from Del Monte Ranch, Questa, N.M., 3 October 1924. *Letters*, p. 623.

page 184

l. 7 D.H.L. to Catherine Carswell from Del Monte Ranch, N.M., 8 October 1924. *Letters*, p. 626.

l. 15 A few days after Lawrence left he sent Ted Gillett to our ranch with a book for Swinburne Hale. "If you will just give that book to Mr. Hale. Lawrence said I must see that he got it." The book was *Birds, Beasts and Flowers*. It was inscribed "To Swinburne Hale from D. H. Lawrence / Lobo 12 Sept. 1924."

l. 18 Frieda Lawrence, p. 152.

l. 19 Ibid.

page 185

l. 12 D.H.L. to Aldous Huxley, Villa Mirenda, 27 March 1928. *Letters*, p. 724. "Goethe *began* millions of intimacies and never got beyond the how-do-you-do stage, then fell off into his own boundless ego."

ll. 12–13 D.H.L. to Aldous Huxley from Villa Mirenda 27 March 1928. *Letters*, p. 724. "Your ideas of the grand perverts is [sic] excellent. You might begin with a Roman— and go on to St. Francis—Michael Angelo [sic] and Leonardo—Goethe or Kant, Jean Jacques Rousseau or Louis

324

Quatorze. Byron—Baudelaire—Wilde—Proust: they all did the same thing, or tried to . . . intellectualize and . . . falsify the phallic consciousness, which is the basic consciousness. . . ."

l. 14 D.H.L. to Edward Garnett from Lago di Garda, 1 Febbraio 1913. *Letters*, p. 106.

l. 17 For Lawrence's ideas on Dostoievsky, see letter to Katherine and Jack Murry from Cornwall, 17 February 1916. *Letters*, p. 329. "He [Dostoievsky] has a fixed will, a mania to be infinitive, to be God."

D.H.L. to Catherine Carswell from Zennor, St. Ives, Cornwall, Saturday, 2 December 1916. *Letters*, p. 387. "Oh, don't think I would belittle the Russians. They have meant an enormous amount to me; Turgenev, Tolstoy, Dostoievsky—mattered almost more than anything, and I thought them the greatest writers of all time. And now, with something of a shock, I realize a certain crudity and thick, uncivilized, insensitive stupidity about them, I realize how much finer and purer and more ultimate our own stuff is."

l. 18 D.H.L. to Harry Crosby from Switzerland, 6 September 1928. *Letters*, p. 759.

D.H.L. to Rhys Davies from Bandol, Var, France, Christmas Day, 1928. *Letters*, p. 778. "Tell your man Tchekhov [Chekhov] is a second-rate writer and a willy wet-leg."

page 186

l. 6 D.H.L. to Catherine Carswell from Del Monte Ranch, 8 October 1924. *Letters*, p. 625.

l. 12 D.H.L. to Witter Bynner from Hotel Monte Carlo, Mexico City, Friday. No date. *Letters*, p. 627.

l. 17 D.H.L. to Willard Johnson from Hotel Monte Carlo, Mexico City, Saturday. No date. *Letters*, p. 627.

l. 26 Frieda Lawrence, p. 146; Brett, p. 163.
"How was it?

" 'I don't remember, except that I said that the most important thing to remember, was that we are all, first and foremost men together, before we are artists, that to be a man is more important. But they didn't understand. They one and all protested that it was more important to be an artist.' Then he added: 'There was nothing but beer to drink.' "

page 188

l. 9 Brett, p. 171.

l. 24 Brett, pp. 164–65. "They want to show they have power over strangers, that's all it is."

page 189

l. 4 Lawrence, *The Plumed Serpent*, p. 49; also Bynner, p. 31. "What awed and fascinated and frightened Lawrence most of all was the Indian's deep-rootedness in the reality of death. 'When you got these dark-faced people,' he writes, 'away from wrong contacts like agitators and socialism, they made one feel that life was vast, if fearsome, and death was fathomless.' "

Bynner, p. 29. "Years later he [Covarrubias] regretted not having known what a great man was with us and that he had failed to make sketches of him. Though he had not seen him again . . . he sat down and nimbly drew a caricature from memory. . . . He gave it to me, signed Covarrubias, and it has more Lawrence in it than most of the photographs."

page 191

l. 3 D.H.L. to Mabel from Hotel Monte Carlo, Mexico City, 29 October 1924. Luhan, *Lorenzo in Taos*, p. 280.

l. 20 Nehls, vol. II, p. 371.

page 192

l. 4 Brett, p. 175. "And that was the only fear that haunted

326

you in Oaxaca; that and . . . tales of unspeakable horrors in the mountain villages; of nameless, incurable diseases that are poured into your ears by the Doctors." The Brett and the Lawrences were the first white people to go to Oaxaca after the revolution.

l. 8 Brett, p. 176.

l. 13 Brett, p. 181. "Chapala has not the spirit of Mexico; it is too tamed, too touristy. This place is more untouched."

page 193
l. 11 Frieda Lawrence, p. 149.

l. 15 Brett, p. 189. "Lawrence was always going to the movies and being disappointed."

See also Brett, p. 166. "You sit through it [*The White Sister*] valiantly, more from astonishment that anything can be so bad . . . and your continuous stream of outraged feeling, the strong language of your criticism. . . ."

l. 21 Frieda Lawrence, p. 149.

page 194
l. 5 Brett, p. 192.

page 195
l. 7 Brett, p. 193. Lawrence loved to paint over other people's paintings.

Nehls, vol. II, p. 271. Also to rewrite other people's work. To M. L. Skinner, with whom he collaborated on *The Boy in the Bush*, he said, "If you like I will take it and recast it and make a book of it."

Nehls, vol. II, p. 272. "I was very unhappy when the book arrived," said Miss Skinner.

l. 23 Perhaps Lawrence's state of terror in Mexico came from the gruesome murders Mr. Winfield Scott described to him in Chapala at Bynner's instigation. Bynner, p. 127. " 'Did Scott know he was scaring him?' I asked Spud. 'I don't think so,' replied Spud. 'But it scared him,' I gloated."

page 196

l. 11 Brett, p. 194.

l. 20 Brett, p. 195.

l. 27 Brett, p. 197.

page 197

l. 6 Brett, p. 197.

l. 10 Brett, p. 198. "A note of homesickness is in your voice, and a great longing."

l. 19 Brett, p. 199.

l. 29 Frieda Lawrence, p. 152.

page 199

l. 5 D.H.L. to William Hawk from Oaxaca (Mexico), 7 February (1925). Moore, *The Intelligent Heart*, p. 338. "This place full of malaria. I've had the doctor, and heavy quinine injections, and feel a rag."

l. 16 Lawrence, *The Plumed Serpent*, p. 338.

page 200

l. 24 Brett, p. 200.

l. 28 Brett, p. 200. "I am appalled at the feeling of hate that pours out of you [Lawrence]."

page 201

l. 7 Brett, pp. 200–01. "What is it that flows from you? . . . How describe the real aristocracy of the heart and mind?"

l. 16 Brett, p. 201.

l. 24 Lawrence, *Mornings in Mexico*, p. 85.

page 202

l. 26 Brett, p. 204.

l. 30 Brett, p. 204.

page 203

l. 1 Brett, p. 204.

l. 4 Brett, p. 204.

l. 11 Brett, p. 204.

l. 13 Brett, p. 204.

l. 17 Brett, p. 205.

l. 22 Brett, p. 208.

page 204

l. 10 Brett, p. 208. Frieda gives Brett a letter. "In it she accuses us, Lawrence and myself, of being like a curate and a spinster; she resents the fact we do not make love to each other."

l. 17 Brett, p. 208. "She [Frieda] says that friendship between man and woman makes only half the curve."

l. 22 Brett, p. 208. " 'But Frieda,' I say, 'How can I make love to Lawrence when I am your guest; would that not be rather indecent?' "

page 205

l. 1 Brett, p. 209.

l. 3 Brett, p. 209.

l. 9 Brett, p. 209.

l. 11 Brett, p. 209.

page 206

l. 2 Lawrence, *Mornings in Mexico*, pp. 53, 55, 63. "Rosalino really goes with the house. . . . He must be about five feet four inches. . . . He works for four *pesos* a month, and his food: a few tortillas. Four *pesos* are two American dollars. . . . He owns two cotton shirts, two pair of calico pantaloons, two blouses, one of pink cotton . . . and a pair of sandals. Also his straw hat that he has curled up to look very jaunty, and a rather cheap shawl or a plaid rug with a fringe."

l. 8 Ibid., p. 63. "His duty is to rise in the morning and sweep the street in front of the house, and water it. . . . After which he walks behind the cook carrying the basket to market."

page 207

l. 13 Ibid., pp. 64–66. "He [Rosalino] has a *paisano*, a fellow countryman to sleep with him in the Zaguán, to guard the doors. Whoever gets into the house or patio must get through these big doors."

page 209

l. 1 D.H.L. to Curtis Brown from Oaxaca (Mexico), 10 January 1925. *Letters*, p. 633.

l. 15 Lawrence, "The Flying Fish," *Phoenix*, p. 783.

l. 28 Ibid., p. 780.

page 210

l. 10 Ibid.

l. 16 Ibid., p. 782.

ll. 21–31 Ibid., p. 783.

page 211

ll. 1–4 Ibid.

l. 7 Frieda Lawrence, p. 150. " 'Let's get under the bed if the roof falls,' I cried."

page 212

l. 17 Frieda Lawrence, p. 149. "I had a local native doctor who was scared at having anything to do with a foreigner and he didn't come."

l. 25 Lawrence, "The Flying Fish," *Phoenix*, p. 785.

page 213

ll. 14–25 Ibid., p. 788.

l. 30 Frieda Lawrence, p. 149.

page 214

l. 2 Frieda Lawrence, p. 149.

l. 9 Lawrence, "The Flying Fish," *Phoenix*, p. 784.

l. 17 Brett, p. 181. ". . . word has been sent from Mexico City that you are to be taken care of."

l. 28 D.H.L. to Curtis Brown from Hotel Imperial, Mexico City, 2 March 1925. *Letters*, p. 638.

page 215

l. 1 D.H.L. to Lady Cynthia Asquith from *R.M.S. Orsova*, Sunday, 30 April 1922. Moore, *Collected Letters*, p. 702.

l. 9 Lawrence, "The Flying Fish," *Phoenix*, p. 784.

l. 19 D.H.L. to Curtis Brown from Oaxaca (Mexico), 10 January 1925. *Letters*, p. 633.

l. 23 Lawrence, "The Flying Fish," *Phoenix*, p. 784.

page 216

l. 6 D.H.L. to Brett from Oaxaca (Mexico), Monday morning (1925). *Letters*, p. 634.

l. 7 D.H.L. to Curtis Brown from Mexico, D.F., care of the British Consulate, 15 February 1925. *Letters*, p. 637.

l. 10 D.H.L. to Idella Purnell Stone from Imperial Hotel, Mexico City, 3 March 1925. Bynner, p. 252.

l. 13 D.H.L. to Curtis Brown from Oaxaca (Mexico), 10 January 1925. *Letters*, p. 633.

l. 17 Lawrence, "The Flying Fish," *Phoenix*, p. 785.

l. 25 About "The Flying Fish": It is my feeling that this unfinished novel—only nineteen pages long—has the veracity and beauty of death itself. It is an actual description of the last moments of consciousness—a poetic revelation. I asked Frieda after Lawrence's death why he had never finished it. "Because he stopped dying," she replied.

See Moore, *The Intelligent Heart*, p. 339. "Lawrence told the Brewsters 'the last part will be regenerate man, a real life in the Garden of Eden' but the story remains a magnificent fragment." Professor Moore is one of the very few who truly realized the greatness and extent of Lawrence's imagination. His books on Lawrence are a monumental achievement.

l. 26 Lawrence, "The Flying Fish," *Phoenix*, pp. 785–86.

page 217

l. 7 D.H.L. to Brett from Oaxaca (Mexico), Monday morning (1925). *Letters*, p. 634.

l. 8 Frieda Lawrence, p. 151.

l. 14 D.H.L. to Curtis Brown from Hotel Imperial, Mexico City, 2 March 1925. *Letters*, p. 638.

page 218

l. 6 Brett, p. 215. Lawrence to the Brett: "I looked so awful. . . . When I reached Mexico City from Oaxaca: just pale green. The people stared at me so in the streets that I could not bear it, so Frieda bought me some rouge. I rouged my cheeks and gave me such a lovely, healthy complexion that no one ever turned to stare at me again. You should have seen me! I used the rouge all the time until I reached New Mexico—until I got past that terrible doctor at El Paso."

l. 10 Frieda Lawrence, p. 151.

l. 17 D.H.L. to Curtis Brown from Oaxaca (Mexico), 10 January 1925. *Letters*, p. 633.

ll. 19–27 Frieda Lawrence, p. 151.

l. 20 Nehls, vol. II, p. 396. "I [Dr. Luis Quintanilla] was with my brother Jose at Lawrence's bedside in the Hotel Imperial, with Frieda, when we called a doctor because D. H. was suffering, at least so we thought from a bad case of grippe. It was then that the doctor took me apart to announce that it was . . . definitely an advanced case of tuberculosis."

page 219

l. 1 D.H.L. to Quintanilla from Hotel Imperial, Mexico City, 19(?) March 1925. Nehls, vol. II, p. 397.

l. 4 Frieda Lawrence, p. 151.

l. 7 Frieda Lawrence, p. 151.

l. 15 Nehls, vol. II, p. 523 (note 98). Richard Aldington said of Lawrence's difficulty with the immigration authorities at the border, "They'd have turned Keats back."

l. 17 Frieda Lawrence, p. 151.

l. 21 Bynner, p. 253. The Lawrences stopped briefly in Santa

Fe (29 March 1925). One would accordingly deduce that
he had crossed the border two days before.

ll. 22–27 D.H.L. to Mrs. G. R. G. Conway from Questa,
N.M., 2 April 1925. Moore, *Collected Letters*, p. 832.

page 224

l. 16 D.H.L. to The Honorable Dorothy Brett from Kiowa.
No date. *Letters*, p. 639.

l. 17 D.H.L. to The Honorable Dorothy Brett from Oaxaca,
Mexico, Monday morning (1925). *Letters*, p. 635.

l. 21 Frieda Lawrence, p. 153. "How grateful he was inside
him! 'I can do things again. I can live and do as I like, no
longer held down by the devouring illness.'"

l. 30 D.H.L. to his mother-in-law from Del Monte Ranch,
15 April 1925. Frieda Lawrence, p. 175.

page 225

l. 5 Tindall, from "St. Mawr," p. 153.

page 226

l. 25 Frieda Lawrence, p. 151. "I think in that play he
worked off his struggle for life—so many different motifs,
giant motifs, in that play."

page 227

l. 27 *David* was produced in London sometime in May 1927.
D.H.L. to Robert Atkins (London theatrical producer)
from Scandicci, 16 October 1926. Moore, *Collected Letters*, p. 941. "Dear Atkins: I enclose the music I have written out for *David* . . . if one can only get that feeling of
primitive religious passion across to a London audience. If
not it's no good. I am wondering what sort of a cast you
are planning."

However, the play was not well received. D.H.L. to E. H.
Brewster from Scandicci, 28 May 1927. Moore, *Collected
Letters*, p. 980. ". . . the impudent reviews of the produc-
tion of *David*. They say it was just dull. I say they are

eunuchs and have no balls. It is a fight. The same old one."
D.H.L. to his sister-in-law, Else Jaffe, from Scandicci, 1
June 1927. Frieda Lawrence, p. 226. "They [the review-
ers] say the play was very dull, that it was like a cinema
with too much talking, that it was boring and no drama in
it, and that it was a very great mistake for a clever man like
me to offer such a thing for the actual stage. A clever man
like me doesn't fret over what they say."

page 228

l. 5 Brett, p. 230.

l. 29 Brett, p. 219.

page 229

l. 19 Brett, p. 220.

page 230

l. 11 Lawrence, *David*, p. 149.

l. 13 Ibid., p. 146.

l. 15 Ibid., p. 145.

page 233

l. 16 Swinburne Hale died in Stamford, Conn., in 1937 and
is buried in Newport, R.I.

l. 19 D.H.L. to author the summer of 1925. Fragment of a
letter now lost.

l. 27 Albert A. Cummings [1865?–1934]. Taos butcher. Mr.
Cummings sold all cuts of meat—sirloin or spareribs—for
twenty cents a pound.

page 236

l. 29 The hook on which Lawrence hung his screened larder
is still there today, but has grown quite high up the tree.

l. 30 D.H.L. to his mother-in-law from Del Monte Ranch, 15
April 1925. Frieda Lawrence, p. 176.

page 237

l. 12 D.H.L. to his mother-in-law from Del Monte Ranch, 15
April 1925. Frieda Lawrence, p. 175.

page 238

l. 9 This painting of the ranch on which Frieda and Lawrence and Brett all painted is now in the possession of Mr.
Saki Karavas of Taos, N.M.

l. 29 Lawrence talked to me at great length that day about
his illness in Oaxaca while he changed his trousers. And
later while I watched him milk the cow. He wanted me to
understand how close to death he had been. It was an intense moment in our friendship. He fixed me with his eyes
a long time as he told me about his hemorrhage, "Thought
I'd die, thought I'd die," he kept saying.

page 239

l. 18 D.H.L. to author the summer of 1925. Fragment of letter now lost.

page 240

l. 31 Frieda Lawrence , p. 151.

page 242

l. 27 Brett, p. 254.

page 243

l. 16 Beal, pp. 376, 390.

l. 25 I wanted Lawrence's opinion of Joyce very much. But
Lawrence always made a face and cast his eyes upward
when he talked about Joyce. They were equally famous
in the early '20s.
Moore, *Collected Letters*, p. 1075. Lawrence said of Joyce:
"My God, what a clumsy *olla putrida* James Joyce is!
. . . What old and hard worked staleness masquerading as
the all-new!" D.H.L. letter to Maria and Aldous Huxley
from Kesselmatte, 15 August 1928.

l. 31 Beal, p. 333.

page 244

l. 23 Beal, pp. 396, 404. "Whitman's essential message was
the Open Road. The leaving the soul free unto herself

. . . which is the bravest doctrine man has ever proposed to himself."

page 245
l. 9 James tricked out his sensibilities *ad nauseum* to Lawrence's way of thinking. *Never* got to the root of the matter.

l. 14 Lawrence, "Surgery for the Novel," *Phoenix*, p. 518.

l. 30 Lawrence liked to roll the "r" in Brett's name.

page 246
ll. 25–26 Brett, p. 234. Brett and her whistle: "We have made a plan that when I come I whistle, in case . . . I am not welcome to Frieda."

l. 29 Brett, p. 246. Brett was very famous in Taos for her angling.

page 247
l. 17 D.H.L to Mrs. G. R. G. Conway from Questa, N.M., August 28, 1925. Moore, *The Intelligent Heart*, p. 343.

l. 19 D.H.L. to Catherine Carswell from Del Monte Ranch, 20 June 1925. *Letters*, p. 644.

l. 23 Brett, p. 254. "You [Lawrence] reading very slowly, very intensely. I can read four pages to your one."

page 248
l. 3 Brett, p. 245.

ll. 17–22 Brett, p. 252.

l. 28 Brett, p. 259.

l. 31 Brett, p. 256.

page 249
l. 7 D.H.L. to Curtis Brown from Questa, N.M., 23 June 1925. *Letters*, p. 645.

l. 18 Brett, p. 249.

l. 24 Brett, pp. 249, 254.

l. 11 D.H.L. to Bynner from New York, care of Seltzer, 5 West 50th St., 14 August 1923. *Letters*, pp. 581–82. Also Carswell, p. 195. Lawrence did not like New York. Yet when Catherine Carswell asked him which he would rather have New York or London, " 'New York,' he said, 'London is locked away, out of touch. . . . With New York one is in touch with the free outer world. . . .' "

l. 6 Frieda Lawrence, p. 133. "Near our cabin two of the young stars had their cabin. They seemed to sleep all day and looked white and tired in the evening. Cases of empty champagne bottles stood outside their cabin in the morning."

l. 22 D.H.L. to Frieda's mother from Palace Hotel, San Francisco, 5 September 1922. Frieda Lawrence, p. 154.

l. 12 D.H.L. to Robert Pratt Barlow from Kandy, Ceylon, 30 March 1922. *Letters*, p. 548.

l. 2 Fifty years later, I met Sara Higgins again. She was old and grey and tired.

"What do you remember about Lawrence? What was *the* thing about Lawrence?" I asked her.

"Lawrence—himself!" she laughed.

How things are lost in time. Perhaps a legend is the only living thing.

"I have read *The Rainbow* many times," she told me. Her skin sags but her eyes shine.

"What is it about *The Rainbow?*" I asked.

"Its plasticity. No one has ever done life's plasticity so well in a book as Lawrence." Sara thought a moment, "I don't remember anything about Lawrence but his Lawrence-ness." Then, "We were all so very, very young in those days," said the little old woman lighting a Benson and Hedges with her freckle-spotted hands.

page 269
l. 28 Bynner, p. 352; Lawrence, *Kangaroo*, p. 175.

page 270
l. 5 Brett, p. 230.

page 271
l. 16 Frieda repeated this encouragement to the author in a letter now lost.

page 272
l. 14 The Hawk house still stands today facing the valley. It is owned by Mrs. Eya Fechin Branham, daughter of the Russian painter Nicolai Fechin.

l. 18 Tindall, from "St. Mawr," p. 153.

l. 25 Brett, p. 247. "You have no idea how difficult it is to write [complained Lawrence]. . . . It is much more difficult than painting."

"Do you ever have a clear vision of what you are going to write?" [Brett asked]. "No" [replied Lawrence], "I never know when I sit down just what I am going to write. I make no plan; it just comes, and I don't know where it comes from."

page 273
l. 8 D.H.L. to J. M. Murry from Spotorno, 4 January 1926. *Letters*, p. 653.

l. 23 D.H.L. to Brett from Inverness-shire, 14 August 1926. *Letters*, p. 676.

page 274
l. 11 D.H.L. to Brett from Spotorno, 25 January 1926. *Letters*, p. 656.

l. 12 Brett, p. 260.

l. 19 D.H.L. to Frieda's mother from *S.S. Resolute*, 25 September 1925. Frieda Lawrence, p. 177.

l. 27 D.H.L. to Brett from Spotorno, 29 December 1925. *Letters*, p. 652. "Nobody encourages me in the idea."
D.H.L. to Bynner from Genova, Italy, 27 January 1926. *Letters*, p. 657. "I might go to Russia. Would you like to go with me? I've even learned my Russian A.B.C."

page 275

l. 4 Brett, p. 261.

l. 5 Brett, p. 257.

l. 9 Brett, p. 252.

ll. 12–17 Brett, p. 236.

ll. 27–31 Brett, p. 258.

page 276

l. 1 Brett, p. 258.

l. 19 Brett, p. 252.

l. 23 Brett, p. 257.

page 277

l. 8 Tindall, from "The Novel," p. 189.

l. 12 Ibid., p. 192.

l. 14 Ibid., p. 193.

l. 18 Ibid., p. 197.

l. 24 Ibid., p. 193.

l. 27 Lawrence, "Surgery for the Novel," *Phoenix*, pp. 517–18.

page 278

l. 3 Lawrence, "Morality and the Novel," *Phoenix*, p. 531.

l. 6 Ibid., p. 532.

l. 8 Lawrence, "Why the Novel Matters," *Phoenix*, p. 535.

l. 9 Ibid., p. 537.

l. 11 Ibid., p. 528. "The novel is the highest example of subtle inter-relatedness that man has discovered."

l. 21 He did, however, give us a copy of Giovanni Verga's *Little Novels of Sicily* which Lawrence had translated.

page 279

l. 7 While Lawrence was changing his trousers he gave me a slight volume to read (McDonald's *Bibliography of the Writings of D. H. Lawrence*). He was very proud of that book. "They tell me it is the first time a bibliography has been done of a living author," he said with his half smile.

page 287

l. 11 Frieda Lawrence, pp. 291–96.

The Lawrence Ranch, now owned by the University of New Mexico, has had various names: the Flying Heart (when Mabel owned it) and the Lobo and Kiowa Ranch (when Frieda owned it). The Del Monte Ranch, where Lawrence stayed the first winter, is two miles away from the Lawrence Ranch and is owned by Bill and Rachel Hawk.

BIBLIOGRAPHY

Aldington, Richard. *D. H. Lawrence: Portrait of a Genius But.* ... New York: Duell, Sloan & Pearce, 1950.

Asquith, The Honorable Herbert. *Moments of Memory: Recollections and Impressions.* New York: Scribner's Sons, 1938.

Austin, Mary. *The American Rhythm.* Boston: Houghton Mifflin, 1930.

Beach, Sylvia. *Shakespeare and Company.* New York: Harcourt, Brace & Company, 1959.

Beal, Anthony, ed. *D. H. Lawrence: Selected Literary Criticism* (Compass Edition). New York: The Viking Press, 1966.

Brett, Dorothy. *Lawrence and Brett: A Friendship.* Philadelphia: Lippincott, 1933.

Bynner, Witter. *Journey with Genius: Recollections and Reflections Concerning the D. H. Lawrences.* New York: The John Day Company, 1951.

Carswell, Catherine. *The Savage Pilgrimage: A Narrative of D. H. Lawrence.* London: Chatto and Windus, 1932. London: Martin Secker, 1932.

Colbert, Col. Herschel M. *The History and Practice of Modern Medicine in Taos County.* Unpublished pamphlet, Harwood Library, Taos, 1966.

341

Curtis, Natalie. *The Indians' Book*. New York: Harper and Brothers, 1907. New York: Dover Publications, Inc., 1968.

Hale, Swinburne. *The Demon's Notebook: Verse and Perverse*. New York: Nicholas L. Brown, 1923.

Lawrence, D. H. *The Collected Letters of D. H. Lawrence*. Two volumes. Edited with an Introduction by Harry T. Moore. New York: The Viking Press, 1962.

————. *Compari. The Complete Poems of D. H. Lawrence*. Collected and edited with an Introduction and Notes by Vivian de Sola Pinto and Warren Roberts. New York: The Viking Press. Copyright 1964 by Angelo Ravagli and C. M. Weekley, Executors of the Estate of Frieda Lawrence Ravagli.

————. *David. The Complete Plays of D. H. Lawrence*. New York: The Viking Press, 1966. Copyright by the Estate of Frieda Lawrence Ravagli.

————. *The Letters of D. H. Lawrence*. Edited with an Introduction by Aldous Huxley. New York: The Viking Press, 1932.

————. *Mornings in Mexico*. New York: Alfred A. Knopf, 1934.

————. *Phoenix: The Posthumous Papers of D. H. Lawrence*. Edited with an Introduction by Edward D. McDonald. New York: The Viking Press, 1936.

————. *The Plumed Serpent*. [*Quetzalcoatl*.] New York: Alfred A. Knopf, 1936.

————. "The Gentleman from San Francisco" (translation with S. S. Koteliansky from Ivan Bunin), in Ivan Bunin, *The Gentleman from San Francisco and Other Stories*. London: The Hogarth Press, 1922.

Lawrence, Frieda. *"Not I, But the Wind . . ."* New York: The Viking Press, 1934.

Luhan, Mabel Dodge. *Lorenzo in Taos*. New York: Alfred A. Knopf, 1932.

———. *Movers and Shakers*. Volume 3 of Intimate Memories. New York: Harcourt, Brace & Company, 1936.

McDonald, Edward A. *A Bibliography of the Writings of D. H. Lawrence*. Philadelphia: Centaur Book Shop, 1925.

Merrild, Knud. *With D. H. Lawrence in New Mexico*. (First published 1938 under the title of *A Poet and Two Painters*.) London: Routledge & Kegan Paul Ltd., 1964. Barnes and Noble, Inc., New York, has granted permission for the American Rights to the above book.

Moore, Harry T. *The Intelligent Heart: The Story of D. H. Lawrence*. New York: Farrar, Straus and Young, 1954.

Murry, John Middleton. *Son of Woman: The Story of D. H. Lawrence*. New York: Jonathan Cape & Harrison Smith, 1931.

Nehls, Edward, ed. *D. H. Lawrence: A Composite Biography*. Volume II with a Foreword by Frieda Lawrence Ravagli. Madison: University of Wisconsin Press, 1958.

Nin, Anais. *D. H. Lawrence: An Unprofessional Study*. Chicago: Swallow Press, 1964.

Russell, Bertrand. *The Autobiography of Bertrand Russell*. Boston: Atlantic; Little, Brown and Company. Copyright 1951, 1952, 1953, 1956 by Bertrand Russell. Coyright 1968 by George Allen and Unwin Ltd.

Tedlock, E. W., ed. *Frieda Lawrence: The Memoirs and Correspondence*. New York: Alfred A. Knopf, 1964.

Tindall, William Y., ed. *The Later D. H. Lawrence.* New York: Alfred A. Knopf, 1952.

Waters, Frank. *Leon Gaspard.* Flagstaff, Arizona: Northland Press, 1964.